Page 143, second paragraph, penultimate sentence should read, "Through the lens of 2022, it seems impossible to imagine that Gwendolyn Brooks won the Pulitzer in 1950 for *Annie Allen*, and then there was a thirty-seven year wait until Rita Dove won in 1987 for *Thomas and Beulah*, and seven more years until Yusef won for *Neon Vernacular*."

T0356638

DEAR YUSEF

Dear Yusef

Essays, Letters, and Poems,
For and About One Mr. Komunyakaa

EDITED BY JOHN MURILLO AND NICOLE SEALEY

Wesleyan University Press   Middletown, Connecticut

Wesleyan University Press
Middletown CT 06459
www.wesleyan.edu/wespress

© 2024 Wesleyan University Press
All rights reserved
Manufactured in the United States of America
Designed and composed in Aller and Warnock Pro
by Julie Allred, BW&A Books, Inc.

Library of Congress Cataloging-in-Publication Data
available upon request
cloth   978-0-8195-0133-2
paper   978-0-8195-0134-9
ebook   978-0-8195-0135-6

5 4 3 2 1

Contents

The Work of Orpheus: Critical Essays and Other Considerations

Translating Footsteps: Poems After Komunyakaa

Introduction

In May 2019, Cave Canem Foundation and New York University's Creative Writing Program, in partnership with the PEN World Voices Festival, held a day-long celebration of the life and work of one of the most impactful American poets of the last half-century. *Yusef Komunyakaa: A Celebration* brought together a veritable "Who's Who" of contemporary American poetry to honor a poet who, it turns out, is as beloved for his teaching and mentorship as he is celebrated for his creative work. This anthology finds its genesis in, and moves in the spirit of, that day-long symposium. It also owes a debt to an earlier anthology dedicated to another of our beloved poet-teachers—*Coming Close: Forty Essays on Philip Levine*, edited by Mari L'Esperance and Tomas Q. Morín for Prairie Lights Books in 2013. Upon seeing Phil's great joy at being able to hold that book in his hands, to read all that his students and friends had to say about him, we knew we had to pay similar tribute to Yusef. Our only regret is that it has taken us this long. While both the Komunyakaa symposium and the Levine anthology predate Covid, our anthology feels like part of a larger trend that seems to have picked up since the pandemic. Now more than ever, it seems, readers and writers are making greater efforts to honor elders and contemporaries while they are here to receive the praise. Recent tributes that come immediately to mind include a virtual reading held in honor of poet and Cave Canem co-founder Toi Derricotte by the Brooklyn Book Festival in October of 2021 and *Trying for Fire: A Tribute to and Celebration of Tim Seibles*, which took place at the Association of Writers and Writing Programs (AWP) conference in 2022. As of this writing, there is an essay collection honoring Sharon Olds in the works by the University of Michigan, and another dedicated to Komunyakaa to be published by the Louisiana State University Press. We say, the more the merrier. Clearly, it is flower-giving time.

If you're reading this, you already know who Yusef is and what he means. But, just in case: Yusef Komunyakaa is the author of nearly twenty volumes of poetry and prose, and his plays and librettos have been performed to international acclaim. His honors include the Pulitzer Prize for poetry, the Wallace Stevens Award from the Academy of American Poets, the Poetry Foundation's Ruth Lilly Poetry Prize, and the William Faulkner Prize from the University de Rennes, among others. He served as chancellor of the Academy of American Poets from 1999–2005 and has taught at Cave Canem's week-long retreat, as well as at many universities, including the University of New Orleans, Indiana University, Princeton University, and New York University, where he served, before retiring in 2021, as Global Professor and Distinguished Senior Poet in the creative writing program. He has taught your best teachers and is most likely your favorite poet's favorite poet.

The word "anthology" derives from the Greek *anthos* (flowers) and *logia* (collection, or gathering). This book, then, is a bouquet. A bouquet for one whose generosity, kindness, and wisdom, whose guidance, mentorship, and friendship have made rich the lives of each of the contributors. It was an honor and a joy to gather these flowers for you, Dear Yusef.

John Murillo and Nicole Sealey
Brooklyn, New York

WHAT COUNTS

Letters and Personal Essays

Dear Yusef,

This is the thing, I'm not sure if I should call you Yusef or Mr. Komunyakaa. And I say Yusef, because the only Yusef, since I first read your work, is Yusef Komunyakaa. You have become the embodiment of the name and turned the name into every part of speech imaginable, including myth and legend and the story we tell in the barbershop about the cat who ran a three-minute mile or leaped and snatched a quarter from the top of the backboard.

The story I tell most often about poetry begins with the hole. A contraband copy of Dudley Randall's *Black Poets* slipped under my cell door in solitary, introducing me to Sonia Sanchez, Claude Brown, Nikki Giovanni, Lucille Clifton and Etheridge Knight and Countee Cullen and all of the rest of them. Less often told is what happened weeks later. Shipped off to a super-maximum-security prison in the gutted side of a mountain, a young brother with dreadlocks and a shank buried on the yard would let me borrow Michael Harper's *Every Shut Eye Ain't Sleep.* He said, Shahid, I think you'll dig this, as if there was something about the way I moved around those circles of incarcerated and suffering men that suggested poetry.

Happenstance is one of those words not used often enough is what I think. But it's all like the happenstance that led me to naming my second son after Thelonious. First hearing the name in "Elegy for Thelonious," I carried it around in my head for years before saving up some change and buying me a Thelonious Monk cassette while in prison. "Untitled Blues," "How I See Things," "Facing It," I know you've heard this before—how some of your words didn't just create meaning for a young'un hoping to spin words on a page, but made them believe such a thing had value. And now we all, after getting hip to your work, have decided that we want to turn image into legacy. That's not all of what I mean though. In the same anthology, Rita Dove writes "if you can't be free, be a mystery" in "Canary." What has always struck me about that line is how you, Mr. Yusef Komunyakaa, have always finessed what it means to be a mystery. The source of the transparency of your mind on paper has always been a kind of elusive—as if your wisdom just happened.

Back then, I had no way of knowing who Yusef Komunyakaa the man was. I wasn't even certain if you were Black. The name Komunyakaa as mysterious as whatever the source of your stories were, except, truly, your stories almost immediately felt like they belonged to me *cause I know I was born to wear out at least one hundred angels.* At least I came to know that after reading "Anodyne" and remembering that it is okay to love the *ragtime jubilee behind my left nipple.* And still, what I mean is that I couldn't place how a Black man came to know all the things in your poems and know himself as Yusef Komunyakaa.

This letter started out as a would-be review of your new book, *Everyday Mojo Songs of Earth.* But lately I've been reading Milton's *Paradise Lost.* Something about this last reading of *Paradise* has me thinking that Milton's problem is that he wanted to workshop God. And he wanted to pull Adam and Eve into it. They resisted after the fall, but Lucifer still had some punctuation he was at odds with. It ain't end too well for him. And me believing that some poets are, at least, prophets, if not the voices of some g-d, I figure I know better than Lucifer and the pair. And so I won't go tinkering with messages from glory. I wonder if you dig Rakim. Generally, I know how you feel about hip hop. But Rakim, nicknamed the G-d MC, always had me recognizing what it meant to want to be more on a page. That's how your work has been, in a way. And so the review wasn't in me. Picking up *Mojo Songs* was more a walk back down memory lane.

You know yourself in ways we avoid. And don't nobody else make the reader fall into that voice until they're becoming more cognizant of themselves. "I want each question to fit me / Like a shiny hook, a lure / In the gullet," you write in "When Dusk Weighs Daybreak." And I'm thinking maybe that's the rub. These lines reveal how to make a man understand himself, and then admit the cost: "I need a Son House blues / To wear out my tongue." A different way of saying all of this is that in those first-person poems, in the space of those narratives, I became somebody else. A wiser, hipper cat with more than just the stories that carried me to prison. And sometimes, in doing all that, I become afraid of what I know. Take the end of one of your new joints, where you write, "To stand naked before a mirror / & count the parts is to question the whole / season of sowing & reaping thorns." Who is brave enough to walk into the world with that knowledge?

I be telling myself how I met you in prison and take solace in that. Cause, like many a young writer, I want to know the man behind the poems. But prison teaches you to give a man his privacy. And so, when I met you years ago at Cave Canem, I was awed. But just wanted to be chill. And maybe I regret this. Now believing that, now deeply believing that part of all this work of art is to spend time listening. Though there is something to be said about what it meant to watch you in a chair alone sipping your drink, having earned whatever rest or weariness you wanted to have, in solitude. I should have told you though, how all those years ago your words were a part of the yarn that I spun into the loudmouthed poet who felt invisible and so needed to be seen that I would have wept if my body knew how. Where I grew up only cowards wept though. And while I was never one for accurately landing a jab or a hook, I knew how to hold my tears. What am I saying? There were things I might have said, but the wild thing is that just watching you chill for a moment made me feel seen and made me know that the accumulation of words that led to that moment meant something. I'm from the generation of Black boys who found their elders in prison cells and mostly forgot them if we were lucky enough to get free. And then your poems turned you into one of the first men who knew my name.

Once, you, while critiquing one young poet's sprawling poem, said something to the effect of, see, the poems ends ten lines up from the period. If there was a lesson in that, I figured it was that sometimes in life you run past where you want to be to land where you need to be. But you also must be able to check and see if you've run too far. First time I realized I could turn to the past and find where I needed to be was in your words. That's the thing so many of us are after, how to return to yesterday to find the scaffolding for tomorrows. And I know, like a lot of my peers, I'm still just trying out your notes. Hoping that the few times I get it right, I'm not afraid of whatever unravels between the lines.

Take care,
Dwayne Betts

Refuge

The first time I entered his office, moments after sitting opposite him, Yusef unceremoniously asked me to read aloud the poem I'd brought. I say unceremoniously, but I don't mean without ritual. This request was, I'm sure, a part of his practice as a teacher. I'm a teacher too, of a different sort—as of that moment, I'd clocked in almost a decade in a public high school. Yusef appreciated that, which isn't always the case in academia. I remember r. erica doyle, a public school administrator and brilliant poet, once telling me, "They think we're stupid." But I never felt that from Yusef. Rather, I felt a sense of belonging.

Yusef makes small, satisfied noises as he listens to his students read poems. He did that in class, and he did that in his office. He leaves space for silences. He's not there to ramble. The silence speaks. If it's filled with meaningless anxieties, then probably the poem needs work. If it's filled with weight and thought and heart, then probably the poem is doing its work. He asks questions that are both precise and extremely open-ended. He repeats a line or a phrase, and asks "Or is it *this* . . . ?" He trusts the image as a form of communication, and aims to get it right. He trusts the image as connection.

He tells me to take the collected works of Muriel Rukeyser from his bookshelves, to bring it home, to read it. I flip to the lines, "I know I am space / my words are air." I keep the book for a month, then buy my own copy because I understand her work as initiation. I return Yusef's book to his shelf, knowing someone else will need it later.

Years later, Yusef and I participate in a reading to launch the *Inheriting the War* anthology. We end up, I'm sure, at Café Loupe, at a post-event celebration. He sits across from me, is kind. We talk about small things. He seems to see people—to look around and gently through—slowly and with tremendous grace. He asks me about teaching. I tell him highlights from my day. He seems content and listens. We don't say much, but everything feels comfortable.

I read Rukeyser, her collected works, and her *Book of the Dead*, on repeat. I teach a workshop to other poets in which we read her gently and repeatedly, aloud together. I think about the simplicity of this practice. The repetition, the care, the patience. An antithesis to our scrolling, short-form culture. I think this practice, in its simplicity, is possible from years of study with my meditation teacher and from briefer study with Yusef. The two people are not dissimilar. A librarian contacts me about Rukeyser's archives. She's heard about our workshop and invites us to visit. My students and I collectively visit, feel we belong. We read her again, in this new space. A slowness and depth, an appreciation for the conversation that happens in the silences between, by being, and being together in the presence of these words.

I don't remember most things he's said to me. Yusef writes "memory's see-through cloth," and he's correct. We likely all connect to this blurred image. I want to say there were several times that Yusef put pressure on a few blurred words of a poem, and everything changed. A sort of alchemy. That first visit, I had brought him a poem about my father, also a veteran of the war in Vietnam. It was based on a story my dad had told me about falling through the ice as a child and being afraid of his mother's punishment. The poem ended: "Afraid to tell his mother, afraid / she'd beat him, or would she offer her skirts for cover?" Yusef understood the fear my father had, and asked, "Is it a question? Or a statement. A fear that she'd cover him." That was the only thing he said about the poem. The line changed, and I repeated it aloud: "she'd beat him, she'd cover him with her skirts." The silence that followed felt full.

A Journey to Kolkata with
Yusef Komunyakaa, January 2008

At sunrise each morning, the sound of rhythmic slapping awakens me. Beyond the open window: the nameless lake—mirroring huts and laundry—where bed linens are struck across the water until they clean. A prayerful singing accompanies the work, rising from the voices of washerwomen. When I close my eyes even now, I can hear this singing.

My journey here had been troubled by a cancelled flight, a suitcase lost forever, a re-routed trip with a midnight stop-over in Delhi, a taxi ride through the night streets from one airport to another, and upon my arrival, the news that the bookfair, Kolkata Boi Mela had, at the very last moment, been cancelled this year "for political reasons." We would not join the expected two million people on the grounds of the Maidan for the largest non-trade book fair in the world, nor make our way through its warrens of book stalls and candy vendors, musicians and singers, writers and poets. It would seem to have been an inauspicious beginning. But not to fear, poet Goutam Datta reassured us, we would create another book fair among ourselves, a band of American poets led by Yusef Komunyakaa and the book lovers and writers of West Bengal. An alternative, smaller fair was already in progress on the outskirts of Kolkata, where we would be welcomed with garlands of marigolds and blue buttons, sprays of roses and birds of paradise, for such is the disposition of West Bengal toward poetry.

The larger book fair, I learned, was held every year in Kolkata beginning on the last Wednesday of January and ending twelve days later on the first or second Sunday of February, coinciding with the Hindu festival Saraswati Puja, named for the Goddess of Learning, and on this day the people pay their respects to books and don't touch them other than reverently. This year, American literature was to have been showcased, but that wasn't the reason for the cancellation. It was said to have had something to do with the rising of dust caused by the footsteps of millions of readers. For years, attempts had been made to find an alternative place for the fair, to prevent the rising dust from damaging Maidan and the nearby Victoria Memorial. This year, *Save the Maidan* protestors prevailed, or so the newspapers announced, and at the last moment, the High Court banned the 33rd Fair from being held on the Park Circus Maidan. But it wasn't the dust, our hosts assured us, as the dust would nevertheless rise. It was politics.

This was my first journey to India, and I had with me the poems of Rabindranath Tagore, whose residence at Shantiniketan we were to visit. The book was in my carry-on bag, and became one of my few possessions during the stay, along with the clothes I had been wearing on the flight, a moleskin notebook, a few pens, and some medicines. As the taxi wended its way from the airport to the hotel, I opened Tagore: "No one will go back / as he came / on this shore of the sea / of India's great humanity." This was from James Talarovic's translation of the *Gitanjali*. Around us swarmed cycle rickshaws, oxen, hand-pulled rickshaws and taxis, three-wheeled cars and bicycles and along the roads, on the banks of the roads, people bathed themselves by pouring plastic buckets of water over their heads while beside them others cooked over small fires and long metal cook-stoves, a blue smoke rising from the whole of it— and women stirred pots larger than any I had ever seen, and every few meters, a supplicant naked but for the blanket she held around herself, reclined or sat upright, gazing as if she were elsewhere—

There were no traffic lanes and yet the procession swerved and wove without collisions, guided by a symphony of horns tooted and blasted in a music seemingly understood by all. I was later told that if my taxi driver were to accidentally strike a pedestrian, I should flee the taxi on foot and not look back. The driver would be beaten or killed on the spot, they said, and his taxi torched. One is told such things, seriously or in teasing. But this particular cautionary advice was echoed several times in West Bengal.

Tagore would be my refuge. It is better than bringing a map with you, to bring a country's poet. The poetry is a better guide. He writes: *May I be able to say this / when I go: / There is nothing to compare / with what I have seen and received.*

Our delegation included Goutman Datta, Ram Devineni, and Catherine Fletcher, and, while I was there, also Bob Holman, Joy Harjo, Suji Kwok Kim, Nathalie Handal, Dante Micheaux, Ed Pavlić, and Yusef Komunyakaa, in whose honor the trip was undertaken. Others had preceded us, including Bharati Mukherjee, Christopher Merrill, and Idra

Novey, but my visit followed theirs, and I was able to do little more than embrace them in passing. As promised, the bookfair was symbolically opened by a delegation of Bengali journalists and writers on January 31st to protest the cancellation, and an improvised fair was scheduled, with "all events subject to change." I missed the readings by Joy and Bob, but arrived in time to read with Dante and Ed at the Bangla Akademi on the evening of February 3rd, and to attend the "Give Peace a Chance" program at the Bengal Club the following night. The next morning, we left for Tagore's Shantiniketan.

The station was teeming with bearers of the tea harvest, and Goutam Datta guided us with exemplary diplomacy toward the train, as if we were visiting from another galaxy, which in a sense, we were. And then the train slid through the farm fields of West Bengal on the alluvial Gangetic plain. The train was filled with people, mostly Hindu, who are people of revealed and remembered scripture, Vedas and Upanishads, the Bhagavad Gita, and there are also Sikhs, Buddhists, Jews, and Zoroastrians, and they are mostly Bengalis, but also Chinese live here, and Tamils, Napalis, Telugus, Assamese, Gujaratis, Anglo-Indians, Tibetans, Maharashtrians, Punjabis, and Parsis, and they are speaking Bengali, Hindi, English, Oriya, and Bhojpuri, a symphony of utterance. The journey took some hours, and when we arrived, we were seated in bicycle rickshaws for the distance to our hotel, and then to the peace of Tagore's house and the world university he founded in Shantiniketan. We were emissaries from America, a war culture, and it was a relief to walk in the gardens of Tagore's residence, and to wander through the quiet rooms of his house: his bedroom, the "modern" bathroom he had installed nearby, the library where he wrote, the kitchen where his *beguni* were prepared. That I was able to sit in his chair, run my hands over the century-old gleam of the desk, hold his manuscripts and drawings in my hands, leaf through his notebooks and look out at his tended gardens through his own open window was a surprising joy. But we did so. That day passed in meditative expectancy. The curator of Tagore's life generously offered us the fruits of his collection. *O my mind,* Tagore wrote, *steadily awaken / in holy pilgrimage.*

A general strike kept us unexpectedly in this place. No one could travel, it seemed, anywhere in West Bengal for the following twenty-four hours. To do so would be to risk one's life. No trains were running. Any vehicle on the roads would be attacked and burned, people said.

So we stayed, and, fortuitously, a traveling troupe of mystic musicians called the Baul arrived and gathered to play under a canopy in the center of the town. *The Baul* are here! people cried out as they hurried to the canopy. *The Baul.* Yusef and I sat on a blanket under the canopy in front of the riser where the Baul had gathered in their saffron alkhalla robes, with their long hair knotted and coiled around their heads, wearing basil beads and cradling their one-stringed *ektara* guitars. Their name comes from the Sanskrit words for "madcap" and "restless," and they travel from town to town, living only on what they are given, singing ecstatic unwritten songs about the soul's sojourn on earth and of the soul's earthly distance from the spiritual world. They also sing of love, destiny, and the mystery of life. They profess no religion, but their beliefs fuse Islam, Hinduism, and Buddhism. They accompany themselves on *ektara*, the *dotara*, a musical instrument from the jack-fruit tree, an earthen drum, chimes and cymbals. As they gather, they greet each other, and there is an apparent gentleness among them. One by one they rise to sing, and without knowing their language we discern from them a spiritual message that reminds us of what it is to be a human being. The Baul call themselves simply Baul. They are the very light and earth of this place, and cannot be separated from what it means to be Bengali. Yusef and I are on the blanket, and after a song, the Baul singer approaches us and takes our hands in his and pours his light over us. The Baul were especially drawn to Yusef.

Later, because the Baul had been told that we were poets from America, we were joined by them under the stars for continued playing and singing. They wanted to accompany the poets from the other side of the world. That went on into the night. We were lifted into their world from ours.

We also visited a tribal Shantal village near Shantiniketan, where we were met by the villagers whose daughters danced for us and with whom we danced, who played musical instruments with us, and for whom Joy Harjo played her saxophone. We had no language in common, but we held hands and embraced and sang and danced as the night fell upon us.

The next morning we walked in darkness along the roads of Shantiniketan toward the train station. Ours was an early train, and there were no taxis. So we groped through the darkness, American poets and Bengali hosts, walking by the light of each other's clothing, calling out to each other to keep our way on the road. I walked by the light of Yusef's white shirt. We knew only that we had to walk straight down the road, and it would lead us to the train station. But when we reached the end, there seemed to be a fence and a construction site. We thought we had become lost. Then one of the poets noticed that to our right was the empty, dark station. On its platform, we gathered with a few Bengalis to await the early train. A man was playing with a monkey there. We danced and talked and softly told jokes to each other. Daylight came slowly just before the train arrived, and after boarding, we settled in for the journey back to Kolkata. The Bauls had left us light-spirited. It hadn't mattered to us if the train had arrived or not. We had entered a region of poetry, light, and singing. *I don't know / if I'll come back or not. // I don't know / whom I'll meet today. // At the landing place / that unknown one plays his lute / in the boat.*

Toward the end of the stay, and after my return to Kolkata, it became for us important to walk along the banks of the Bhagirathi-Hooghly river toward the ghats. Why? It did not seem enough to read poems at the Bangla Akademi and the Club Bengal, as beautiful as those gatherings were. My clothes were filled with dust by now, my only clothes, and around us the city of Kolkata pressed, waiting to be met in fullness by our hearts. *No more barriers / remained in my life. / I dashed out toward the world.*

We hired a taxi that took us from Mahatma Gandhi Road to the Strand Bank Road and then we left it and walked toward the ghats, the funeral ghats where cremations were performed, where the ashes of the dead were passed into the river, and the bathing ghats, and beyond them, the sadhus making their way, mendicants wrapped in blankets, merchants and beggars and soon we were surrounded and followed but we kept walking until Joy Harjo was stopped by a persistent blackbird that perched on an incense stall and began chattering at her with great persistence. Joy kept her attention on this bird, and a conversation ensued between Joy's gaze and the bird, which would not leave her alone. She had been singled out by this bird, and it had a message to deliver in a bird-tongue along the banks of the Hooghly. In one of her poems, some time ago, she had written: *We cannot be separated in the loop of mystery between blackbirds and the memory of blackbirds.* The men and women on the banks of the river braided flowers for the dead, hauled baskets of fish, lighted incense in mourning, disappeared into hunger, sold breads and images of Hindu gods, and we walked among them on the dirt roads behind slow trucks, ox carts, rickshaws, and other walkers, until the whole of it surrounded us, humankind on the banks of the river, and a lone beggar chanted behind us: *I have nothing. You have everything.* And Tagore wrote: *It is only right / that You walk behind all, / beneath all, / among those destitute of all / where there live / the poorest of the poor.*

When it was time to leave Kolkata, I couldn't bring myself to go. Now I traveled lightly, having lost my luggage forever, having spent these days washing my clothes in a basin, carrying the poet with me in his words. I was tired, and ragged I thought, and I had too much worried about my lost possessions, but the Baul were singing in my heart, and I knew that what Tagore wrote was true: *Day and night and every day / carefully gather and store these flowers / as a garland in your consciousness— / and consider yourself blessed.* It was Yusef who made this journey possible, whose tranquility of spirit entranced the mystical Baul, and whose towering presence guided us along the crowded train platforms and through the gardens of Tagore, and if I saw and felt the world differently there than in any place before or since, it was because of him.

with gratitude to Yusef,
Carolyn Forché

BRIAN GILMORE

Chasing Yusef (for Kenny May)

After finally meeting up with the poet Yusef Komunyakaa and my friend
Kenny May in New York City, back in July 2017, this is the email I sent to
Yusef, at his invitation, a few months later.

Hello Yusef
I would first like to say it was a pleasure to be able to hang out
in NYC this past summer. As it is often unusual for me to make it
to literature conferences, and readings, in NYC, etc., I always enjoy
shooting the breeze with poets and artists. It reminds me of the days
when we would travel from DC to Newark, New Jersey, and hang
out with the late Amiri Baraka. I was especially enthused to talk
with you and my old friend, Kenny May, who I met 20 some odd
years ago, struck up a friendship, and then only saw him again,
when I saw you. I can only imagine the level of endorphins that
must have been released in those few hours. I also wish I could have
come to Trenton with you and Kenny and checked out the club. I
had to get down to DC, and my family, and especially my daugh-
ters. Of course, that is the reason why I felt compelled to write you
anyway because of your own poem about daughters that I read
in Poetry *recently. I have now read it a few times and the poetry*
spoke to me particularly strong being the father of three daughters.
It seems to be a poem about daughters but also women in society
and it had some quite clever language and nuances that urged me
to drop this note. The language seems casual at times, colloquial on
some level but also rich, and exact, which is something difficult to
tackle sometimes in literature. The poem also seemed specific to me
and abstract and that too is something missing from a lot of poetry
I read. Poems are often always specific, but they very often are
abstract, and the poet disappears (Barthes says we disappear any-
way, I've read) but this poem has abstract moments that still feel
specific to your experience. The "rib" line is especially clever and,
the poem seems to be in two parts, an introductory portion, slowly

setting up the more personal end. Well, I could be wrong about all of this, but it is a powerful poem for me. I am reading your book, "Taboo" right now, trying to catch up on literature that has escaped me over the years.

I do hope our paths will cross again soon, and perhaps, I can see that club in Trenton. You, Kenny and I owe it to the universe to reconvene one day in the future. I am sure I won't take a bicycle cab to meet you guys next time. It was still a great time. —Brian

The rickshaw bike dropped me off at a bar in New York City not far from the Village. Yusef was working at NYU at the time, and he chose the spot. This was months in the making. My friend, Kenny May, who I had not seen in twenty-one years or more, and who was an expat artist in Korea, told me, meet me in New York. I am hanging with Yusef one day this summer. One day. It was worth it.

I am not sure why, other than it was an unknown quantity. Kenny and I had met more than twenty years ago in Atlanta at the Association of Writers and Writing Programs conference and hung tough. And, of course, there was also Yusef Komunyakaa.

The poet of a distinguished mystery. He was quiet. I would read his work and hear him read, but could not figure him. He was so deep on one level and communicated the very essence of the human experience. He was also elusive, radically withdrawn—but also dedicated. He felt more like a jazz pianist than a poet. But perhaps that was the point.

I was in Michigan at the time, when the moment arrived to try to hook up with Yusef and Kenny. I worked in Michigan, but I was headed east to Washington, DC, my real home. It was doable. So I went for it.

As soon as I got off my plane at the Thurgood Marshall International Airport in Baltimore, I jumped on an Acela train to New York City. When I arrived at Penn Station I jumped in a bicycle rickshaw because it was pouring down raining. I didn't even think; I should have taken the subway.

When I arrived at the spot where Yusef and Kenny were hanging, the rickshaw driver said I owed him like $110. I gave him everything I had in cash, which was about $75. Kenny and Yusef came outside the eatery to see if I had enough money. I told them I thought I did.

Yusef, as I recall, laughed the hardest when he heard what I paid. Then we stepped back in, sat down, and like three sailors on leave who had landed in America again, began chopping up the two things we mutually loved: music and poetry. It was cool, I remember thinking.

One of those moments when time stops. Kenny May, of Korea now, by way of Indiana, and the poet, Yusef Komunyakaa, citizen of the world. Poet of the world.

I first encountered Yusef Komunyakaa in Philadelphia in February 1996 at the twelfth annual Celebration of Black Writing in Philadelphia. Yusef was a poet in high demand and though I had never heard him read, he was well known to me just by reputation.

He had just won the Pulitzer Prize in 1994 and everyone wanted a piece of him. He was like a rock star that weekend in Philadelphia. His workshop was jam-packed and later, when he read at the Painted Bride, a venue for artists in Philly, it was SRO.

I sat in on his workshop on writing and was intrigued. I remember one specific thing he said that still sits with me today and continues to drive me. Always have several manuscripts going at the same time, he said. I remember he said "four."

I felt challenged. Was I pushing myself enough? Why didn't I have several projects going? As a result of that little bit of talk from Yusef, more than twenty-five years ago, I now always have various projects going.

When I saw him read at the Painted Bride that night, Joel Dias-Porter and I were right up front. Kevin Young, the great poet, read with Yusef.

As Yusef read, he didn't smile, or laugh. He also rarely made any comments about the poetry. He didn't try to do introductions, or set-ups. Try to tell us what he was talking about before he launched the word. I loved that. I don't like doing that too much either. Let the audience decide what they are hearing. Let the words carry the audience wherever it goes.

That's what he did. He just read his poetry from his many books. Here was an artist, I remember thinking. Like a painter. He just showed you what he painted. It is up to you to find your meaning.

Yet I still found Yusef hard to figure. That was a good thing. What was I feeling as I heard him read, his deep, grounded voice, rooted in the humanity of ordinary lives?

I encountered Yusef again many years later at the Hurston/Wright Legacy Awards in 2015 in Washington, DC. He was now well past his "hot period" following the Pulitzer. He was more in the legendary status.

Yusef was, in fact, the world when it came to poets by then. He was like Ellington, "Beyond Category." He commanded attention even though he wasn't like Duke at all.

He presented an award that night and read a poem about Richard Wright, as I recall. I was there as a nominee for an award. Afterward, I was lucky. I cornered him and at last, after many years, we talked quite a bit.

He asked me what I was working on, and he even told me he enjoyed one of my other books, a book on Duke Ellington I had written. This was cool.

When readers like your work, it is magnificent. But when another poet likes your poetry it is even more so. And then there is acknowledgement of your elder writers. These kind of tributes are the very best.

When we finally settled into the bar after my madcap excursion in the skies and railways and roads of America, I thought about what Yusef had said once about when he met Ornette Coleman, the legendary free jazz saxophonist: "We just talked . . . I was in awe of him."

I was in awe of Yusef, of course. But I also remembered what my friend, the poet Kenneth Carroll, always used to say—act like you belong. So I did, and dove right in asking Yusef, over red wine, about the poems he wrote for Charlie Parker years ago, for a publication called *Brilliant Corners*, which publishes poetry about jazz. I remember reading Yusef's work and wanting to get published in that publication immediately. I did submit once, but no dice. I didn't keep pushing.

His Charlie Parker tribute in *Brilliant Corners* is alluring. Yusef dives deep into Bird's life and art, and his piece was one of the first extended poetic portraits of a jazz musician. I read it when the issue came out in 1997. I was personally immersed in writing poems about Duke Ellington. I didn't know where I was going with my stack of Ellington poems, but after reading Yusef's fourteen-part tribute to Bird, I knew for sure. I would write until I felt I had my say. He had done fourteen parts on Bird; maybe I would write just as much on Duke. I eventually finished a whole book of poems that did get published. I had done what he had suggested. I got several projects going all at once.

I also asked Yusef about writers who wrote in this idiom, and he was on top of much of it. Amiri Baraka, Jayne Cortez (he mentioned her), and Albert Murray (I brought him up). We also talked about the difference between writing about jazz—sounding like jazz, but also, how to make your writing jazz itself. Structurally pushing your writing to become a jazz composition with themes, and heads, and solos, and improvisation within the work itself.

It was probably the richest concept on this kind of writing I have had since my days of going up to Newark to read poetry in the basement of Amiri Baraka's house. Baraka was one of the only poets I met who also spoke of trying to make literature become jazz.

Then Yusef told us about a jazz club he was hoping to open in Trenton, New Jersey. I could see his eyes light up as he talked about it. Rarely had I ever seen him bright-eyed like this over the years. I could tell as he spoke how much he loved the music, and the artists, and the idea of a space for the art.

I also spent much of the time that day asking Yusef about his forays into drama. By 2017, he had written many plays and had some of them staged. I asked him why it was that many poets were pivoting to drama.

As is customary with Yusef, he took his time to respond. He said many things about my question. But mostly, he thought it was the brevity of poetry that helped poets write theater. Poetry, as a form, has certain expectations and efficiencies, and it works as well for drama.

At the end of the evening, as darkness descended upon the city, and the red wine and cold grog wore off, Kenny and I strolled slowly with Yusef back to the campus of NYU. We continued to chit chat and chop it up.

Mostly, the topic was Yusef's club that might soon open in Trenton, New Jersey. He urged us to come by once it was open and we promised we would try to make it. We also talked about getting together the following day to go to the Louis Armstrong Museum that had just opened in Queens.

Sadly, I knew I could not attend. I had to get back down to Washington, DC early the next day. Kenny and Yusef did go, and it was nice to know Yusef was looking for me when they hopped on a train to make their way over there.

That next day, when I was back on the Acela train headed home, I felt again something come to me about Yusef Komunyakaa. He seemed to embody the jazz voice itself of a musician. He always spoke carefully like he wanted to be sure what he had to say. His hesitations created these silent spaces, the quiet in between the notes, but nevertheless, meaningful. I still feel that today. His voice so deep, yet also quiet and soft. It created a dissonance that defied meaning, in a way.

On November 26, 2017, Yusef did email me back. It was like we were again talking about jazz and art in New York City.

Dear Brian,

Good evening. How are you? I'm here in Trenton at the moment, still attempting to keep the faith with possibility. It was great to hang for a moment with you and Kenneth in the Big Apple. You were indeed brave to take that damn rickshaw; I can't even imagine hopping into one. Brian, I was at the American Academy in Rome for a month, and I've been trying to finalize a new play. I owe Kenneth a holler across the ocean. Thanks for commenting on "A World of Daughters"; it will open my New and Selected: "Everyday Mojo Songs of Earth." What are you working on these days? Yes, let us keep in touch. Take care and keep the faith.

Best,

Yusef

I am still hopeful there will be another meeting of our trio.

The Forty-Fourth Poem

It was 1996, and I'd just landed a new teaching gig as instructor of Eng-L205: Introduction to Poetry, a correspondence course offered at Indiana University, where I was a graduate student pursuing my MFA in poetry. It sounds quaint, *correspondence course,* a class conducted entirely by postal mail. By handwritten, sometimes typed words on paper, folded into an envelope, addressed and stamped. Even then, I remember finding something pleasingly old-fashioned about the idea. It felt—because it was—part of a much older activity, one of the things poets did before the now-ubiquitous creative writing workshop had been invented. It made me think of Keats's letters, or Rilke's to a young poet, or Dickinson's. (I suppose that tradition still continues, but at the moment we call it, alas, "asynchronous instruction.")

I had been given some official envelopes to use, as well as the course reader and assignments, a spiral-bound volume students purchased that broke the course down into units, the units into lessons. These lessons and all the course materials had been recently designed by the previous instructor, who'd been paid to update the course. I'd been hired merely to continue to teach the course as it existed, not to invent my own version. It can be challenging to teach a course the way someone else designed it instead of the way you might conceive of it yourself. On the other hand, teaching it, especially at that moment in my life, was essentially to be a student in the class myself, working through the lessons and units just ahead of, sometimes right along with those enrolled in the course. The units and lessons covered the usual elements of craft: image and metaphor, line and rhythm, sound and form, culminating with a unit that reviewed the previous lessons while also undertaking the close reading of a book of poems. The collection chosen for this purpose was *Dien Cai Dau.*

If one were to read a single volume to represent the last fifty years of American poetry, one couldn't do much better than *Dien Cai Dau.* Pronounced "Dinky dow," the former instructor had written, the phrase was Vietnamese for "crazy in the head." It was a term Komunyakaa, like other American GIs, would have heard the Vietnamese muttering about them under their breath. And it *is* above all a book about madness: not only the madness of the war, the *dien cai dau* of "a world [that] revolved / under each man's eyelid" in the opening poem, "Camouflaging the Chimera," but also the madness to be confronted within one's own country and culture. "There's more than a nation / inside us," Komunyakaa writes in "Tu Do Street," where "black & white / soldiers touch the same lovers / minutes apart, tasting / each other's breath." In one of the most chilling poems in the volume, "The One-Legged Stool" (even the madness of a one-legged stool!), a prose monologue spoken by a Black prisoner of war, madness emerges as the exceedingly valid paranoia of being betrayed by one's own comrades:

You're lying. Those white prisoners didn't say what you say they said. They ain't laughing. Ain't cooperating. They ain't putting me down, calling me names like you say. Lies. Lies. It ain't the way you say it is. I'm American. (*Pause.*) Doctor King, he ain't dead like you say. Lies. How many times are you trying to kill me? Twice, three times, four, how many?

Although there's also an inchoate hope one reads between the lines that it's the war itself, the temporary situation of it, that is the cause of the madness that occurs throughout, and that such madness might evaporate or abate, the final and extraordinary poem, "Facing It," confirms that *dien cai dau* will remain, only now as post-traumatic stress disorder, as hallucination. In "the black mirror" of the Vietnam Veterans Memorial back in Washington, DC, years later, the speaker catches himself thinking that "a woman's trying to erase names" from the monument. "No," the final line of the volume self-corrects, "she's brushing a boy's hair."

Even as *Dien Cai Dau* abounds with contextual details that convey the specificity of a time and place, so many of these poems nonetheless stand shoulder to shoulder with some of the greatest lyrical poetry about war in the English language. One example is "We Never Know," a gorgeously understated lyric that describes the killing of an enemy soldier. Who does the shooting is unclear, but Komunyakaa notes that "[o]ur gun barrels / glowed white-hot." Komunyakaa draws from our traditions of religious and metaphysical poetry which often traffic in paradox and conceit: "There's no other way / to say this," he writes. "I fell in love." In the final gesture of the poem, the speaker turns the body over "so he wouldn't be / kissing the ground." Likewise, another poem drawing from traditions of religious poetry is "Thanks," which operates both as litany and prayer. A catalogue of moments where the speaker escapes death reveals how little stood in those instances between him and "a sniper's bullet" or booby trap. "What made me spot the monarch / writhing on a single thread / tied to a farmer's gate, / holding the day together / like an unfingered guitar string," writes the speaker, "is beyond me." The speaker's only sure knowledge is that he was surrounded by danger, not how he actually survived it: "I know that something / stood among those lost trees / & moved only when I moved."

Imagery, conceit, paradox, litany, and also the viscerally registered rhythm throughout: these are the visual and sonic elements of form that Komunyakaa so deftly employs to make his poems seen, felt, and heard. Robert Frost, in an effort to define or describe what he famously referred to as "the sound of sense," wrote that "One who concerns himself with *it* more than the subject is an artist" [emphasis mine]. It is one formulation of many versions of the same notion, namely that there is not only a distinction between form and content, but also that poets are those most concerned with the former over the latter. I have been told as much by writers and teachers for my entire life, and often enough, I've repeated versions of this same assertion myself. There are valid reasons, historical as well as contemporary, that an insistence is made to concentrate on formal choices when discussing or evaluating a poem. Content, I suppose the thinking goes, is intractable, territorial, personal. It is the *given*, not the *made*. But the notion that form and content are separable and distinct, and especially that the former is somehow more important than the latter, is a construct I've never felt happy with. It is hardly a radical thing to say, and yet sometimes it bears repeating: the content of poems matters in a primary way. To borrow an aphorism from William Blake, it is the "fire" that "delights in its form."

A powerful (and literally incendiary) example is "You and I Are Disappearing," in which a speaker describes witnessing a young woman burned in a napalm attack. The emphatic syntactical repetition of "she burns" accrues the power of incantation while each comparison evokes differing, even contradictory senses. She burns like paper (instantly consumed and crumbled), like foxfire (glowing eerily), like oil on water (inextinguishable), like poppies in a field (flame-colored). She also burns like a sack of dry ice (evoking body bags preserved to be sent home), like a banker's fat cigar (recalling the greed of those waging this war), like a glass of vodka or dragon smoke (alcohol and heroin, the self-medicating soldiers), in a "thigh-shaped valley" with a "skirt of flames" (evoking the erotic), like a burning bush (suggesting God, the supernatural). By the poem's end, so much additional content steadily accretes that one not only imagines the woman burning, but also the context and setting of Vietnam itself, the psychic toll of those who witnessed "with [their] hands / hanging at [their] sides," and, once again, the madness and cognitive dissonance of the war.

I suppose another way of thinking about this question of form and content is to acknowledge that we separate them as a way to ponder how they are fused and mutually supportive in a poem itself. I am fond of quoting Robert Creeley's assertion that "Form is never more than an extension of content," and in the ways I've just suggested, "You and I Are Disappearing" supports that well-loved assertion. But form, to put it slightly more insistently, does more than extend; it redoubles content. It is also that special content of the poem that is about poetry itself.

When I first encountered *Dien Cai Dau*, I was trying to write my own first book, comprised more or less of all the best poems I'd written thus far in my life. It was, in other words, a grouping motley in nature, a mash-up of trying my hand at different styles, received forms, subject matter, talking back to different poets and poems I'd read, and also trying to tell the story of my own life and landscapes. That summer I'd attended my first writers' conference, Bread Loaf, where I'd heard someone pontificating about the concept of a book of poems, something I listened to with great interest. If you had twenty-five poems, said this writer, the book of poems itself was the twenty-sixth poem. This way of thinking about a book as a book resonated with me; it likened the writing of a book of poems with the writing of a poem itself—as if every poem in the book were a line in that hypothetical twenty-sixth poem. I don't actually remember who even made this claim, but I do vaguely remember that they were quoting someone else whom I also don't remember. Having heard it at Bread Loaf, for many years I had concluded it must have been Robert Frost. But in recent years, reading and thinking about Frost more deeply, I've come to doubt it and have never managed to locate the quote in his work or anywhere else.

Dien Cai Dau is comprised of forty-three poems. While each of these poems stands on its own individually, and while so many of these poems also seem to hold conversations with other poems in the tradition, it is also undeniable that they build off each other, proceeding in a single sweep, without even the need for sections to separate or organize. They make a whole world, a specific setting, and in that setting, they tell the story of an individual speaker, a community, two nations at war, and the history of racism, capitalism, sexism, violence, popular culture, and art, among other things.

The first student in my correspondence course who completed the final lesson on *Dien Cai Dau* was, like many students in that course, incarcerated in the Indiana State Penitentiary. In his essay, he wrote that *Dien Cai Dau* was the first book of poems he'd ever read. He'd been so taken with the experience that he'd proceeded to read poems from it aloud to his fellow inmates, after which they'd exchanged stories about being in the military, about Vietnam. He wrote about what it was like to witness violence. About what it was like to be numb, or to want to be numb. About what it was like to be in the constant company of men. He wrote about desire, the way the men "inside" talked and thought about women. About the relationships with women "outside" that had fallen apart because of distance, as the soldiers in the poems had experienced. He also wrote about appreciating beauty, especially natural beauty, and of an awareness of gratitude for some grace that had nonetheless kept him alive, about how the poems still gave him hope. *Dien Cai Dau* had had a profound effect on him. At the end of his essay, he apologized for not talking enough about the form.

This student may not have tallied the imagery, pointed out the recognizable craft elements, but he had nothing to apologize for. He'd gone straight to the power and impact of the book's content. The resonances he described were those of the forty-fourth poem of *Dien Cai Dau*, content that in fact could never be exhausted. For me, that forty-fourth poem also included a new, more nuanced understanding of the inextricability rather than the distinction of what we think of as "form" versus "content." Encountering this book brought me closer to being the kind of reader, writer, teacher, and reader that I aspired to be.

Everyday Mojo Letters to Yusef

A series of creative reflections on why Yusef
Komunyakaa remains one of our greatest living
writers and what it means to be a Black Jazz Poet

START OF THE SIXTEENTH DRAFT
OF AN EXCESSIVELY WORDED DOCUMENT TITLED
"EVERYDAY MOJO LETTERS TO YUSEF"

Dear Yusef, I was thinking I'd write about your star in the genre of the
Black Jazz Poet, but I keep changing what I mean by Black and Jazz and
Poet. Such words come boxed in metaphor. Ken Burns, for example, said
the word "jazz" was derived from the scent of jasmine on prostitutes
when Louis Armstrong was a boy in New Orleans. The poetry of a Black
man gets romanticized and boxed in the same way. The difference be-
tween the jazz of Louis Armstrong and the jazz of Miles Davis says how
useless it can be to describe the spirit of jazz or Blackness or manhood.
To call you a Black jazz poet is to call you an elusive, walking metaphor.
I nod. Was it John Coltrane who said, "I don't play jazz I play John Col-
trane"? You are not simply writing "jazz poems" at this point, you are
writing "Yusef Komunyakaa." Duke Ellington was clearly playing Duke
Ellington. Maybe Quincy Jones comes closest to extending Ellington's
poise. "Jazz has always been a man telling the truth about himself," Jones
said. (A Black woman can be heard saying, *That might be why jazz is
dying, Quincy.*) Gordon Parks simply said jazz was inherently elusive:
"The meaning of it is as evasive as silence." I love Gordon Parks.

Like "jazz," the word "mojo" is one of those words that got its roots
clipped or crisscrossed during the Middle Passage. I read somewhere it
can be traced back to the West African medicine man. The root doc-
tor carrying cures for the body in a mojo hand. I know the griot's gris-
gris wards off griefs and ghosts. In the first poem in this collection, "A
World of Daughters," you write "one glimpses what one did not know"
and the sense echoes across the pages. I made evidence of it.* What does

*As a cento composed of twenty iterations of twenty years of knowing in *Everyday
Mojo Songs of Earth.*

it mean to *know* in *Everyday Mojo Songs of Earth*? It sounds less fixed than "knowledge." It's the kind of "knowing" that is glimpsed; it is insistent and fixed as a refrain. "A World of Daughters" makes me think of something you said about "Requiem," the last poem of the book, on the Poetry Society of America website: "I knew I wanted to attempt to capture a continuous motion, looping and winding, dredging up and letting go." Starting with new poems that lead back to new poems makes any reading of a selected poems "a continuous motion." For example, the intimate and allegorical pitch of "A World of Daughters" returns later in "Requiem." Or how the book feels wonderfully framed in prayer when I read "Prayer for Workers" in the new poems and later return to "Prayer" in *The Emperor of Water Clocks* (2015). The collection is also framed by those ghazals, "The Mountain" and "Ghazal, after Ferguson." In my most perfect world there would be a forthcoming collection of Yusefian jazz ghazals.

> "one glimpses what one did not know" "We know the men from women by the colors they wear" "He knows 'We Shall Overcome' & anthems of the flower children" "& the Angel knows defeat" "But I know when the question flew Into my head" "I need to know if iron tastes like laudanum Or a woman" "These ghosts know the power of suggestion is more than body language" "There's a pain inside of me, but I don't know where" "I know laughter can rip stitches, & deeds come undone in the middle of a dance" "I know all seven songs of the sparrow" "I mean, I also know something about night riders & catgut. Yeah, honey, I know something about talking with ghosts" "I've known of secret graves guarded by the night owl in oak & poplar" "I know all the monsters lurking in Lord Byron's verses" "I know, I also said I'd kiss the devil" "I know time opens an apple seed to find a worm." "I know the scent of belladonna" "I know hearsay can undo a kingdom." "I, too, know my Hopkins (Lightnin' & Gerard Manley)" "I know a dried-up riverbed & extinct animals live in your nightmares" "& now I know why I'd rather die a poet than a warrior, tattoo & tomahawk."

MOJO LETTER AFTER ERIK SATIE'S INSTRUCTIONS
FOR PLAYING *GNOSSIENNE* NO. 3

Dear Yusef, after Ed asked me to write about this new book, I dug out an interview we did in New York in the spring of 2002. I remember trying to get you to say things you hadn't said before about your influences, your ambitions, yourself. I have been circling back to one of my questions:

> In *Blue Notes* you said, "It is difficult for me to write about things in my life that are very private, but I feel I am constantly moving closer to my personal terrain, to the idea of trying to get underneath who I am." What are you doing to get closer to this more private terrain, and how do you draw the line between the Private and the Public, as a poet?

You slyly did not answer the question. I also dug out a brief, mediocre review of *Talking Dirty to the Gods* (2000) I wrote for the *Xavier Review* when I taught in New Orleans. I was so embarrassed when I read it, I decided to write you a letter of apology. I shuddered at my critiques of what I called your "leaps of obscurity" in the book. The tiny eyes of a young poet. Icarus critiquing the wings of Daedalus just before takeoff. I've learned to embrace the confusion I sometimes experience inside a poem. (Our young poets will ask for an example and I will say find your own damn example of confusion.) *Everyday Mojo Songs of Earth* got me thinking about the continuous motion between learning and knowing. I've spent the last two months poking at Erik Satie's *Gnossienne* No. 3 between poking around your poems. Satie's coinage of the word "gnossienne" is rooted in *gnosis*, the Greek word for knowledge. Satie's use of the word is not incidental to his interest in Gnosticism, but the original *gnosis* suggests the kind of circular, lyric, *open* knowledge that helps me think about you.

I've learned to look forward to the things I don't know—the room left inside a Yusef poem—the way I look forward to the room Satie leaves me in his compositions. His first and third *Gnossiennes* share similar motifs and patterns, but are written without bar lines or time signatures. The third is easiest, so I figured learning it would make learning the first easier. The waltz of the left hand is a dressed-up kind of blues minimalism. A "dressed-up kind of blues" works as a jazz definition sometimes. Satie, a famously weird dude, was, I suppose, afraid folks would not get the mysteries/obscurities of the *Gnossiennes*. He left a set of instructions specific to playing each piece. For *Gnossienne* No. 1, he advises the player to "wonder about yourself." I haven't started learning that one yet. For *Gnossienne* No. 3, he advises the player to "counsel yourself cautiously," and "be clairvoyant," "alone for a second," "Very Lost." I am still learning to feel clairvoyantly self-counseled in poems.

I don't believe we have ever actually talked about poems or poetry in all our years of hanging out. For our first poetry conference nearly twenty-five years ago, we listened to jazz with the wiry widow of an abstract expressionist amid the kayaks and canoes she rowed across Provincetown. Listening to music with you and Pat is on my list of top ten ecstatic life memories. Listening was feedback. You, Larry, Radi, and me listening to live jazz at the Candlelight Lounge is also somewhere on that as-yet unpenned list.

Readers will not be wrong, exactly, to highlight the presence of jazz in this book, but "The Candlelight Lounge" is as concerned with community as it is with music: "Faces in semi-dark cluster around a solo." Readers will not be any more wrong to highlight the presence of jazz in your poems than they would be to highlight the presence of jazz in the poetry of Michael S. Harper or Al Young. Y'all are as uniquely oriented— or about as harmonic in your love of jazz—as a room of uncles debating which song should be played at the Black jazz poet family reunion. Poems like "The Candlelight Lounge" measure the impact of the music as much as they track its construction. *Talking Dirty to the Gods* marks the transition to a kind of poem that can invoke jazz poetics with or without concerning itself with jazz as a subject. I could write about you and the genre of the Black Jazz Poet, but you keep changing what it means.

MOJO LETTER CANNIBALIZED BY A FAILED UNBOXING
VIDEO SCRIPT FOR *EVERYDAY MOJO SONGS OF EARTH*

On YouTube you can find a whole genre of these videos of people unboxing new stuff. I've seen a few smartphone unboxings, and a few sneaker unboxings, an unboxing of a compact automobile. I watched a few before writing my own unboxing script. The book arrives in a real box. "You want to come at it from as many angles as possible," I say, cutting into the cardboard where it is held by tape. Inside the book inside the box, I begin removing lines of poems and holding them up to the camera. The lines echo with innuendo and throw shadows. The lines look like electric transparent eel-shaped sentences evaporating at the mouth. "Yeah, honey, I know something about talking with ghosts." Everything in the box is useful. The top and bottom perspectives held up by four sides of perspectives. Make something with the box. Even if you have no glue and scissors, you can turn it into a legible surface or fortress or sculpture. Throw nothing away. "Do not necessarily subscribe," I say as I lower myself into the box of poems. I begin to hear sideways piano. Sometimes I will just sit and read Komunyakaa poems out loud in the unboxing video. These poems make a vintage entrance and provide vibrant everyday interactions. Inside the book inside the box, find poems never before seen by readers old and new. Storms, crows, gunmetal drones, shouts, circadian incantations, mantras of healing expand in the box. The liberty and music of musing & muscling mischief out of melancholy is packed into the box. "Great Ooga-Booga" almost rhymes with "didgeridoo." Inside the box a room of belladonna and jasmine mingle with a humid afternoon in New Orleans. "There's a pain inside of me, but I don't know where." "I know laughter can rip stitches, & deeds come undone in the middle of a dance." "I know all seven songs of the sparrow." Inside the box the brothers, sons, and nephews of James are not gone. "The mojo is a talisman and practice, a noun and action, and you, Reader," I say, shouting up from inside the box, "are privy to the everyday mojo songs of a psychic blues historian like Zora Neale Hurston and Sterling Brown. Yusef Komunyakaa is one of those fortune-tellers born of soothsayers who raise griots who live as teachers," I say, vanishing between the lines.

MOJO LETTER IN THE SPIRIT OF
THE YOUNG POET'S LETTER TO RILKE

"Go into yourself," Rainer Maria Rilke advises the military cadet and aspiring young poet, Franz Kappus, in *Letters to a Young Poet*. (I don't know if that's a thing a real poet needs to hear. It's incredibly useful for a reader though: instruction to "go into yourself" as you read.) There is no wrong way into the self. Kappus was a nineteen-year-old at the time he wrote Rilke, who was himself twenty-seven. The exchange might be more like undergraduate student to graduate student than mentee to mentor, were we not talking about Rilke. The other day I was shocked when one of our well-read young poets did not know your poem "Venus's-flytraps." That should be standard Komunyakaa canon by now. I dropped into your baritone: "I am five wading out into deep sunny grass." I played a couple recordings I have of you reading the poem. I directed him to my Vimeo bootleg mashup of you reading the poem over the railroad scene in Andrei Tarkovsky's *Stalker* and scenes from *Kirikou and the Sorceress.* Fanatic-fan-in-a-pandemic shit. I know almost no body of work better than I know yours. Or it may be better to say no body of work is more deeply in my blood than yours.

I remember when I was a young poet hearing your name for the first time. When I was nineteen or twenty, poet Judson Mitcham said what sounded like a foreign spell with a magical drawl. I knew only the poems of Black poets I found in literature anthologies when I was in college. Gwendolyn Brooks, Robert Hayden, Etheridge Knight, Amiri Baraka, Audre Lorde. I don't even think Rita Dove or Lucille Clifton were in some of those textbooks yet. When Mitcham visited my tiny, maybe-2,000-student-bodied campus in Hartsville, South Carolina, I got to sit with him and talk poems. At some point he wrote your name in fine southern cursive on a torn slip of paper. Not long after that, I bought my first poetry book, Jorie Graham's 1990 edition of *The Best American Poetry*, because I spotted you beside "Facing It." That poem rearranged my mind. (I think actually *Good Night, Willie Lee* was the first poetry book I bought, when I was fifteen, but it was because I had a crush on Alice Walker, not because of those very good poems. Someone should do a retrospective of Walker's poetry.)

Debates over *the* key Komunyakaa poem always include "Facing It," "Venus's-flytraps," "Anodyne." This new book only makes the debate more impossible to resolve. And the poem "Fortress" is reason enough to reread everything I've read before. How did I miss that poem? I shudder to think how much beauty is covered by blind spots. "Fortress" feels like some of the poems from *Magic City* carved down to nectar. When you write, "I see the back door / of that house close to the slow creek / where a drunken, angry man stumbles / across the threshold every Friday," the father reaching for a can of Jax at the opening of "My Father's Love Letters" echoes in my heart. You write, "I see forgiveness, unbearable twilight, / & these two big hands know too much / about nail & hammer." Hands open and reach across your poems. I could have found enough references to hands here for another mojo hand cento, but I stopped myself.

The last of my questions during that 2002 interview was: "When you think about being fifteen years old, what do you remember being obsessed with?" You answered: "Strangely enough, I was obsessed with building a greenhouse. I had drawn up all these elaborate plans and I thought that's what I would really do." Rilke tells the young poet to find his reason for writing: "confess to yourself whether you would have to die if you were forbidden to write." You say late in the book, "now I know why I'd rather die a poet than a warrior, tattoo & tomahawk." The work of the hands was to be part of whatever path opened before your clairvoyantly counseled fifteen-year-old self. I rejoice that they make such poems.

MOJO LETTER IN THE SPIRIT OF
VINCENT VAN GOGH'S LETTERS TO THEO

The distance between a café in Paris and the asylum in Arles may be in no way comparable to the distance between New Orleans and Bogalusa to the few souls on the planet to visit all four. Possibly only Yusef Komunyakaa has seen and said more about such worlds. All who dare summarize a poem must then be forced to summarize Thelonious Monk, *The Starry Night*, joy and shame. One of the plantations on the outskirts of a town somewhere has been converted into a spa of psychiatric poetics. But "psychiatric" it seems is metaphor for nightglow, psychokinetic, audiovisual sentences where what is seen and said of the world is music. The ghost of Professor Longhair plays a legless piano in a Van Gogh painting above the chameleon couch where the doctor's patients rest their eyes. The doctor has the patients read Komunyakaa poems as answers to their plights. All who dare summarize a painting must then be forced to summarize mojo, vibrato, bravado, taste. I love the singing double-talk between "ignis fatuus" and "fata morgana," the blue dementia of Orpheus at the gate between worlds. The photographs of Van Gogh's paintings projected on the walls of a museum somewhere in the distant future or far back as the cave of Plato, let us remember, are not the painter's paintings. I shudder to think how much beauty is covered by blind spots. With my eyes closed below the painting talking to the doctor, I begin to hear sideways piano. Music emanates from the painting when I look at it with my eyes closed. The ghost of Professor Longhair plays piano on the floor in a museum with walls covered in projections of Van Gogh's colored brushstrokes. The great Bogalusa poet has returned to town. A poem arrives every time Yusef Komunyakaa comes round.

MOJO LETTER IN THE SPIRIT OF
JAMES BALDWIN'S LETTER TO HIS NEPHEW

Dear Yusef, for the last month I have been circling back to the spirit of James Baldwin writing his fifteen-year-old nephew and namesake in 1962. Weren't you around fifteen in 1962 too? You talked about discovering Baldwin as a teenager during our interview in 2002. At the time I wondered whether those private essays in your files and yellow writing pads would ever see the light of day. They need not. The poems themselves are a response to the unspeakable grief shadowing those years. Poetry makes every day some kind of song. I am a witness. I imagine you a Black fifteen-year-old greenhouse dreamer reading Baldwin's letter to his namesake in the Bogalusa library. He might as well have been speaking to you. My father, James, was born four years after you. I guess you already know the name "James" is common among Black folks of a certain generation. You might be part of the Baby Boomer generation had you grown up middle class, safe, and White. Your generation heard word of Emmett Till's murder in real time. Baldwin means to instill in the younger James a sense of self rooted in the tangled realities/histories/impulses of America. He articulates, to my mind, an unprecedented expression of love for you in 1962. There are few other literary expressions of a Black man's love of another Black man, and most of those also are found in the writing of Baldwin. (I have been reading you in months following the riot of racists who raised a Confederate flag inside the Capitol. I mean who could have imagined it? ((Octavia Butler maybe. We'll discover she's the boss when we get to heaven.)) The riot surprised even our ability to imagine how much White people can get away with in this country.) 1962 is also the year Sonny Rollins released *The Bridge*. Do you know the story of his twelve to fifteen hours of practice a day on the Williamsburg Bridge? The title track reminds me of a manic, possibly panicked, lyrically frantic Bird accompanied by drummer, double bass, and Djangoistic guitarist. It's terrific, so live. Then it's followed by this mellow "God Bless the Child." Sometimes music is as close as we can get to prayer. Does the nephew write his uncle back? Was his name even really James? I could find nothing about him online. I imagine the Jameses pausing on the bridge where Rollins plays. "You come from a long line of great poets," Baldwin says in the letter. You are the kind of great poet he means, Yusef. You cross the bridge carrying the song.

MOJO LETTER IN THE SPIRIT OF
THE LETTER TO BOB KAUFMAN BY YUSEF KOMUNYAKAA

Inside the box my father's father's name waits to be found in a marvel of marble and stone erected inside your baritone warble. Emily Dickinson knew every poem is a letter to someone because every letter is a poem and said so because she had blackbirds for eyeballs. I say she was reborn as Bob Kaufman. The cries of Dickinson when she was alive sounded like hymns because the only songs she knew came from the Bible, whereas the cries of Kaufman continue to reverberate as silence. Two or three years before Kaufman transforms again someone drives him home to New Orleans for a final passage of respects, voodoo, and song. I read you as you read him and dance the Calinda with yourself like a poet from New Jersey. A house of stairs and shadows where you dream a spell for the root worker. Inside the box the brothers, sons, and nephews of James are not gone. Bob was right next door, God as my witness, floating two or three inches from the floor as he improvised a poem.

Off the Rim

Layups. Fast breaks.
We had moves we didn't know
We had. Our bodies spun
On swivels of bone & faith,
Through a lyric slipknot
Of joy, & we knew we were
Beautiful & dangerous.

Yusef Komunyakaa, "Slam, Dunk, & Hook"

1. *Layups. Fast breaks.*

When I was a freshman in college the only thing that mattered as much to me as playing basketball was watching basketball. Indiana University in Bloomington was at that time home of Bob Knight, Calbert Cheaney, Assembly Hall, and five NCAA Championship banners hanging in the rafters. It was also home to a monolith called the HPER—an acronym for School of Health, Physical Education, and Recreation. But for me, it was the name of the first indoor basketball facility where I could play as long and as often as I wanted for free.

The HPER is miraculous: fourteen regulation-sized basketball courts, and at any time of any day, there were people playing. Most days those people included me. Addressing Bertrand Russell's question: "Can human beings know anything?" in Philosophy 101? Bertrand Russell was no Bill Russell. Calculus quiz today? I'll be quizzing some scrub on how his ankles feel after I show him the chain rule of my crossover. Barely staying in school? That's okay, my three-point shot is like butter now, and that's got to count for something.

Literature was the only subject I managed easily because of the capaciousness of interpretation. Once sentence diagramming and *Animal Farm* were no longer the coin of the realm, I excelled. Poetry offered special opportunities for me as I stretched the narrow paint of my mind into something more extravagant. The exception was the class that should have been the easiest: Introduction to Creative Writing.

2. *We had moves we didn't know / We had*

Creative Writing was a class populated by variations of the same students who still turn up in Midwestern workshops today. Not as stereotypes, exactly, but those students for whom creation's particular gravity can exert itself: A nervous young woman who wrote diary entries about death and being sideswiped by love. A mumbler with long hair and a Black Flag tee concocting phallic similes involving coffins and lipstick. A football player looking to leapfrog Shakespeare for his English credits by writing haiku about the rigors of the field. Me, solo minority with a pen, fulfilling the quota.

I was the personification of William Matthews's poem: ". . . I was seventeen, / and so I swung into action and wrote a poem, // and it was miserable . . . " Even though the instructor said I was "well spoken," I didn't know anything about poetry. My high school English teacher skipped the poetry lesson because she assumed we wouldn't understand it. As far as I could tell, a line break may as well have been the rest between wind sprints.

But just like in basketball, everything fundamental is built on something creative and recognizing that was something you either had or did not have. Like knowing when to cut to the bucket or fade to the top of the key. Like the difference between Michael Jordan reversing on Shaq in the playoffs and a "reverse layup." Cannonball Adderley called it "hipness" when he said "Hipness isn't a state of mind; it's a fact of life," but what he was really talking about is creativity and I was drawn to that fact of life. The thing that differentiated my poetic moves from others in the class was that my writing was somehow spiced with Black Arts rhetoric. I was the token in class, just as I was the token in nearly every space in Bloomington except the basketball court.

It was my workshop leader who first suggested I speak with Yusef Komunyakaa. When I asked how to spell his last name, she said, "Don't worry about it. Everyone calls him 'Yusef.'" Honestly, I was ready to understand what Komunyakaa was doing poetically. My favorite poem at the time (which is still in my top 5) was Etheridge Knight's "Feeling Fucked Up," a poem that diverges from Komunyakaa's aesthetic in most ways except the deep insistence of jazz and blues. So when I read Yusef's poems, they reminded me of my uncles talking about Al Green while they shared a bottle: old school before I recognized how good old school can be.

I later realized Yusef's poetry has a polyphonic swing, a lyrical motion through narrative that is so incredibly intricate that it seems effortless—the same way a layup isn't all that impressive until you consider how many thousands of coordinated muscle movements are necessary for success.

3. *swivels of bone & faith, / Through a lyric slipknot*

I hadn't been to a professor's office yet, and I didn't know anything about the etiquette of office hours or appointments, so I didn't understand how inappropriate it is to demand an audience with a faculty member. I hadn't written more than ten pages of words—poetry or prose—either, so when I banged on that wooden door and an intense man opened it, I was not intimidated or impressed: a poet doesn't seem poetic until you know what poetry can be.

Yusef very politely told me to wait my turn, and I agreed to do so. It makes me laugh to recall that one of the reasons I stayed is because he mentioned the Lone Ranger—my favorite black-and-white television character when I was a child—in one of his poems. There was something rumbling in his words—and his accent, which was the verbal equivalent of a '70s strut—that made me think that talking with him might be a good thing.

It's exactly right that Yusef was working on the concept for *Talking Dirty to the Gods* while in Bloomington. The book both glorifies and questions the underbelly of mythology (poetic or otherwise), and there was a mythos surrounding him at Indiana University, even before he won the Pulitzer.

His appearances never caused anyone to cancel class like one of Bob Knight's open practices, but his free readings at the Runcible Spoon became social events more like concerts than poetry readings. The readings were meant to help the coffee shop stay in business by bringing in the coffee buyers, and getting there early was a must: a few hours in advance for a seat, at least an hour early for a spot inside. Latecomers were relegated to the outside, where speakers that sounded like someone was holding up a phone to a jukebox amped whatever was going on in the back room. But they'd stay out there, listening, whether the snow was shoveled or not.

Appreciating none of this at the time, I returned to his office after a cup of coffee at the Runcible Spoon, having reread my fistful of poems. The first thing I said to him was, "Yusef, when you read my poems and see how good they are, will you kick one of the students out of your class so I can be in?"

I was so intent on delivering my loud-mouth declaration that I didn't even notice that his office hours were already over; that he was in the middle of writing a poem when I banged on the door; that I didn't really believe my poems were that good; and that creative writing workshops at Indiana are not merit-based. Unlike pickup ball, the classes are filled on a first-come, first-served basis, without consideration for skill. I couldn't see any of this because I approached writing and talking about poetry in the same way I approached basketball: In order to get picked up for a game, you have to act like you can play.

It was only in retrospect that the validity of Yusef's looking at me at first as if I owed him money became clear. But then he smiled and said simply, "You know . . . everyone thinks they're good," and asked if I had poems to show him. "No, not with me," I said as I backed toward the door thinking, "This old man just punked me out."

4. & we knew we were / Beautiful & Dangerous.

I spent the next three years working on my poetic chops. I was going to show Yusef who was good. I cut my basketball playing down to roughly four days a week. I rarely went out with my friends on the weekends. I spent hours listening to The Pharcyde, Fela Kuti, and Miles Davis, trying to find a way to distill music into words. I read and reread *Magic City*, looking for the right words to distill. I'd show Professor Yusef Komunyakaa the difference between somebody with game and somebody who thinks he has game.

During that time, I learned a bit more about poetry and about the uniqueness of Yusef's poetic statements. I learned how a poem's logic can tattoo itself into the brain so that "She burns" must be followed with "like a burning bush / driven by a godawful wind." Or why it just makes sense that "August is a good time / for a man to go crazy," especially in the Midwestern humidity.

But no amount of reading or admiration for the power of his poetry could slow my urge for a rematch with Yusef. Even if I did hide behind the first available tree every time I saw him walking across campus, scribbling in his notebook. Even if I couldn't figure out how to write a poem about basketball because "Slam, Dunk, & Hook" said all I had to say about hoops.

In the fall of my senior year, I was ready: with a sheaf of poems in my clutch, I registered for Yusef's workshop. He'd just won the Pulitzer for *Neon Vernacular*. When I walked into his class, ready to re-present, he wasn't even there. Roger Mitchell, the head of the MFA program, was the last-minute replacement because Yusef was on sabbatical. He didn't return until after I'd graduated.

But in 2002, I had the good fortune to finally study with Yusef at Cave Canem, a writer's retreat for Black poets. It was the first time I had spoken with him since I ran out of his office eleven years before. He had just finished judging the Bakeless Prize, for which my manuscript was a finalist but didn't win. So I still felt the need to show him that I had poetic skill.

Even before I'd turned in my hoop gear for good during graduate school, I had come to realize how impressive a writer Yusef is. His poetic rockings between demons and drums make their own unique lyric and narrative concoction—one whose complexity has both confused and invigorated me more than any other poet's. What I mistook at nineteen as being old-school aesthetic was, in fact, Yusef breaking poetry's ankles.

When I caught up with Yusef on the first day of Cave Canem, after several years of reflection on how I'd disrespected him, there was a whole lot more hat in my hand than there had been at our first meeting. He somehow remembered our brief encounter, though not as graphically as I did ("Did I say that?" he asked with a smile), but his response to my questions about my manuscript was more detailed.

We talked for about two hours, and he spent that time pointing out some of the fundamental things in the manuscript that weren't effective—from the opening poem to the arrangement of the sections. We talked about approach and intent, writing rhetoric and the basics of poetry. One of the most important suggestions he gave me was about the working title, "The Nature of Skin." Yusef told me straight up, "Change it. There are too many books of poetry around with 'skin' in the title." Later that week, he compounded things by pointing out that "a bad title is like a dunce cap on a poem." I'd spent a very long time trying to come up with a poetic title for my book, and an equally long time trying to come up with a poetic sensibility for myself. But Yusef's dunce cap simile reminded me of an experience at a basketball camp I attended as a teenager. Steve Alford—the hardworking jump shooter who would lead Indiana University to an NCAA title in 1987—preached to us the importance of persistence, of addressing the fundamentals.

He said, "Practice free throws and jump shots every day. You never know when you'll get the chance to shoot a layup, but you can always shoot a jump shot." I wasn't even trying to hear what Alford was saying; in my mind, jump shots were for people who didn't have enough game to take it to the cup. But what was impressive about Alford's talk was that he wasn't a disembodied lecturer, detached from his subject matter. The whole time he was speaking, he was also shooting free throws— one hundred straight without a miss, "Nothing but a hot / Swish of strings like silk."

Like Alford, Yusef is a teacher, practitioner, and walking example of tenacity. Asked what he wanted his work to be remembered for, Yusef said, "Persistence." Indeed, his success can be attributed in part to his relentless follow-through: his refusal to turn away from any of the possibilities in poetic invention, whether manifested as freewheeling verbs, imagistic improvisation, or trochee'd aggression. That poetic persistence creates possibility is something Yusef unconsciously introduced me to in Bloomington and reiterated at Cave Canem. It may be true that everyone thinks they are good, but Yusef Komunyakaa's poetry—his willingness to share and instruct—proves time and time again that he is the one who truly has game.

Dice in a Hard Time Hustle
Yusef Komunyakaa & Etheridge Knight, 1988–1991

I am this space / my body believes in
    Yusef Komunyakaa, from "Unnatural State of the Unicorn"

His time is not my time / but I have known him / in a time gone.
    Etheridge Knight, from "He Sees Through Stone"

Roots and All

At the beginning of my first Free People's Poetry Workshop in India-napolis, in the summer of 1989, Etheridge Knight rolled his eyes up to the Heavens and arched them from left to right until they landed on me with a glance, "We ain't in this workshop to give no A's & B's." Just a little more than a year and a half earlier, I had been encouraged by a creative writing friend at Indiana University, "You should apply for Yusef Komunyakaa's poetry class next semester." Going into that next semester, it should have been my final senior semester. Academically, though, I was barely a sophomore. Debt towered so high I feared that not even discovering a shipwreck of Spanish doubloons could pay it off someday. So, in January 1988, my goal was to take one class that would save my life.

Yusef's poetry class that semester was in the evening, a 400-level class; therefore, one needed to submit poems beforehand in order to earn admission. During the afternoon of that cold January day, I found his office in Ballantine Hall and slipped three poems under his door with a note: "Dear Professor Komunyakaa, I hope to join the class; here are three of my poems. I will go to the classroom ten minutes early for your response. Thank you for your consideration." When I arrived at the classroom fifteen minutes early, he was already there sitting comfortably with his materials. His presence took me by surprise. Most professors would have arrived on time or a minute tardy. He motioned for me to sit and I sat down on the same side of the long table that he was sitting on; he pushed an enrollment slip forward with two fingers. With no other students in the room, he made small talk, "Where are you from?"

"Indianapolis," I replied.

"Indianapolis has a rich jazz history," he countered. Fortunately, during high school, my best friends, Mike and Osho, were in the all-city high school jazz band. Just being around them blessed me with a sense of Indianapolis jazz history and its icons like Wes Montgomery and his brothers, Monk and Buddy, J. J. Johnson, Freddie Hubbard, Slide Hampton, The Hampton Sisters, and the legendary Indiana University jazz educator and cellist David Baker, who performed with my friends as part of his quest to teach jazz at all academic levels across the Hoosier state. Yusef may have thought me peculiar compared to IU students interested in hits or underground bands. That semester Yusef complimented my imagery and lifted the blinds covering the windows of a poem's possibilities. He gave me a B+. It didn't matter. My light was lit. Poetry connected and distilled everyday life and in that discovery the entire trajectory of my life changed.

Amorphous and Cumulative

Prior to petitioning for Yusef's course, I had read his poems in *The Morrow Anthology of Younger American Poets*. Once in his workshop class, acquiring his collections became a mission. *Copacetic* set my synapses on fire. *I Apologize for the Eyes in My Head* sliced the threads anchoring down my dreamworld and painted a whole new surreal terrain. The closing lines, "I am this space my body believes in," from the poem "Unnatural State of the Unicorn" became somewhat of a mantra. Delving beyond Yusef's poetry, the interview "Lines of Tempered Steel" conducted by Vicente F. Gotera proved instructive. I underlined the sentences until the whole thing was different colors of ink. A couple points Yusef made resounded into psychic detonations:

"At one time, I saw all of my experiences in a negative context; that's probably true of most of us. But I see those now in more of a positive framework, and that's good for me. It's liberating, necessary for growth." In the same interview, while responding to Vicente Gotera's question about his definition of poetry, Yusef replied: "Poetry is so difficult to define, I think, because it's constantly changing, growing. It's becoming something else in order to become itself—amorphous and cumulative until it forms a vision."

Poetry: amorphous and cumulative. Life: amorphous and cumulative.

The phrase "amorphous and cumulative" and the idea of seeing one's experiences in a positive framework in order to be liberated from them was like being given a magic prescription. One of my earliest questions for him was "How does one avoid living as a victim?" He pursed his lips, shifted his jaw and answered, "Essentially, one has to change the title in their head." So, while driving around Indiana, in my desperation to discover a life, I imagined positive thoughts pasted onto the highway billboards. I ended up taking twelve credit hours with Yusef by the time of graduation, four different workshops or literature courses and two independent studies. There was one other class but it doesn't appear on my university transcripts. In the spring semester of 1989, not too long before meeting Etheridge Knight, I enrolled in another poetry workshop with Yusef but was cut when the dough for tuition couldn't be raised. I kept attending anyway. Years later, in 1995, when Yusef did a brief residency and reading at George Mason University, while I was in the creative writing program there, I asked him if he had ever noticed the absence of my name from that final roll. He replied, "I was curious about that."

Kah doom / Kah doom-doom

After having failed to pay for tuition that 1989 spring semester, I went into that summer resigned to drop out of university for an extended hiatus that likely would have become a black string of days forevermore. I left Bloomington, scurried back to Indianapolis, and scraped up one job as a server and another landscaping and excavating. To hold onto a thread of poetry, I attended the open mic poetry readings organized by the Indianapolis Writers' Center at the famed Slippery Noodle Inn, a blues bar which once was a station on the underground railroad and a hideout for the John Dillinger gang. The Writers' Center held their open mic readings there every second and fourth Tuesday of the month. So, on August 8th, 1989, after finishing a closing shift at the restaurant, I bounced into my 1989 Hyundai Excel and sped through a mess of yellow lights straight down Meridian Street from the northside in hopes of squeezing into one of the final spots before the event concluded. Upon arrival, the reading was going on. I whispered to the host stationed in the back, "May I do a couple poems?"

Her first answer was polite but firm, "I am sorry we just have one more person."

"Please, I just drove all the way across town after work."

"OK," she said. "You can go after Etheridge Knight."

Etheridge sat with a small squad of eclectic folks at the front. They congealed into a vibrant oil painting. Etheridge's work first circled into my life via his appearance in the Donald Hall anthology *Contemporary American Poetry* and the Dudley Randall anthology *The Black Poets*. By the time this evening came along, the covers of my *Essential Etheridge* and *Poems from Prison* were already frayed. Etheridge took the stage. He said several poems, including "Hard Rock Returns from the Hospital for the Criminally Insane" and "He Sees Through Stone." At this point, Etheridge had not yet discovered that he had cancer. He had recently returned to Indianapolis from Philadelphia to be near family and to get regular medical care at the local VA hospital after being struck by a car while crossing the street. His leg was severely and permanently impaired. Despite his pain and suffering from the injury that I didn't yet know about, he was in playful spirits, and closed with "Last Words Sung By Slick." Knowing I was next as a last-minute add-on, my Adam's apple slid down my throat until it kahdoomed itself in my stomach like a cannonball.

Etheridge garnered an electric round of applause; the host said, "We have one more reader tonight who just showed up and his name is Kenneth." The first two times I had been to the Writers' Center readings, which were my first-ever performances, Etheridge wasn't there. I read off paper. The pages shook in my hands like hummingbird wings. Consequently, I decided to ditch the paper and commit poems to memory in order to diminish the appearance of anxiety in front of an audience. When I summoned the gumption to peek at Etheridge, entrenched at the table directly in front of the stage, his glasses were at the tip of his nose and his eyes were double full moons lasering through my skull. His mouth was ajar. That cannonball churned in my stomach. I worried that it might go farther south and I almost pissed down my leg faster than Karl Amorelli in the woods. It was intimidating and confirming at the same time. Retreating from his gaze, I scanned the room and spied the back corner near the host and glimpsed a beautiful woman.

Once the poetic festivities concluded, everyone mingled. I drifted towards Etheridge and his crew. In his mix were painter Stephen Stoller, poet Francy Stoller, poets Sonny Bates and Michael L. L. Collins, and prose writer Herman Salinas of Indianapolis. Warm and enthusiastic greetings flowed. Laughter abounded and smiles shone all around. They mentioned their Free People's Poetry Workshops and that "You should come." Etheridge said something like, "I was impressed that you knew your work." Little did I know that right there in that small group were three of my future six poetry and art mentors—Etheridge, Stephen, and Francy—and even less did I know that the host that night, poet Elizabeth Krajeck, would become a fourth, and that the beautiful woman I glimpsed from the stage and who departed amidst a mountain range of heads and shoulders turned out to be her daughter, and that the two of us would fall madly in love at the next open mic two weeks later, but that's a whole other story.

The Free People's Poets

Etheridge Knight and the Free People's Poetry Workshop became an instant part of my life. I quit playing sports. In the years after Etheridge's release from prison in 1968, he held workshops in Indy at a place called the Bluebird Café. Twenty years later he's back in town and another workshop has sprung up around him. For the rest of that August of 1989, my time vanished while working at the restaurant and at construction sites, or hanging out with Etheridge and the Free People's at the Slippery Noodle, the Denouement art gallery owned by the Stollers, Mugwumps Café (where workshops were held), the Chatterbox jazz bar, or at Etheridge's apartment, 18-J, in a building affectionately referred to as the Triple Nickel because it sat at 555 Massachusetts Avenue. Soon after, poet Elizabeth Gordon McKim whizzed into Naptown like a comet from Boston. She was Etheridge's beloved at the time. They called each other "elizabethridge." They worked diligently on a book-length interview manuscript during this period, called "Freedom and Confinement." Elizabeth became the fifth of my six mentors.

With Etheridge coming fiercely out of the oral tradition, the Free People's Poetry Workshops were conducted quite differently from university ones. First off, everyone in the workshop was of vastly different ages. Secondly, more cultural diversity sat at the table, and attendees came from every occupation and financial stratosphere. The most glaring difference: no one passed out photocopies of poems. Poems were said, listened to, and not read. We began from the left of the workshop facilitator, from the side of the heart, and went around to the right.

Poems were workshopped orally. Sometimes poems were recited again or parts of them were repeated and those parts were workshopped more heavily. If someone didn't have a poem to share, Etheridge would still encourage them: "Go ahead. Say your piece." And the group would talk about what that person expressed.

This method of workshopping led to different kinds of critique. Discussion would encapsulate when to take a breath, or where to emphasize a word or phrase more or less intensely, to find, in all the poem's phrases, the rhythm of a river and the natural music in language. Poems were workshopped for content, imagery, music, theme, etc., but also for performance, especially how to "take the space" (embrace the moment) on stage and deliver the poem to an audience with confidence. He once said, "The poet's job is to enlighten and entertain."

Ultimately, his critique was about putting more tools in the poet's poetry and performance toolbox. He declared, "Someone told me I shouldn't use rhyme in my poems. That's like asking a carpenter to throw away his hammer." Everything about the Free People's Workshop added up to Etheridge's credo: "The Poem/The Poet/The People." It was the poet's job to relay the poem to the people, whether or not you were Etheridge Knight or his neighbor Chuck White, the alto sax player who hadn't blown a riff in years, but who tried to compose a handful of words one night from the ashes in an ashtray into lines that would charm Medusa's snakes.

The absolute and ultimate core of the Free People's Workshop consisted of Etheridge Knight, Elizabeth Gordon McKim, Steve and Francy Stoller, Sonny Bates, and Michael L. L. Collins. Sonny and Michael were pallbearers. When Etheridge became sick, then sicker and sicker, they were the ones who cared for him the most (apologies to anyone who is left out of my memory). Sonny Bates ran countless missions and drove Etheridge everywhere around Indy in his convertible brown Jeep with the top down.

Etheridge and Steve Stoller collaborated on an exhibition called *Freedom and Fame*, a celebration of painting, poetry, and music. The event had a number of civic sponsors, including the Indiana Pacers, via Stephen's friendship with then-Pacers general manager Donnie Walsh, the two of them being NYC transplants in the Hoosier state. Those of us in the workshop performed as part of the undercard. The two-night event unveiled Stephen Stoller's epic painting of "Etheridge Knight & The Free

People's Poetry Workshop." Stephen commented that he started out trying to do an individual portrait of Etheridge, but it failed to capture his total essence and embrace; therefore, he decided to paint the portrait of Etheridge with the Free People's Poets in a workshop setting. The painting hung for a long time at the Indiana State Museum. The painting remains in the possession of the Stollers. A phrase from one of Elizabeth Gordon McKim's poems, "We are all scared and we are all sacred / We are all sacred and we are all scared" became another mantra for most of us.

The Heart of a Poem

So much happened so fast in three weeks. The autumn 1989 semester loomed ahead, and boosted by the Free People's, falling in love with Elizabeth Krajeck's daughter, and thinking of connecting with Yusef again and telling him about the month spent with Etheridge Knight, I decided to move out of my apartment and into my budget car, a 1989 Hyundai Excel with a broken air con, a faulty tape deck, and a dented right side. I stopped paying monthly rent to a landlord and applied those funds for tuition during the course of the semester.

In a year and a half since first meeting Yusef, the line of students waiting to confer with him during his office hours went from nonexistent to stretching down the hall and almost to Detroit. When I told Yusef about meeting Etheridge Knight and workshopping with him for the last month, it caught him off guard. He paused for a moment and mentioned a letter he received from Etheridge about poetry and music. The letter can be read under Etheridge's bio in *The Jazz Poetry Anthology*, which Yusef co-edited with Sascha Feinstein. We talked a little more about my experiences with Etheridge. I mentioned to Yusef that Etheridge knew he was my teacher and offered to arrange a meeting between them. Yusef said, "Yes, that'd be great."

Besides changing colors, the trees that autumn were waving hello and goodbye at the same time. Sleeping in my car at construction sites, the restaurant parking lot, friends' homes, and the Indiana University Memorial Union, or wherever became normal. Everything shimmered. Then unsettling news hit: cancer had darkened Etheridge's lungs. Prospects were grim. Etheridge had recently workshopped Sonny Bates and I all night. He poured us two tall glasses of warm vodka. No ice. No water.

No tonic. He drank his. We sipped ours. Etheridge advised about building a body of work, "If I look at a poet's body of work and I don't see a poem about their momma and their daddy and their family, then I don't trust them!" He also commented that when he was released from prison he was simply released into the larger prison of society. Etheridge decreed, "It's your divine right to travel the world. Don't let anyone tell you that you can't see the world. Borders are just bigger prisons. In my sixtieth year, my dream is to travel the world with Elizabeth," but now with the cancer diagnosis that dream was floating off like a yellow balloon.

I shared the jarring cancer news about Etheridge with Yusef. A meeting between them hadn't even been arranged yet. By this point, I stopped visiting Yusef's office and joined him at Mother Bear's Pizza for Thursday's Jazz Fables series featuring players from the Indiana University jazz program. Jazz cellist and educator David Baker, whom I had seen perform with my high school friends years prior, often played at these sessions. The musicians played the entire jazz songbook. Once, when the Duke Ellington song "Prelude to a Kiss" was introduced, Yusef leaned across the table and whispered, "Good title." Another time, poet William Matthews visited IU. Yusef ushered him straight to Jazz Fables. I sat there with them both, kept my mouth mostly shut and listened to them discuss jazz, poetry, and everything else! At one point, I asked a question about improvisation and revision. Yusef gave a wry smile and replied, "You have to be careful not to polish the heart out of a poem."

Winners Already

Yusef doesn't drive. He has never driven a car. So when the date was arranged for Yusef and Etheridge to meet in Indianapolis, it was the first of countless road trips we would take together. Usually, I picked him up at his home on tree-lined Washington Street in Bloomington. Over the years, we drove through Indiana and the Midwest for various readings of his and other events. We saw Terence Blanchard spit sirens through his trumpet and sweat through his clothes at an outdoor show hosted by the Indianapolis Art Museum. We caught Gwendolyn Brooks at the Madam Walker Theater on Indiana Avenue, the traditional heart of the African American community in Indianapolis and from where all the Indy jazz legends sprang. At the end of Gwendolyn's reading, Yusef and I stood in line for her signature. I was next to last. For me, she inscribed her famous lines from "The Second Sermon on the War-pland," from her collection *In the Mecca*: "Conduct your blooming in the noise and whip of the whirlwind." Yusef was last in line. She signed the books of hers that he held in his hands. I drifted from them so they could have a private moment. From what I could tell, they had a gentle and polite chat.

A road trip that those who went reminisce about often is when we journeyed to the Chicago Art Institute for the exhibition, *Degenerate Art: The Fate of the Avant-Garde in Nazi Germany*. The general feeling and belief from our group that day was that America likely would not relapse in such a way as Nazi Germany, but, you never know. Thirty-one years later, now we know. That evening we checked out the famous Poetry Slam led by Marc Smith at the Green Mill Cocktail Lounge. Sonny, Michael, and I signed up for the open and slam sections. Yusef signed up for the open section only. No one recognized Yusef, even though *Dien Cai Dau* had been published to acclaim. He even wrote his name on the signup list as "Yusef." In the open section, the order was Michael, me, Sonny, and Yusef, who read some *Magic City* poems. After Yusef stepped off the stage, Marc Smith exclaimed, "Hey, these guys from Indianapolis are pretty good!" In the slam section, with no local support, the three of us didn't make it past the second round, but we were winners already. We were with Yusef.

Summit at the Triple Nickel

Highway 37 between Bloomington and Indianapolis cuts through a swath of land famous for Klan activity. My cousins lived there during my youth. On the way, I told Yusef the legend about Etheridge some old geezer hawked one night at the back end of the bar at the Chatterbox: "Etheridge had a Cadillac on a Friday and over the weekend sold it to three different suckers and left town driving it on Monday." Yusef is on record as saying that you can go from sea to shining sea collecting Etheridge stories. Etheridge is like Charlie Parker in this sense. Around Indy, discovering a new Etheridge story was like running into the same person all over town. Everyone had an Etheridge story, but with Etheridge it could feel like you were hearing about a different person. Some legends stretch to say that Etheridge never served in Korea. Once, when I chauffeured Etheridge to the Slippery Noodle, he hunched down and tilted sideways into my Hyundai Excel and commented in a tone that was question and answer, "This here is a Korean car."

"Yes," I replied.

"Americans don't say it right," he continued. "It's not 'HYUN-DIE.' It's 'HYUN-DAY.'" Years and years later, after I moved to Busan, South Korea, I learned that Etheridge was right. Americans say it in American English. Even as a seventeen-year-old soldier, in Busan during the Korean War, before he discovered poetry, Etheridge possessed a sensitivity to language—in this case, Korean language. He remembered the music of it, and Americans were getting the music wrong.

Yusef and I pulled into the small parking lot outside Etheridge's building. Sonny Bates had arranged Etheridge's apartment through his job doing living-assistance placement. Etheridge's monthly rent was nine bucks. We swung the car doors shut. Yusef surveyed the neighborhood and looked up at the building and beyond it into the sky. The security guard spied me nearing the electrical panel with Yusef and buzzed us in before I could press the button. We took two steps in, and before the door could clang and lock behind us, Etheridge lumbered across our path towards the cigarette machine with its levers and handles. "Oh, Etheridge," I said, hesitating a couple beats so Yusef could maneuver from the doorway and line up directly with Etheridge, "Etheridge Knight, this is Yusef Komunyakaa. Yusef Komunyakaa, this is Etheridge Knight."

Several hours of respectful talk passed in Etheridge's apartment before heading across the street to Mugwumps Café and Bar for our regular Free People's Poetry Workshop. Etheridge sat on the chair that served as his throne. Yusef reclined on the sofa. The immediate kinship between Yusef and Etheridge was sewn before they met. They had already traded letters. Places like Mississippi, Louisiana, Korea, and Vietnam were sewn into the fabric of their human fiber. They displayed a quiet admiration of qualities and experiences the other embodied. Etheridge, the so-called street poet, played an honorable host, and Yusef, honored academic, comported himself as a homespun guest. Etheridge talked the most, and we listened. Yusef chimed in with remarks like closing notes in a ballad.

Etheridge expounded about being videotaped: "If I let myself be videotaped then these schools don't need me to show up and do a reading or talk, and I don't get paid." This partly explains why there are not a lot of

Etheridge videos out there in the world. After being released from prison in 1968, Etheridge lived off "poeting." Etheridge also discussed how poets can be from different directions, "The Chinese and Japanese poets are the East. Their poetry is a poetry of nature. It's where the sun rises. In the north, you have the academic poets, because their poetry is associated with the mind. Walt Whitman, Allen Ginsberg, and the Beat poets are poets of the west, going out with their long lines across America. Poets from the south are poets of the belly."

The workshop Yusef participated in was heavily attended. Everyone knew he was going to be there in advance. The respect and reverence Yusef and Etheridge had for each other in the apartment carried over into the workshop, and it trickled down from there into everyone. Yusef, as he often did in his university workshops, mostly laid in the cut. Everyone else made comments first, but he was mindful to slip in his illuminating critiques when he was sure that Etheridge would have the last word before moving onto the next poet and poem. At this workshop, I shared a linked haiku poem consisting of five haiku. Etheridge loved haiku, and haiku was an essential element in his work. Michael L. L. Collins is on the verbal record as saying, "Everything Etheridge did was based on haiku and five syllables." "We Free Singers Be" and "Born of a Woman" serve as two of his five syllable examples. About my haiku Etheridge commented, "A haiku needs four things: it has to have something living, a sense of season, motion, and a cut of going from one place to another."

Yusef's visit with Etheridge went over so well that Etheridge lent his grace again and opened his home the following weekend to a group of Yusef's students that I mixed in with Free People's poets Sonny Bates and Donita Parrish. We did some free association. Etheridge instructed us to close our eyes and say whatever popped into our heads. So we closed our eyes, but the six of us were way too nervous to begin. How can anyone say anything before Etheridge? The silence elongated. Kevin and I broke the rules and opened one eye, looking at each other like "WTF!" Finally, Etheridge broke the dam and his line wiggled in the water: "My heart is beating." Dying of cancer and surrounded by young aspiring poets he barely knew, or had just met, and he exhibited his capacity to be intimate with anyone by saying, "My heart is beating." The next verbal contributions from us were, "the darkness is all around," and "I pick it up in my hands," and "It's new." The last hour produced an exquisite corpse poem called "A Poem By All of Us" that Etheridge titled. Etheridge wrote the first three lines. The paper was passed around the circle from the side of the heart as usual. It came around to the right, and I had to write the last three lines. It took a while. Sonny exhaled, "Goddamn, Kenneth." Etheridge said, "The last lines are important. Take your time." Jenny Okeon, from Memphis, read it. When she finished, Etheridge levitated up from his chair, saying, "The sand boxes and monkey bars at the end go back to the buildings and the lights of the city at the beginning."

On and Off, On Now

From the time of their first meeting to Etheridge's death, there were several hang outs which included both Yusef and Etheridge. April 19th, 1990, Etheridge's last birthday, stands out. That night Etheridge gave a reading at Butler University with Carolyn Forché. In the days prior to the reading, Etheridge said, "I am so happy to be reading with Carolyn on my birthday." He adored her as kin in the struggle for poetry, justice, and betterment. Fans, friends, and students packed the large lecture room. They stood in the back and along the sides. They sat on the steps in the aisles between the sections. We found seats in the middle. Carolyn read first, and after listening to her read I decided to apply for George Mason University's MFA program, where I eventually studied with Carolyn, Peter Klappert, and C. K. Williams, who had once taught Yusef. Etheridge summoned all of his powers at this reading. He sang, "Willow Weep for Me," read and said poems from the *Essential Etheridge*, and closed with his favorite poem at the time: "Where Is the Poet?" by Melissa Orion, the only poem by someone else that he wished he would have written. The only known surviving photo of Yusef and Etheridge together was taken at this event by Alexander Mouton.

Yusef and I hung out more often, too, sometimes at the Runcible Spoon, a coffee roastery with a brunch menu that was popular with alternative crowds. On May 29th, 1990, a Tuesday, we met for coffee. I presented him with my worn paperback copy of *Copacetic* and asked him to sign it. He replied, "Hmm, is it okay if I give this back to you next Tuesday?"

"Sure," I replied.

The next week, I show up early and he's already there again. He hands me back my copy of *Copacetic*. "Here," he says. Only, it's not mine, I think. It's heavier. It's a hardback. Awareness washes across my mind: "Ah, he switched out the paperback for a hardback." Opening the hardback, his elegant signature crests across the page:

For Kenneth—

The shape of our lives
Go into who we are
willing to become.

Peace,
Yusef

with admiration &
respect.

The date: June 5, 1990. This inscription inspired me to continue finding an identity and life in the world of poetry and art. In Bloomington, Indiana, inspired by Yusef and Etheridge, I started organizing my first-ever poetry and art events, including one at the Runcible Spoon where Yusef was the feature poet, while poet Kevin Elmore and myself served as supporting readers. Kevin expressed nervousness and Yusef deadpanned, "Sometimes you have to face the crowd."

On New Year's Eve, 1990, we gathered at the home of Sonny Bates for Etheridge's last time to witness the year change. The night began with cheerful tones and musical tunes. No one talked about Etheridge's cancer much, openly. Folks talked poetry. Despite their age differences, Yusef and Etheridge could talk to each other across the decades. They had so many similarities—both African American men from the deep South, both war veterans and poets, both able to code-switch and play the game of life that appeared in the heat of a moment. Just before midnight, Yusef and I spotted Etheridge sitting in a chair alone by the cracked-open window. Etheridge moaned and swayed. Sweat sparkled on his temples and thin tears streamed down his cheeks into tributaries. We looked at each other and decided to let him be. Etheridge finished his meditation, I think, when Elizabeth retrieved him in time for a round of hugs before heading home.

The Tribute Reading for Etheridge

A massive six-hour tribute reading attended by over seven hundred people was held in honor of Etheridge during the last week of January in 1991 at the American Cabaret Theater in Indianapolis, right there in the middle of Etheridge's walkable universe near his home. Writers' Center leader Jim Powell sliced lots of red tape in civic budgets to make it happen. Renowned poets flew in from all over the country. Galway Kinnell and Sharon Olds. Samuel Allen and Jared Carter. Donald Hall told the story of learning about the word "funky" from Etheridge. Dudley Randall read. Indianapolis resident Mari Evans, who sometimes joined the Free People's mix, performed. About her friendship with Etheridge, from the stage, she said, "The quality of a friendship can be measured by the number of quarrels it has endured." Robert Bly chanted Etheridge's "kah-dooms," and reminisced about a time when he saw applause pass right through him: "He didn't hold it." Haki Madhubuti delivered Gwendolyn's love from Chicago and spoke with his good teeth. Christopher Gilbert read. So, too, did Coleman Barks, and Etheridge's beloved Elizabeth Gordon McKim.

On the way up from Bloomington to Indianapolis in the car, Yusef asked, "Kenneth, are you reading?"

"No, there's not enough space," I said. "Etheridge called me earlier in the week and said there wasn't space. Sonny, Francy, and Michael will represent Free People's. Etheridge told me he was sorry, but he wanted me to know that he had considered me. I thanked him and told him that I understood and that it was no problem."

Etheridge sat at the big round table right at the front. Yusef and I sat with our party right behind him. Etheridge moaned throughout the night but his groans were groans of approval as all the poets paid tribute to him. In hour four, Yusef took to the stage. Before he said his third poem, "Facing It," he announced, "I'm just going to do one more poem and then call Kenneth May to the stage to finish for me." I wasn't expecting that at all. Yusef knew that I knew my work from heart, so he knew I'd be able to say some poems despite calling me to the stage unexpectedly. With Gulf War 1 active in everyone's thoughts, "Facing It" carried even more weight. Yusef prefaced it by saying, "There is always a war and this poem is about another war." Yusef delivered the last line and the crowd went into a collective gasp before applauding. And then they applauded his generous gesture to share the space. I got up from the table in a daze. Yusef and I locked into a fist-handshake and embraced on the stage steps off to the side. I recited two short poems and finished with a poem based on Etheridge's poem "Belly Song":

> This song is for Sonny
> who can hold your attention in a hailstorm
> This song is for Donita
> who believes water is worth more than the asking
> for Herman's daughter
> who said she is as quiet as a marshmallow
> For Etheridge & Yusef . . .
> This song
> This song

Fran Quinn, who hosted that night, said in reference to Etheridge, and to Yusef's sharing of the moment, as I weaved back to the table, "Great poets and poetry create community." Etheridge read last that night. As he did at the Butler University reading, he shared Melissa Orion's poem, "Where is the Poet?" Second, he told his favorite slightly obscene joke. Third, he recited his signature poem, "Circling the Daughter," written for his daughter, Tandi. She ascended to the stage as he finished the last refrain, "You break my eyes with your beauty: Ooouu-oo-baby-I-love-you." They held a long embrace while the entire audience stood, clapped, and shouted approval.

The Funeral, The Cemetery, The Party

Etheridge died on March 10, 1991. The house I temporarily moved into by this time didn't have a phone. On a pay phone across the street, I called Yusef to check in for an update and he told me that Etheridge had made the ascension. Father Boniface Hardin, who founded Martin University in Indianapolis, gave the eulogy. Before Etheridge passed, Martin University awarded him an honorary degree in American poetry and criminal justice. Etheridge and Father Boniface Hardin had a substantial history. Etheridge used a quote from Father Boniface Hardin to serve as an epigram for his poem "We Free Singers Be": "If we didn't have music, dancers would / be soldiers, too, holding guns in their arms, instead of each / other." Father Boniface solemnly took to the podium, paused behind the microphone and began: "Etheridge boogied!" Yusef chuckled, "Oh, no." Father Boniface repeated, "Etheridge boogied!" But Father Boniface was great and the eulogy worked. To reference Yusef's poem, "Blue Light Lounge Sutra," Etheridge had let the devil use his head as a drum. The solemnity had been brightened.

A single large hill within Crown Hill Cemetery is the highest point of land within the Indianapolis city limits. At the top of that hill is the tomb of Hoosier poet James Whitcomb Riley, a rival to Mark Twain on the nineteenth-century lecture circuit. Besides some family and other friends of mine, the cemetery is also the final resting place for notable people from Indiana history: Wes Montgomery, President Benjamin Harrison, bluesmen Yank Rachell and Leroy Carr, Charles Gatling (the maker of the Gatling gun, America's first AR-15), and the Depression-era bank robber John Dillinger. As we drove into Crown Hill Cemetery, I mentioned to Yusef that this was where my mother had taught me how to drive a car, "because you can't hurt anybody here," she said. He suggested I write some poems about the cemetery—and I have done so.

We parked and walked toward the tent over Etheridge's casket. I thought of Riley's tomb with its ten columns up on the hill and Etheridge buried along the roadside. We approached the wide circle of folks. Etheridge's mother Belzora sat front and center. There was a military guard and an American flag on the coffin. Yusef stared at that flag, leaned over to my left ear and murmured, "I gotta think about that." I understood that when he said, "that" (about the flag on the coffin), he meant "THAT," in all capital letters despite his hushed tones. The symbolism of the American flag is entwined with complications for African American persons, especially for military veterans. They fired the military salute, folded the flag, and gave it to Ms. Belzora. As we drove the curvy road out of the cemetery, Yusef revealed that Etheridge's funeral had been the first one he had attended since he was very young. The respect he felt for Etheridge compelled him to break the promise he had made to himself about not attending funerals.

The reception, at a small church, consisted of family, friends of family, and poetry friends. Yusef and I faded to the bottom of a stairwell near the bathroom. A voice from inside growled and out lurched Robert Bly, who had flown in for the funeral despite also having participated in the tribute reading six weeks earlier. He saw Yusef and bellowed, "Oh,

Yusef! And your young friend from the tribute reading." Yusef chatted to Robert Bly and then turned to me and said, "Kenneth, say a poem for Robert." So I said a short poem about a young boy joyously riding a roller coaster before he is matter-of-factly scooped back to his wheelchair by his mother. Robert Bly cocked his neck back, squinted his eyes, and probably not even referring to my poem, commanded, "Kenneth, never forget your dark side. Etheridge never forgot his dark side." He shook Yusef's hand. He clasped my shoulder and trudged up the stairs and departed.

In the early evening, everyone arrived at Etheridge's apartment in waves for the party. We didn't have many snacks but there were lots of cans and bottles. Bottles were shared and swapped since there weren't enough cups. A festive mood filled the room like it was a second New Year's Eve. Indy Free People's and out-of-town Free People's, like Boston-based artist Deta Galloway, cozily cramped into the large section of the kitchen and living room. We stayed out of the bedroom where Etheridge had died a week prior in Elizabeth Gordon McKim's arms. Good talk, laughter, and singing colored the air indigo. No one used any hot words. Maybe Etheridge was better off now, somewhere making an angel in the snow. Elizabeth pressed two bloodstones from the dish of bloodstones she and Etheridge had accumulated into my hands, "One from me and one from Etheridge," she said. To close the night, we went around the circle and everyone said a poem, sang, or had their say, including Yusef, who spent the whole night standing up, back pressed against a sliver of wall, engaged in conversations with everyone. We didn't leave until the clock hands pole-vaulted midnight. We drove south down Highway 37 from Indy to Bloomington exactly at the speed limit through the deep, dark heartland, bleary-eyed and listening to Mingus's "The Black Saint and the Sinner Lady."

Lucky

Two months after Etheridge died, I graduated. In a year and a half, I completed three years of university credits while being mostly homeless, working two and three jobs, being in love, hanging out with Yusef and a Bloomington crew and Etheridge and the Free People's in Indy. I ended up with a double major in English and African-American Studies, which may have been the first major of its kind at Indiana University, because there was no official system in place other than pursuing it through the Independent Studies Program. Living in my car for much of this period turned out to be an advantage in maximizing my time with everyone. Yusef attended my graduation party. My mom and her second husband had recently climbed out of financial stress and had bought thirteen untamed acres in Plainfield, Indiana, about forty-five minutes from the Indiana University campus. We threw the graduation there. No house sat on the acreage, but it had a barn, a couple horses, and fencing. For recreation, folks rode the horses. Even Yusef saddled up. How did he look on the horse? Like a natural, of course! Once again, we had a poetry circle to end the gathering. Yusef, not wanting to read his own work, read Etheridge's tender and overlooked poem, "I and Your Eyes," with a cadence that invoked Miles's *Kind of Blue*.

A high school friend who attended knew I was assembling a chapbook at the time, so he asked Yusef, "Do you think Kenny should have a chapbook?"

"Yes, I think it's a good time for that," Yusef replied.

"Well, you gotta milk life for what it's worth," my friend said.

And Yusef, pausing for a moment, replied, "If you're not careful, it'll end up milking you."

The coolest thing was Yusef and my mom getting along like neighbors from an old-timey era. My mom, who didn't finish high school, and Yusef, the great poet, who can fold the darkest night between a butterfly's wings, chatted it up. At one point, Yusef pointed to my mom's white husky and asked, "What's his name?"

"Lucky," she replied.

"Why Lucky?" Yusef queried.

"Well," my mom said, "We found him abandoned by the roadside. So, he's lucky he has a home!"

"That's right," Yusef confirmed.

Realizing how much my life had evolved from digging ditches and hustling tables to swimming in poetry and something still not entirely known, I felt pretty lucky, too. After the party ended at sunset, Yusef returned to Bloomington via a ride with another party-goer. Three friends piled into my car and we barnstormed west on I-74 to St. Louis for additional celebrations in the coming days. We parked on the Washington University campus and traipsed in the shadows talking way too loudly, found an unlocked window on the first floor of an administration building, and after climbing through it, crashed on the carpeted office floor until sunrise.

We Free Singers Be

We live in a day when once again being nice and being helpful is being militant. When I think back to the onset of meeting both Yusef and Etheridge, what comes through is their helpfulness. Here I was, nobody's nobody, and they took an interest and lifted me into a new sense of being. From 1992 to 1996, Yusef and I continued to hang out, but over a wider distance, still in the Midwest on occasion, but also on the East Coast anywhere from New York to Washington, DC, and any place in the vicinity since I was at George Mason. The bulk of our close friendship actually happened during those years.

The last time we spent time together before I relocated to South Korea was at the AWP Conference in Atlanta in April of 1996. In the months before, he floated the idea of opening a café, but I was broke and had not yet been overseas. A group of us in the Washington, DC area, including poets Joe Ray Sandoval, Brian Gilmore, and a young Ta-Nehisi Coates, piled into a van I commandeered for free from George Mason University as a perk of being the poetry editor of *Phoebe*. On the way down, Ta-Nehisi instigated a discussion on Yusef's poem "The Cage Walker." We must have had eight people in our van and hotel room those two nights.

In those days, Yusef regularly dedicated a poem to me from the stage if I had made the journey to one of his readings or helped him get there, usually "Slam, Dunk, & Hook" or "Letter to Bob Kaufman." At his AWP feature reading, he did the same, for what he knew would be the last time for a very long time, since I was departing for a life in Busan, South Korea a couple weeks later. Extremely honored that I always was, I always felt unworthy, because he had given so much I could never repay. Paying it forward seemed like the best way to pay the debt of gratitude. So I did my best to combine the lessons gleaned from Etheridge and Yusef and combine them into curating community arts in Busan, South Korea.

Our correspondence over the last twenty-one years has been steady and regular, and when I went through a traumatic time about ten years ago and reached out to Yusef for his wisdom, he advised, "Don't let it corrode your soul." The root of that advice harkens back to his comment in the interview with Vicente Gotera to accept our experiences for what they are in order to be liberated from them.

Whenever I visit the states, it's three or four days in New York. Each time, I think, "Well, Yusef is busy, a little older now. Maybe we can hang out twice for a little bit." We end up hanging out most of the day every day. As the years passed, I suggested doing NYC activities that he hadn't yet done. In 2014, we went to a Yankee game. Looking at the memorial plaques of Yankee greats, it was impossible to not think of the color line in baseball and America, and how Negro League superstars like Josh Gibson were denied opportunities to compete on the playing field and challenge Babe Ruth for the title of Home Run King.

In 2017, we visited the Louis Armstrong House and Museum in Queens and participated in the forty-minute tour. We were hoping Brian Gilmore could join us, but weather circumstances detained his arrival. Yusef and I stood in the kitchen, at the rear of the pack, just like when we were at the end of the line for Gwendolyn Brooks, when the tour guide pointed to a horizontal cabinet built into the countertop wall. She said, "Louis loved to customize the house. Can anyone guess what this is for?" Yusef spoke up from our small group, "Bread."

"No, that's what everyone guesses!" the tour guide beamed.

I couldn't help myself and suggested, "Paper towels." The tour guide, flabbergasted, asked how I knew, and I referred to working in restaurants. Maybe, back in the day, Satchmo snatched the idea for a horizontal paper towel dispenser at his own home while walking through kitchens on his way to the stage? Anyway, it's very rare to know or outguess Yusef! So, I'll keep just this one!

A year before Louis Armstrong's death, in 1972, he had a bar area built in the side yard. Yusef and I shot the breeze out there, in front of the bar and behind it, and imagined all the jazz cats who might have gathered around it during a party. Yusef uttered his signature phrase for when something is obvious, "Yeah, man." The next day we made the journey to Trenton by train. We checked out a property he purchased with the aim of opening a café and lounge dedicated to performance and the arts. Although he already had several great ideas, he encouraged suggestions about the interior and how it could come together in menu, atmosphere, and function. He asked about my restaurant experience and experiences of hosting community events in various public venues of Busan. He wanted to know what could work and what wouldn't work.

We even came up with the name for the dessert section of the menu. Afterwards, we attended his beloved jazz jam at the Candlelight Lounge. I met the incredible folks in his Trenton community. During the jam, someone asked Yusef, "How was the Louis Armstrong House?"

Yusef replied, "It was pretty cool."

Yusef is the sixth mentor to be named in this memoir, but he is the first one. He made meeting the other ones possible. In recent years, Yusef has connected me with several of his New York University MFA students: Jihyun Yun, Nicole Lachat, and Emily Yoon, who is from Busan. I saw in them the radiance he inspired in my generation of students. His positive touch endured the decades. They have performed in our art events in Seoul and Busan. They have made new friends and connections in Korea and have inspired writers younger than them. What Robert Bly said about Etheridge can also be said about Yusef: applause passes right through him; he doesn't hold it. On the day he found out that he won the Pulitzer, he taught his students and did not even mention it to them. Consequently, his attention is free for whatever matter is on hand, whether it's working with students or collaborating with artists, encouraging meditation and experimentation along the way. Once, when we were cruising along, the Tom Waits song, "Diamonds On My Windshield," strutted through the speakers in its jazzy, beatnik style. Yusef pointed to the tape deck. "Hey, man. You can do this." And I've performed poetry to music ever since, often with odd combinations of instruments and multiple voices.

The life of an artist is very hard. Yusef is a tremendous example that before our art can be art our lives must be art. The system jostles artists off their paths and if an artist finds a path then that path remains loaded with peril and pitfalls. Sustainability is undermined at every turn. Artists without sustainable lives can't have stable communities and stable relationships. And then how do the ideas of the artists carry forth through future generations? In the early twentieth century, Émile Durkheim described "collective effervescence" as the synergy and serenity individuals sense in a group when they share in a moment of enlightenment, and how that moment of enlightenment inspires the individuals to become creators with a broader sense of shared purpose. Yusef and Etheridge have that power to provide folks with a feeling of collective effervescence that propels them forward. Speaking only for myself, they provided the entire foundation for how I engage community arts in Asia, and, within a context of expatriates who've left friends, family, and familiarity behind, I come across folks at our events who need encouragement or space to grow. The ideas, spirits, aesthetics, and embrace of Yusef and Etheridge have passed into hundreds of artists these last twenty-two years in Asia. To not share what they gave would be to betray the gift.

My gratitude for Yusef and Etheridge continues to expand. Sometimes, when folks ask me what it was like hanging out with them in those days, I want to riff about Etheridge's creed of the poem/the poet/ the people, how his poetry resonates with people who like poetry and people who don't like poetry, how he was a Korean War veteran, a walking haiku, a jailbird of the Heartland, the rugged man whittled down to shoulder blades, who one night after workshop, on the frozen sidewalk, beckoned, "Kenneth, come over here and give the old man a hug." I feel compelled to assert that Yusef is the Duke Ellington of American poetry (they share the same birthday) and how there should be a symposium comparing the trajectory of Yusef's and Duke's works, how Duke and Yusef evolved, over their careers in jazz and poetry, from short songs and poems in their formative years into long suites and librettos in their later years. These are the things I try to express about Yusef and Etheridge when asked, but sometimes, memories swirl through a kaleidoscope of appreciation and joy, and all I can say is, "Yeah, man."

Bloomington

In September of 1988, during my first month in graduate school in Bloomington, Indiana, a few of the university faculty gave a reading at a local elementary school on a Saturday afternoon. I walked over with some other graduate students. The reading was in the school's small lobby, an industrial tiled floor with some twenty folding chairs set out. Yusef Komunyakaa's *Dien Cai Dau* had just been published, and this was, I believe, his first reading from it. Jon Tribble, the editor of the *Indiana Review*, who, I'd already discovered, loved to talk poetry, had told me that the book was extraordinary.

Sitting in my metal chair, among classmates who had yet to become friends, I heard Yusef read "Facing It," his poem about confronting the Vietnam Veterans Memorial. I had to listen hard to understand his southern baritone, and I was too young to realize how rare great poems were, but I felt this one lodging itself in me. It is the poem that has guaranteed Yusef a place in the history of American literature. Roger Mitchell, who also read, had a poem about the memorial, too. He acknowledged before reading it, with simple frankness, that it was "nowhere near Yusef's." That unforgettable final sentence: "In the black mirror / a woman's trying to erase names: / No, she's brushing a boy's hair."

———

That first semester, I took a playwriting course. In it, I was reworking a play I'd drafted the previous year that was set in Vietnam. Though I knew no vets, the war had been central in my thinking about my life. My parents had protested the war when I was young, and the idea of resisting war was, early on, embedded in my consciousness. Still, I was just twenty-three. The war had ended when I was nine.

When I met Yusef at a party before classes began, I leapt into a discussion of contemporary poets, no small talk. Rather than being turned off, Yusef invited me to lunch with him and his wife, Mandy, at the Trojan Horse in downtown Bloomington. With the ignorance and bravura of the young, it took less than half an hour for me to blurt, "You were in

Vietnam? What was it like?" He and Mandy exchanged a brief look, we ate some more hummus, and the topic changed.

Later he did share a bit of his experience, but only obliquely. He recommended books: Michael Herr's *Dispatches*, Wallace Terry's oral history *Bloods: Black Veterans of the Vietnam War*, and Frances Fitz-Gerald's *Fire in the Lake*. He seemed especially interested in PsyOps, the way governments aimed for your heads. "*VC didn't kill / Dr. Martin Luther King*" reads a leaflet aimed at Black GIs in "Report from the Skull's Diorama."

He also offered to read my play. He pointed out how many times characters said each other's names, a rookie mistake. I remember cleaning up the script, deleting all the awkward instances of "Willie" and "Johnny." Yusef nominated the play for a local award from the National Society of Arts and Letters. He may have seen something in me that I didn't recognize in myself: I could write dialogue. Sometime in my second year in Bloomington, he proposed we write a screenplay based on the life of James Beckwourth.

Beckwourth was an elusive character. When I read about him, I was struck by how uncertain the facts of his life were, in part because he was given to self-mythologizing. He was mixed race, one of the early mountain men who explored the West in the mid-nineteenth century. He lived with the Crow Nation and became a Crow chief, took a Crow bride. He also served with the US army and was a fur trader. Some said Beckwourth couldn't be trusted, his allegiances too complex.

Looking back, Yusef seemed most interested in this complexity, a man who can't commit to the culture he ostensibly is told that he belongs to, although he doesn't exactly—as a Black man, he was an outsider. I may have been more drawn to the varied narratives about him—who could I trust?

We each drafted a scene or two. Yusef sketched the beginnings of a love story between Beckwourth and the Crow woman. But I was in the middle of too many projects, and I needed to be the one to take the lead. It foundered.

———

I broke his antique chair.

Yusef let me and my girlfriend (now wife) Eileen stay in his house for two summers while he went to Australia. There were two mourning doves in a cage in the kitchen, and, as instructed, we'd drape a cover over their cage at night. The doves would remind us to remove the cover every morning, cooing from behind their veil at the sunrise.

The first summer I revised a poetry textbook for Indiana University's correspondence course, a class I'd inherited from American surrealist poet Dean Young, who had attended Indiana a few years before I had. I'd work at a tiny desk in Yusef's front room, and when I needed a brief break from composing, I'd lean back in the small chair planted in the plush maroon carpet, balancing on just two legs, doing what mothers tell children not to do. One day, a crack—and the back had broken. I was younger than my years, clueless about property and value. I just told him it had broken when he returned and offered to pay for it. And that was the last I heard of it.

One evening, after Eileen and I had minded the house all summer, we had dinner with Yusef and Mandy. As we sat on his wide, wrap-around porch, Mandy said that the house was haunted. "I've seen a ghost," she said. A ghost? I expressed some incredulity. I didn't believe in ghosts. "He has, too," Mandy said, gesturing at Yusef. Yusef nodded. He said he'd seen his grandfather.

———

In May 2019, at a day-long celebration of Yusef at NYU, there were several reminiscences about the experience of being Yusef's student. Nicole Sealey recalled how there was always a line of students outside his door, how she was grateful for the hour or two she got to meet with him over the course of the semester. Back in those Bloomington years, Yusef wasn't in demand. Occasionally there would be a student meeting with him in his office, but just as often, I'd walk in and we'd start talking. I talked more than I should have, listened less.

What did we talk about? We only discussed my work a little, his hardly at all. I talked about what I was reading—Beckett's *Endgame* shook me up, Baldwin's *Giovanni's Room*.

During the buildup to the first Gulf War in 1991, I set about educating myself about the Middle East. I went to the Bloomington Public Library burning with anti-war fervor and read a couple books about the Palestinian conflict. One was about Yasir Arafat, "peacemaker." In one meeting in Yusef's office, I railed against Israeli cabals and double-crosses. Yusef listened carefully. "Where did you read this?" he asked.

Given his own fascination with history and politics, his query was a gentle way to remind me: always consider the source.

This is not to say that Yusef wasn't against the war. One memorable night in February of 1991 at the Bloomington Public Library theater, Yusef, David Wojahn, and Roger Mitchell, along with me and other graduate students, gave a protest reading. "Every war poem is an antiwar poem," Yusef has said.

———————

In Bloomington, the graduate students had a weekly basketball game. On the day he'd returned from Australia and I was moving out, loading up my stuff, Yusef picked up my ball and slapped it in his palms, ran them over the seams. I sensed he was enjoying the feel of it. His hands, I noticed, were much bigger than mine. "You play?" he asked.

"We've got a weekly game," I said, "if you want to join us."

He gave a look as if those days had long passed; he was in his early forties. A few weeks later, sitting at the Runcible Spoon Café, he slid a new poem of his across the table to me, "Slam, Dunk, & Hook," which would eventually appear in his book *Magic City*, about his 1950s Louisiana childhood.

I was excited by the poem. The instant energy of its sentence fragments ("Layups. Fast breaks.") hooked me, as did the unpredictable diction, his "neon vernacular," and the physicality of it all. The poem sweats. I know that I borrowed the way Yusef used the lingo of the court when, a decade later, I wrote a lyrical paragraph of fragments about basketball for my essay, "Spin Moves."

When I read the poem that first time, I felt that Yusef had actually borrowed from me. One of my earliest published poems included a moment in which the speaker shoots baskets at odd hours, alone, to process the grief of losing his brother, and in Yusef's poem, Sonny Boy plays "nonstop" when his momma dies.

> We had moves we didn't know
> We had. Our bodies spun
> On swivels of bone & faith
> Through a lyric slipknot
> Of joy, & we knew we were
> Beautiful & dangerous.

These last sentences of "Slam, Dunk, & Hook" seem some of Yusef's finest lines, and this has nothing to do—well, maybe a little to do—with my own attraction to basketball. The sentence holds so much—the emphasis on the body, and on movement ("spun" and "swivels") that makes the endeavor feel musical, a dance. Like Dickinson, he gives abstractions shape; the swivels are "faith" and joy is "a lyric slipknot." The word "slipknot" reminds me—jarringly—of a noose, but this is one that the bodies spin through, a balletic drive that finds a space to get to the bucket, to, somehow, and perhaps only briefly, escape. While it's not at all self-conscious, it's an escape into self-knowledge—the players "knew" what they were.

In Yusef's poetry, it is the body that gives us definition. He has faith in the body, not in some Herculean sense, but in the sense that the body can contain identity that resists messages of society and culture.

> My initials aren't on a branding iron.
> I'm standing here in unpolished
> shoes and faded jeans, sweating
> my manly sweat. Inside my skin,
> loving you, I am the space
> my body believes in.
> "Unnatural State of the Unicorn."

I've always felt the force of the line, "My initials aren't on a branding iron," but only in typing them for this essay did I think of how Yusef changed his initials when he changed his name, and how "YK" would be very unlikely initials for a slave owner. Y? Yancy? Yorick? Yale?

The celebration of the body's truth, its individuality while being something we all share, finds its full expression in Yusef's paean to the body, "Anodyne." "I love my crooked feet . . . made to outlast / belief," he writes.

In the recording of the poem by Yusef, David Cieri, and Mike Brown, the piano and bass find their way toward a blues melody, drums shimmering, and Yusef takes his time, words falling like clean rain:

> I love this body, this
> solo and ragtime jubilee
> behind the left nipple,

because I know I was born
to wear out at least
one hundred angels.

———————

In 1998, when Yusef came to Salem State, the university where I ended up teaching, he visited a contemporary poetry class. Someone asked him about the images in "Facing It." Were "the red bird's wings / cutting across my stare" something in the past that's being remembered, or in the present?

He said the poem was about "reflections," but didn't get more specific than that. It seemed that he wanted the images in that poem not to be pinned down to a place or time. They existed, solid as facts, but they also hovered in the space between reality, memory, and consciousness, the skull's diorama.

Since our class focused on American poetry, I asked "Do you consider yourself an American poet?" I was probably thinking of the themes of the class rather than his particular life and work—did he see his work following in an American tradition, and, if so, how?

I still don't know exactly what was behind the look he gave me, but I won't forget it. He paused, looked at me as if he didn't want to answer, or didn't have an answer; maybe there was surprise or irritation that I'd asked. Maybe he just needed to think.

Yusef's essay "A Needful Thing," in *Condition Red*, celebrates Frederick Douglass and Robert Hayden, and says that ultimately Douglass is a greater influence. This isn't surprising, given that Yusef rejects the modernist idea that the writer must be an outsider. Given his sense that writers can speak to the communal and can be, at times, a griot, writers are only outsiders when they can't abide the injustices of society. They don't sacrifice their individuality, or their ties to community.

Yusef's recent contribution to *The 1619 Project*, "March 5, 1770," a poem about Crispus Attucks, the first colonist to die in the American Revolution, shows, perhaps, that he wants to complicate the title of the project by emphasizing Attucks's implicit claim to citizenship. "What was interesting to me about this individual," he says, "is that he seemed so ordinary, but yet he was an escaped slave. He had a certain kind of spirit and tenacity that he could push against things . . . he knew what freedom was."

The poem suggests that multiracial class solidarity was behind the first deaths of the American Revolution, those who are "sharing a grave" had "laid a foundering stone." The poem sees intersectionality as not just an idea to understand oppression, but as a tool to resist. It also suggests that this force has been denigrated by those in power. In an "echo of the future," it's John Adams, a founder of the early republic, who defends the British soldiers in court by labeling the resisters a "motley rabble of saucy boys, / negroes & mulattoes, Irish / teagues & outlandish jacktars." In a project emphasizing 1619, this poem nudges attention toward 1776, making us reflect on the real promise and real failures of the American Revolution.

I wonder now if Yusef's look regarding whether he was an "American poet" was more a look of astonishment that I had to ask. He was. He'd been in Vietnam; he'd endured the sting of American racism. He was Louisiana-born. Despite his bohemian allegiances, his respect for rebellion, he was as American as Frederick Douglass, as Crispus Attucks.

———

Eileen and I left Bloomington and spent a year in Madison, Wisconsin, then Greencastle, Indiana, before ending up in Salem, Massachusetts. While in Greencastle, I drove down to meet with Yusef, who was soon to leave Bloomington for Princeton. He asked me if I had any poems. He was editing an issue of *Ploughshares*. "What have you been writing?" I sent him five poems. He chose one poem for publication in a local magazine, and one, a piece about the last basketball game my friend Mary played with our co-ed group before she began chemo. And he chose another, "On, Wisconsin," for an issue of *Ploughshares* that he was editing.

"On, Wisconsin" was more formal than many of my poems. Yusef suggested a few small edits, which I took, but I remember one I didn't. He wanted me to cut the word "heat" from the line "fanning themselves in August's heat." He proposed "fanning themselves in mid-August." I said no, explaining that I wanted the word "heat" for an exact rhyme, but his suggestion nagged at me. As a poet who valued concision, I knew that "heat" was unnecessary, and the subtler slant rhyme of "mid-August" was, I came to feel, more mature. When I published the poem in my first book, I changed it.

At that meeting where he invited me to send him poems, I mentioned a student I had who impressed me, Gil Durán. Yusef asked me to send some of Gil's poems along with my own, and he ended up selecting one of Gil's for *Ploughshares*. Gil was exceptional, but I was impressed that Yusef sensed that from just a few of his poems. Gil didn't pursue poetry, but went on to become a communications director for Dianne Feinstein and press secretary for Governor Jerry Brown.

After we both had left Indiana, Yusef and I would cross paths at AWP, or I'd drive in to hear him read in Boston. Always, he's gracious and expresses joy at seeing me. We tend to go for drinks or dinner, and we talk for a long time, until I realize I'm imposing on him. Our conversations are usually about literature and history, with just a little autobiography (mostly from me). He rarely talks much about his work, at least not directly, though, I'll realize afterwards, the topics that came up were often what he was writing about.

I'd always admired Yusef's poem, "Blue Light Lounge Sutra . . ." It channeled the energy of performance poetry. It was a showstopper at his readings: "let the devil / use your head / for a drum." I recorded the poem with the musician Phil Swanson on a CD that blended music and poetry, and we performed the piece whenever we gave concerts. One night about a decade ago, I drove down to Wesleyan University to hear Yusef read. Phil and I were performing in western Connecticut the next night. At the reading, Yusef read the poem. He read it twice as fast as I remembered him reading it, and twice as fast as I had recorded it. I was surprised, and I went online and found recordings of him reading it. I discovered two versions, and, weirdly, one was almost exactly twice the length of the other. The next night, when Phil and I rehearsed before our show, I suggested we double the pace of that poem. We did. It sounded better.

At that celebration for Yusef, Sharon Olds talked about how he created "mental images without slides." I understood what she meant. His poems illustrate themselves, and to add photographs to them (as, I suspect, hundreds of undergraduates have done in "projects" for "Facing It"), doesn't add anything. The poems are so vivid in their mix of image and metaphor (and, occasionally, dialogue) that to try and enhance them through additional visuals feels like diffusing their leanness and precision, what Yusef's former student and personal assistant, Dante Micheaux, identified as his "scalpel kind of eye."

Micheaux added that Yusef's eye "eschews hierarchy." I took this to have several meanings. First, simply that Komunyakaa, while fascinated by power dynamics, did not accept the accepted order of things. He viewed himself, as Tyehimba Jess put it that day, "as part of a long stream of humanity," and gave respect to those "in unpolished / shoes and faded jeans." More specifically in regards to his aesthetic, I took Micheaux's comment on how, with his emphasis on imagery, Yusef divests the world from the pomp of rhetoric.

Yet his emphasis on proportion does not feel like a surrealist effort to "derange the senses," to deliberately skewer conventional scale through distortion, like, say, Dickinson or Szymborska. Reading his work, I'm not disoriented as much as I am exhilarated at the feeling of life (elusive life!) being nailed down. Undoubtedly, from his long love affair with jazz, the poetry is musical, but it also feels built, hammered together, groove sliding into groove. Before academia reeled him in, he'd been planning to become a carpenter, and I always have a sense of the lines being laid down, one after another, deliberately and precisely.

I scribbled notes all that day.

Hermine Pinson saying Yusef "makes erudition cool as purple silk." Nicole Sealey saying that Yusef made her realize that "Abstraction was a way to hide." Soren Stockman describing him nurturing "what moved in opposite directions in poems." Kevin Young saying he learned from him to "get you a good hat."

Javier Zamora quoting Yusef: "The ear is the best editor."

Alysia Nicole Harris quoting him: "How can you write poetry and not listen to jazz?"

John Murillo quoting him: "If you don't do what I do, don't do what I do."

———

That day at NYU, waves of images from Bloomington crashed on me, and the feeling of being young and making art in a sunlit college town welled in me, even as I could see how far away those times were, thirty years, eight hundred miles. Since then, Yusef had gone on to inspire and support many writers. Looking around me, I could see they were mainly writers of color. It was an impressive legacy. I wondered if what he gave to me was different than what he'd given them. I was a White middle-class kid fascinated by American history who was lured by those ancient sirens, truth and beauty. And he wasn't the celebrity poet yet. He seemed grateful to have company during his office hours, to meet up for coffee at the Runcible Spoon Café and talk literature and history.

I think what I received from him then was similar to what he gave his future students. His encouragement, and the line of his thinking that I trace in his poetic achievements, applies to artists of different generations and different hues. He knew what freedom was, for humans, *and for artists*, and, with integrity and wisdom, he gave that to us, freely.

———————

"I don't know," my friend said when I told him I was writing this essay, "Yusef's a pretty private person." It's true. At that day of celebration at NYU, most of the anecdotes of him were from an appreciative, admiring distance. A memory of seeing him on the dance floor at an early Cave Canem party, some nugget of wisdom ("You could be writing right now") from a classroom. My memories aren't any more revealing, but they come from a time before Yusef became a household name in the poetry world.

Here's one last memory: in the spring of 1994, just before Eileen and I left Bloomington, we were coming out of the small woodsy area on the IU campus and saw, from afar, Yusef walking down the west walk with Mandy. We both were struck by Yusef's animated talking, so unlike his usual sober self. We discovered later that evening that he had won the Pulitzer Prize. He must have just found out.

That moment, the late afternoon sun slanting down on him and Mandy as they made their way under the ginkgo trees toward Kirkwood Street, Bloomington's main drag . . . For the first time in history, the US had awarded a Black male poet a Pulitzer. I didn't know that then, but seeing—even feeling—the astonishment in his body, I knew that something had changed.

Office Hours

As a student of Yusef Komunyakaa's, I met with him weekly, during office hours. If, for whatever reason, I was late to sign-up and all the slots were filled (as they often were), I'd stalk the sign-up sheet for cancellations or stand at the ready, outside his office in case there were day-of no-shows. And I wasn't alone in doing so. It was that serious. Time with Yusef that precious.

I was *poetstruck*, to say the least. It was nerve-racking, especially at first, sitting across from the man who wrote "Blue Light Lounge Sutra." We spent hours thinking through early drafts I'd normally be too shy to share. But I knew that having Yusef Komunyakaa's eyes on my poems-in-progress is like having Denzel Washington run lines with a beginning actor. Of the drafts shared, "Undone," one I could neither shake nor break open, comes immediately to mind.

> i wish the day
> hadn't . . . dawn has claimed
> yet another sky, its birds.
> the clouds, too,
> have gone, dissolved—
> christ-flesh on the tongue.
> this always, which is itself
> and has no reason,
> this always, which is myself
> and has no reason,
> contains so little.

Before I knew better, abstraction was a tool I'd use to hide the fact that I didn't know what the hell I was doing. In office hours, however, there's nowhere to hide—it was the three of us: my teacher, the poem, and me. Yusef, in his quiet way, questioned: *What else? What more? What next?* Over the course of our meetings, he'd help me land on a new title ("Instead of Executions, Think Death Erections"), realize the first three lines were the ones worth keeping and decide to end on an image.

> I wish the day hadn't.
> Dawn has claimed
> another sky, its birds.
>
> I watch from my burning
> stake the broken necks.
> Once, this lot
>
> allowed wildflowers—
> nothing worse than bruised
> wildflowers. Darling
>
> dawn, death mask
> to which I've grown
> accustomed, show me
>
> one pretty thing
> no heavier
> than a hummingbird.

I can't imagine how many thousands of office hours Yusef has spent in service of his students' poems. I can't imagine how many thousands of poems Yusef has midwifed. There are not enough *thank yous* in the world. To my dear teacher Yusef Komunyakaa, I offer the above poem, which is as much yours as it is mine.

Dear Yusef,

I find myself writing more poems about love, friendship, and tenderness these days, which is a turn from my first manuscript, a book driven by sorrow. Maybe because the world is in pain, I want to enact survival through poetry. Maybe poetry feels like a way to love the world, to hold my people closer.

I think, you would say reading my draft, *this poem is longer*. Which I understand to mean, *Keep looking. Keep looking at what your poem is telling you to sing*. You would also say often, *Keep the faith*. For so long I did not know that poetry allows me to access a more truthful, bolder, and wilder part of me. When you taught, you listened for lines underneath the page, waiting to be called. In your office hours, you always said: *But tell me. How are you doing?*

This is all to say, you taught us, gave us warmth. My memories learning from you all point to this. The framework of your class was always care. Because you cared for us, we cared for one another. From then on, my poetry was always about love, even when it spoke through ugly histories, because I wanted to love the people in those narratives. Now I am just trying to exercise acceptance for all the ugliness, fears, and desires in my poems.

The last time we saw each other was three years ago, in Vermont, at Bread Loaf. I sat with you all night outside the Treman Cottage, with other writers also sitting around us. The Vermont sky had the most stars I had seen, making me dizzy from constantly looking up and giving wrong names to them. That night, I had felt bad that I never gave up my seat next to you, but now I am glad that I was selfish. We talked about my research, the Vietnam War, the Korean War, jazz, horses. You laughed at my silly jokes about McDonald's Filet-O-Fish being fancy. Yusef, my NYU friends were so jealous of my time with you there. Yusef, if only you knew how much we miss and love you, how much you changed us. Yusef, I hope you know.

Yusef, I am keeping the faith.

Love,
Emily Jungmin Yoon

August 2022
Honolulu

INSUFFICIENT BLUE

Poems for Yusef

Colonial Album

They saw mirrored
in the gleaming teeth
everything they had always wanted
but were afraid to speak of,

lifted loincloths and peeked,
loved and beat the help alternately,
as required. There were parks
now on the islands where the vines

had been chastened and the trees
pruned. But inside the Masters,
the overgrowth burgeoned out
of control into endless expanses

of troubled dreams. You cannot
imagine their suffering (though
they lived long and were not sick),
nor their despair. Yet daguerreotypes
were made in which the Master
and his family were luminous
and impeccable with all
their brass buttons, the servants

shadows that broke off
like black lightning and fetched
things from the margins of the frame.
Bats caught in gauze curtains.

And the terror bled out over silver bowls
of floating rose petals.
In the background the fruits
grew heavy on the branches

and if you gaze at the photo
long enough you will see them drop
to the ground and rot, ooze nectar
and be covered with wasps.

Stay longer still and you will see
the grand costumes stiffen
and stand by themselves, empty,
echoing bird cries and the wind

tunneling through the immaculate sleeves.
The jungle grows up through them.
Vines invade the manor house
and the well scums over. Finally,

the statues fall over by themselves
and the children play on them as if
they had never been more than piles of stones.

What Walking Brings

Mercy, please, rock me.
     Yusef Komunyakaa

Dear Yusef, how do you handle despair?
I have wept under a weeping willow
     where I prayed for one eye, mourned the other beyond repair.
Imagine the only window
     boarded up: a nightmare no one should have nor bear.
          I need not imagine a fist nor oily grit
of gay-bar parking lot, nor the humility
     of living with parents to afford surgeries in Mississippi
where I have seen desperation in a gas station
     checkout line: a man shoplifting Vienna sausages
to buy a Colt 45, a poor drunkard's breakfast.
          I have imagined a limb for a limb, old law satisfaction,
when mourning a treetop the power crew
     cut down. All for nought, I thought, bemoaning
a downgraded cyclone,
     yet praising the lovely disaster of pine needles strewn
about roads before spraying plum trees festooned
     with worms writhing within tents of silk, a pestilence
for sure but a world of joy for a boy wielding a stick.
          I have walked on Mississippi's Sargasso Sea,
kudzu flowing like the mighty Mississippi,
     kudzu hogging sunlight from fields once corn & sugarcane,
crops forgotten, fields unmaintained.
          I have misplaced my optimism on a creek bank,
or did I
     lend it to the man I sideswiped on the meat aisle,
a man I loved gone to love a plumber in Dover,
     Delaware, nowhere near my reflection changed by tadpoles

& a maple leaf I followed downstream,
    a leaf later held between seen & unseen streams
spinning a leaf in its place of wisdom:
    Breathe with me awhile, the leaf whispered.
        The nearby blackberry bushes picked clean,
I have called in sick to walk in the rain,
    a youthful delight of many returns:
like the simplicity of pork-rind currency
    & mud-pie bake sales on pond banks: a time
that lingers ——— like my fear of going blind.
    If my left eye goes, I must walk that road.
        "A worthy idleness seeks Beauty & Grace,"
I should have told the alcoholic looting a vacuum machine,
    slinging a hose against pavement
only to dislodge gum in a whiskey receipt, or so
    I thought, until a daddy longlegs fled the hose.
        If I am a part of all I have met, my dear Lord Tennyson,
what am I to learn from the man
    who glued then screwed a Mercedes-Benz
ornament to a Chevrolet Nova's hood mangled
    by a deer, antlers stuck in the grill? Am I a man
allowing pride & loss to guide me so long as I exist?
    I have stared into the soapy abyss
of a crockpot until I heard God: *Once you sew that fist
    in that quilt, will you close that door & let me in?*
I said, "Yes," yet I still dwell on my misgivings
    & my regrets. ——— I admire straw fires that ignite
as fast as they die out, a burn that does not linger unlike
    my fear of going blind. If my left eye goes, I must walk that road.
        Have you watched the sunset through bullet holes
of a cattle-crossing sign? Thrown an engagement
    ring that rolled after someone on the stairs? Relationships
outweigh solitude, allegedly,
    nonetheless, happiness or despair either way,
a joyous or wretched river in us, a sea all about us,
    a cliché within a cliché, my dear Eliot:
better to float in hope than drown in misery.
        I could allow briars in my fig tree

or jog the valley to greet the breeze atop my hill
　　where I have watched swallows feeding
above the dust of bush-hogged fields.
　　　　　Why not ignore the sign, *Bridge Out Ahead*?
Even dead ends lead somewhere:
　　I found an armchair once, so I ate a pear, I read
Baudelaire. J'adore the *taken elsewhere.*
　　　　　I love to count the leaves that waltz across the streets.
Have you noticed such peace?
　　Although I admire the graceful rage of asphalt pavers
so stern each day, I prefer the minnow
　　that quakes the lake, the bug that skates such waves.
Then there's the crane that stands in the shallows
　　along the bank, hours on end, if need'th be, so still
　　　　　unlike the sun crowning my hill
where I have knelt, where I kneel
　　to consider my fields, —— my soul among tilled rows,
walking where irises shall grow.

Dear Yusef,

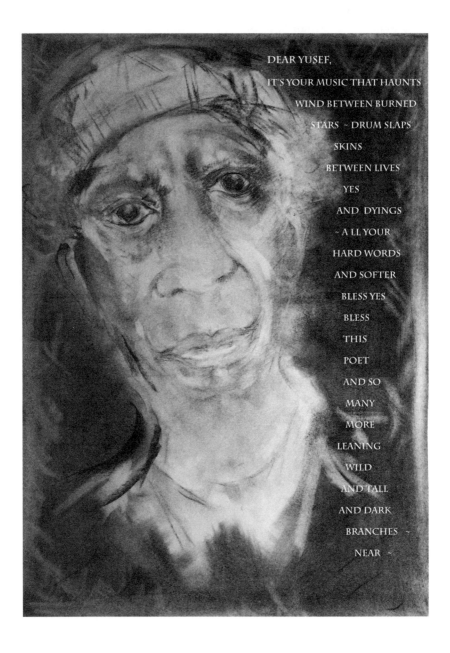

DEAR YUSEF,

IT'S YOUR MUSIC THAT HAUNTS

WIND BETWEEN BURNED

STARS ~ DRUM SLAPS

SKINS

BETWEEN LIVES

YES

AND DYINGS

~ ALL YOUR

HARD WORDS

AND SOFTER

BLESS YES

BLESS

THIS

POET

AND SO

MANY

MORE

LEANING

WILD

AND TALL

AND DARK

BRANCHES ~

NEAR ~

Yusef's Lessons

1. *New Orleans 1977*

First memory—

Hot night in the dark, stage
of stacked wood boxes,
rows of folding chairs, my parents and their friends—
The First Backyard Poetry Theater
in the Bywater. The other kids in a back
bedroom playing Truth or Dare.

I watch the poet take the stage
to read: *Daydream the fat belly of life.*
Daydream a lilacbush in May
Daydream the smoke the curls
back to eat itself.

The heat diaphanous, the language settling
over my body like a dress.

And now here is a hinge in the world that divides past and present.
I want to step into adulthood, into language, into poetry—

2. *New Orleans 1982*

Long workshop table in my arts high school   slow whirring fan
windows open to humid green   he is a poet in the public schools   he
reads our poems   we are fifteen   we are sixteen   there are seven of
us around the table   he regards our work as worthy of his attention
I am a quiet girl but when he speaks I write everything down   later I
will understand how he teaches us what making means

3. *Atlanta 1996*

Walking to class, I'm a grad student,
copy of *Dien Cai Dau* slipped
in my bag. Today my students and I will discuss
"Facing It"—*I'm stone. I'm flesh*—
Today we will step out of
a Georgia winter and enter
the night he creates for us, all smoke
and jungle and grief.

4. *New Orleans 2010*

The fifth anniversary of the storm: reading
to mark Katrina's ruin of this city and the coast.

He reads from "Requiem"—*the Crescent City was already shook down to
    her pilings,*
Her floating ribs, her spleen and backbone.

And suddenly I empty myself completely then fill again with his music—
the bloom of it. The shock and flush of it,

the moment I realize that if no one ever again writes
a poem about this city and what it's lived through
his poem will be enough.

His music blooms—another world to drop into.
The poem illuminates a circle of light.

5. *New York City 2015*

Another stage   the 92nd St Y on the east side of the city   I inter-
view the poet and the actor on stage   I introduce   nervous till I'm not
till I forget myself and listen: *what we can risk—dreaming—is the most
important.*   I sit beside him   I can't write anything down   I commit
his words to memory—

Voices embrace each and make each whole.

CURTIS L. CRISLER

Superheroes Born by a Black Nerd

A two-headed giant booms through hotel's golden gates—
an open portal to Asgard—my first sighting of you, not on book

jacket, not on website, but with son balanced in wrap-around:
his arms clamping your neck like a buoy, your strong right bicep

and forearm strapping his thighs—a snug band, as you swing left
arm like you're back humping—humping passed Dak To and Khe

Sanh, full in your swagger—a yellow huge laugh sashing around
you both. AWP in another big city eats up what we feed to wallets.

I pray for a father placed in my grasp through your eyes, thinking
of hundredth time to write new poem, but not 'til Coleman Hawkins

dirges "Soul Blues" on poutful Tuesday morning, and I manscape
soul-patch with razor dawning four blades that can take all the skin

like a tax. Your bass spurts "Gary, sounds like a boy's name" in CC
workshop, to words I'll spill on 70 pages of white #20. I hear funk,

hear you've processed "Chocolate City,"—my essential contact.
For you I revise title. It's you who changes how I look at wordsmith's

strut by taking the sink out a young poet's lifting of heavy language.
The truth hitched to you. I see your son as Thor, and you are Odin,

and I am outsider who'd love to be a Loki, to be a grumble inside
the cauldron of your voice. I want an Odin too. It's the nucleus

at the center of our moment that every child wants—*that* smile.
That smile a son wears like thunderclaps. You burned *that* in him.

Seven Songs of the Sparrow

(for Yusef who already knows)

a pinky print
on the side of a pail
blackberry moon

melody
of the **ice cream** man
red bird on a branch

dark water
a man wades away from
a plantation's name

a Bloomington fog's
idea of ancestry
ether on a ridge

burning beyond
the bonewheel factory
the Southern **Cross**

fifty-eight thousand
grunts in black granite
blood moon

Not Words But Hands

We have no words for you.

The poets hear the news,
this death unspeakable as the babble
of an auctioneer at the slave market.

There are no words in our language to say this.
We are singers who moan,
prophets with tongues missing
like the clappers of empty bells.

In your poems there are singers, prophets, slaves.
You hammered words for all of them.
But we have no words for you;
there is no name for the grief in your face.

We only have our hands, to soap your shirts
or ladle soup for you, grip your shoulder
or dim the lamp so you can sleep with visions
of the ball field by the lumber company
wars and wars ago.

And this, this poem,
this is my hand.

Komunyakaa at the International Center for Photography, June 11, 2007

Hoodoo pounding the tight drum in his chest, he
confessed the photo of Mary Lou Williams urged
him to read *My Father's Love Letters*. His voice,
all roar—kicked up Bogalusa dust. His tongue split
the air between syllables, stirred long & short vowels
into rhythms. Pure sound pushed consonant clusters
out of hibernation, pulled at the memory of his father's
bib overalls & carpenter's apron, his mother's imagined

laughter. No dropped letters, no compressed
accent, his cadence, richly blued by the decades.
At times, he bowed his head. Eyes closed, he never
looked at the page. When he opened them, his gaze
lit like a plumb line through the audience as though
he just troubled a knowing from his last utterance.

The French Quarter

Over powdered beignets,
over a demitasse of chicory
near Royal, I came to grips I am the lonely sort,
for I am ever seeking an education,
my head sideways, a book winged
in my hand, its words like a concert,
the fried dough going cold and congealing,
the passing tourists drowned out,
a sullen look on my face. It is when I most
want to make love.

Dostoevsky was a way out of my confusion,
as was Baraka whom I gave my reverence freely.

Nothing I believed stayed and thus my melancholy
deepened though banjos and clarinets played
all over the streets through late afternoon rain,
Black Bottom Stomp, eucalyptus and live oaks
aging against arpeggio runs.

I suffered a great pity, and the gypsies
were all too quick to augur behind cardboard boxes.
Stubborn cats mewled in and out around café tables
and pigeons sprang from gothic balconies
on the square. If I were one to make concessions,

my life was a streak of quandaries and doggeries
with quaint and hospitable inscriptions
on doors, every chapter a tempest or escape hatch
at some back table where I read alone
in faint light, a thin band of gold hops
at the bottom of a beer mug.

It is good everyone is having a good time
on the world's piazzas. I am harnessed in the questions
I have made a home. Were I a character
in a novel, I would be assured change was around
the corner, perhaps a priest careworn like me
in this crowd, who likes driving country roads
in winter while thinking gloomy thoughts.

Copacetic Judy

You don't know what it's like to watch somebody you love
crumble away bit by bit . . .
     Judy Garland in *A Star Is Born*

In the *Bleu Bleu* after hour
every chair's upended—meaning
late & early. The b'tender's turned
each bulb to *crepuscule,*
the meanest light. & Judy tunes the muted
trumpet with her *alma imortal.* All of thirty-two,
& worn with knowing, with belting. Shoving
those bangs off, "With hope
you burn up!" (Gosh. Golly.) Why
should anyone bother with a "comeback"
come back high? ('Cause genius turns up!) &
why that dress? Bow at the throat, midnight *azul*
cutting her at some dreamt up waistline,
not her waistline. But—she's torching

Arlen & Gershwin like a copacetic Frances Ethel,
like Woman. She reminds me of Sylvia Plath.
Callous on the voice. Bitter
self-killer. Queen Contralto. Ugly duck.
A kind-of jazzy *fado.* He's there, in the shadow
of the bar, dark liquid—The Man
That Got . . . Her Dave, Vin, Sid, Mark, Mick, etc.
stand-in. My father/brother stand-in—I've the scene
on repeat. I saturate & tune, &: "Art & life bleed
into each . . ." as you say, dear Yusef.
We saturate in what we want
drawn out. Like an Epsom bath pulling at
atomized shrapnel. Your surface stings, as the hard
love of the deeper wound comes clean.

Laugh

Even if you don't believe it.

    Laugh.

When your tears have formed a river.

    Laugh.

If anger and self-pity threaten to take
    you in their undertow.

    Laugh.

Even if it is a hollowed out, plastic sound.

    Laugh.

Practice it. Fake it. Perfect it.

    Laugh.

When the world sings you praises.

    Laugh.

When it denies you.

    Laugh.

If it silences you.

    Laugh.

If everyone has left you alone.

Laugh.

If they should return in a dream.

Laugh.

It is our only salvation.

Why I Keep Coming Back to It

When Yusef speaks about the letters
he received from his father's hands, blood
orange with the memory of violence, my own
childhood spills like a drum of crude oil,
staining the sand below the playground swings
with memories I dare not speak. Although
the act of violence committed is not the same,
there are spiders in my veins that recoil
from touch. Even the soft hand of love
sometimes too much, a fork discovering
the transformer in the radio I took apart
trying to understand why things work.
Not how. Only why. Physics tells me the sky
one day will shiver into nothingness.
An envelope of gases we have never laid
eyes upon suddenly letting go. A breath held
as long as possible before surrendering
to ghosts. It will not matter in that moment
how the mechanism moves towards unlock,
only that the final draught leaves the lips
blue with its absence. A poem, sometimes
has a kinder hand than love.

Because Wouldn't It Be Cool if He Were the Father of the World

This man,
Who stole roses & hyacinth
For his yard, would stand there
With eyes closed & fists balled,
Laboring over a simple word, almost
Redeemed by what he tried to say.

    Yusef Komunyakaa

The first time I read Yusef Komunyakaa
the dog wanted to go out
to do its dog business
but I was too up in my head with his poem
"My Father's Love Letters,"

in it somewhere towards the end
he writes about his dad stealing hyacinths and roses for the backyard,
which is where I gotta get the dog

but the poem is pulling at me, pulling me back
into the treetop of my own old man,
holed up in some nursing home on 72nd and York
I gotta get to him
but I can't even get the dog out of the house,
can't even get my mind out of the humidity
of this world
that burns with blue, broken, boozed, and brave fathers

I wish I was one
even though I am one

and when I saw Steve Harvey on the YouTube
talking crying wilting about his dad
I wished I had a dad
that stole roses and hyacinths to put out in the backyard
so I could go there at midnight and weep
and say, *my father made this*

my dad didn't put anything in his backyard
even though I have to love him
and I love him
and I love Komunyakaa's poem so much
it's tearing my hands off
at the wrists
so I can't turn the knob to the back door
to the backyard
to the best part of *Get Back*
is Billy Preston on the organ
but I've said that already

and the world needs a father named Yusef,
like Lateef and Dayes
but mostly Komunyakaa
because wouldn't it be cool if he were the father of the world
and all of his love letters were our love letters
and we could read them to nothing
in the backyard
with the dog and alone with the roses and hyacinths

where I finally find myself, freed from his poem, never freed
from his poem.

Dear Yusef, Dear Komunyakaa

Why you so sweet?
Cause I am

I only know you through your work,
which is enough, which my father
hipped me to when I was a young man.
He pointed you out at the conference
and, proud older brother, confided
He's the real deal. Yours was the reading
I couldn't miss. I have his copy of *Copacetic*
and a much-thumbed *Neon Vernacular.*
And there's your two-way conversation
about jazz and poetry revisited every few years.
But it's "Facing It" I turn to now:
the Vietnam Vet who *lost his right arm*
inside the stone and a woman stroking
a boy's hair inside a chiaroscuro of names.

Hieroglyphs for Yusef Komunyakaa

Slower now the words, cold
molasses poured from the blue jug

of your breath. In your mouth
every our's an *over*, every hour a *hover*,

your Bogalusa tongue spilling secret v's
in the middle of ours & hours—

arrow of geese writing across the white.
How many hovers left for you, gentle

teacher, over future. Now, you falter
over your own hieroglyphs, translations

of prayer, over oracles ordering
scapula & plastron into clouds.

When, one day, the sky goes dry,
your birds will hour in over mouths.

The Conjurer's Apprentice

Being able to recognize the chicken scratch
that flowed from his pen as magic,
was not listed as a desired skill
but certainly made it easier to usurp
this gig from my predecessor
—bugeyed ambitious & so much less effective
than I at everything. Maven of imitation,
I hit the ground running: epistolary mensch?
Check. Charm Offensive specialist? Check.
Punctual as my grandaddy's wound-up pocketwatch.
The Master, however, has so much deepdown smooth
that I found myself on a learning curve.
First lesson: syncopation: speech sung
in its bass notes as if never split from song
—his, a kind of sonic elixir.
He seldom speaks,
speaks few words when he speaks at all.
I walked behind him once at dusk,
quiet as I could keep, & watched him snap his fingers
to some cerebral art song establishing its tempo,
lifting his forearm to bring the metronome
of pollex & digitus secundus closer to his ear.
Then there was improvisation, & its nuance
of not spontaneity but conversion of the eye
into a prism that transfigures an old nail on the sidewalk
into a stigmatic tool of the Holy Ghost
&, a few lines later, into a behind-the-scenes critic
of Modernist flatwork.
He says the public has to come to the artist,
otherwise a disadvantage to both
& maybe that deft phantasmagoria
is the lure of his lyric—

which brings me to another assignment:
the Master's idiosyncratic catechism of lust,
woven through the conjure and the man;
as precise as pulling a flying insect from the air by one leg,
he whispers the word "nightcap," to no one in particular,
& every woman in the room turns her head
& he already has told anyone who would listen
that his palette is an array of wild colors.
Come to think of it, an elective on structural engineering
snuck up on me: each image is a stanza
so each stanza contains multiple stanzas that build
a single rhapsodic landscape, a literary mise en abyme.
This, of course, should have come as no surprise.
His prowess as a spellcaster is legendary,
staunch with all manner of erudition,
but I was playing catch-up,
because he never simply laid it out for me
in plainspeak;
I had to look for the instruction in his example
& look I did, beyond inspiration to discipline,
into the utter maw of language
to find my sacred symbol, again,
& all the power it contains.
The Master revealed its alchemical properties:
deadly hush; beguiling diction; & the incantation
of an effigy written down—
what most would describe as poetry:
the washed and dried innards of the tulip tree
spun into yarn, a whole self
whelmed in an umber beauty.
The studies went on this way for several years.
Time by time, he would chant about a great storm
then stop; thought he discovered an anodyne
to quell the war record, playing always
off somewhere in the distance;
& when he came to a particularly difficult mojo,
say, to trap a duppy for interrogation,
mend memory that was not his,

con all the steps in a dance of the broke shoulder,
or measure the distance between nightmare and bliss,
he would turn to me, though this was rare,
with a solitary request from an entire arsenal
of aesthetic weapons.

Soul's Edge

In New Orleans
when the green-suited
oracle at Gert Town

predicted I'd be a poet,
my father wanted
to burn down Xavier

University. Use
his military expertise
to torture me

into confessing
whether or not I'd joined
a cult. The water moccasins

had my back when
I said that a career
in counting pills

made me conjure
thoughts of writing
my last words on a paper

flower. Petals adorned
with tears. But I flirted
with academic probation

after she'd spotted
me reading *Magic City*
when I should've been

cramming for my mid-term.
Behind her bangs
was a diamond-studded dome-piece

reflecting the faces of Professor
Longhair & Snooks Eaglin:
artists we blended skins

to while my roommate
pledged a frat that cherished
pyramids & intellect.

After our moans died down,
I tapped into a wavelength
that carried me to a Prismacolor

pen & an endless scroll.
On my couch, I waited
for a metaphor's giant steps

to clear out the weed
smoke & emerge
like a chord progression.

Dear Yusef,

Again last night, I caught Medusa
    sitting in my living room.
Not the devil. Not the dog
    in the shadows, made of shadows.
Not the old translucent maroon
    sharpening his machete. But
Medusa, lighting a spliff, spreading
    Tarot cards across the floor.
I didn't startle when a door slammed,
    but half expected a black cat
to run over my shoes. She wore
    the same red lipstick as the night
before, Yusef. Same black teddy
    with the skinny strap slipped
from her shoulder. Singing to herself,
    her voice split in two—contralto,
baritone: balladeer stroking the braids
    of a woman everyone knows
he beats; the woman singing *Yes*
    and *It's alright* . . . Sequined sleeves
hiding every track, a disco ball
    scattering shards of light along
some drab and peeling wall—Medusa
    cut the deck, relit the spliff, flipped
one card, then another. Took a pull
    so long I thought she'd catch fire.
You've not always been a good man,
    she said, showing seven cards,
coughing hard. There was something
    she wasn't telling me. She liked
that I didn't ask. Liked how I watched
    her dusting ashes from her thigh.

I see trouble finds you easy, hey boy?
    I pulled her onto my lap, or I slid
myself, somehow, up under her
    —I can't remember which—
she singing *Yes,* and *It's alright . . .*
    then slipping the joint, fire side first,
between her lips, she took my face
    in her hands, and shotgunned a cloud
into my open mouth. Some nights,
    Yusef, the serpents curse my name.
Some nights, they tell me secrets.

Y is for Y U S E F K O M U N Y A K A A,

U is for the Ubiquity
    of feeling in his work, no thought without emotion,
    no feeling without thought—the Union
    of music, emotion, beamwork, and thought.
S is for the Sensual,
    no thought or feeling without the felt,
    thinking, singular and seminal body.
E is for Energy, the tensile momentum,
F for the Freedom of Form, Freedom of
    each poem, to invent its living
    form, the living craft of his work.
K is for Kinetic—like a strong wine
    his poems have legs, and the legs move
    the poem, and the moved reader, along.
O is for Omigawd, how does he do it?!
M is for Music, M is for Many Musics.
U is for Universal—his specifics never
    limit who the poem can be singing to.
N is for Gunpowder—the explosives of the
    Nobel family which should come full circle as
    fireworks for books like *Dien Cai Dau*.
Y is for you and me, and for N. Y.
    U. and N. Y. Me, that we get
    to hear him tonight, in his new home.
A is for a sigh we breathe now
    together in anticipation.
K is for Komunyakaa—
A aaaaaaah,
A aaaaaaahhh.

Cento for Yusef, Whose Words
Led Me to Mine

Bloomington, 1989

As a way to stay alive in our world:
this is how I learned your language.

It was long ago. It was springtime.
You were a quiet man

with sweet words.
I tried to weave my own,

pencil pressed against paper
with one foolish hand.

I never asked how you
moved me beyond who I was

when we first met. Each memory
a shoot, a tendril, the tip of a wing.

I close my eyes & can see
you're here again, old friend,

waving to me across the years.
If it weren't for you, I wouldn't be

facing it:
the unknown, what remains unsaid,

the silence between birds
telling each other secrets.

That spring I'd learned
branches cluster with mouths ready to speak.

3/4 Jazz

I am subsumed by how it horns
into obsidian and how it's held up
ever-captive, on the streets where
Coltrane still lives I love the teak
and teak and teak of it, the hand
drum that recognizes me dark I
adore my ebony as it strides the F
key in Lateef's flute & my ten toes,
coal-colored, can outwit every lyre
as well as didgeridoo of aborigines,
coupling jet and the raven Agogô
bell. I'm sable & magical powers &
exhaust at least one hundred cymbals

A Poet Is Addressing My Loneliness

after Yusef Komunyakaa at the Beinecke

A poet reads his poem. Forgive my heart & penis, he says,
but don't forgive my hands. Beside me a listener scribbles some formula
on a piece of paper: letters, numbers, symbols, equations.

I'm alone in this listening crowd
as I think of places I forget.

If I brought a piece of stone or a handful of earth
from the far country where I come from, will I have been forgiven?

There's no forgiveness & the poet
who reads his poem & talks about dangerous beauty
is addressing my loneliness.

I'm an exile & I must forgive myself. Forgive the heart
for loving my self. Forgive, too, the happiness
that the late sunlight, which fills my room opening onto a view
of the outlying sea & the trees that live in silence, makes true.

There's that haunting voice in the hall again,
a poet I love whose face I can't see, reading.

How I long for the hands that nestled
on my back in those days in my country.

But in the distance lies my life, like a lighthouse.

No peace awaits me who must love anew,
& everlasting, the art of leaving.

William's Shoes

William Bush, d. 1898

Some say I mailed myself in a crate
to freedom's doorstep in Indiana.
Others declare I arrived on foot.
Even if I flew, what you need to know
is I came with blacksmith shoes
carved from tupelo.
      I could have continued
to Canada in those sweet-smelling shoes
but "to those whom much is given,
much is expected"—words my father heard
when his father handed him Ogun's bellows.
"Iron is a living thing," Baba said.
"It's in our blood and in earth's rocks.
Our work is to set it free."
    So I stayed in that Quaker town
forging axles for the false-bottom wagons
conductors drove. My hammer's song
called the Old Ones from the village of my fathers.
As I carried freedom seekers to the next station
with a posse in pursuit or waiting in ambush,
they added their sledges to iron's
heartbeat pounding in my chest.
      A blacksmith's stock-and-trade
is the power and knowledge of his forge.
I served as protector of Newport,
seeing in dreams when slave-hunters
with torches drew near. I doctored
people and animals with herbs from the forest
and when deadly smallpox struck,
carried the lesion-crusted bodies,

dug the long row of graves, paid each life
its pennyroyal of silence.

              What is left to say?
If you would know me, go to my village
and there before a glass case consider
what's left of the shoes I filled.

THE WORK OF ORPHEUS

Critical Essays and Other Considerations

Notes

(1) I heard the rhythm as an undergraduate. One of the first poems Dorianne Laux introduced us to in Introduction to Creative Writing was "Facing It" by Yusef Komunyakaa.

(2) I would have to return to "Facing It" many times, gaining a new language to see and hear the poem. I continue to return, this time making a map of rhythm.

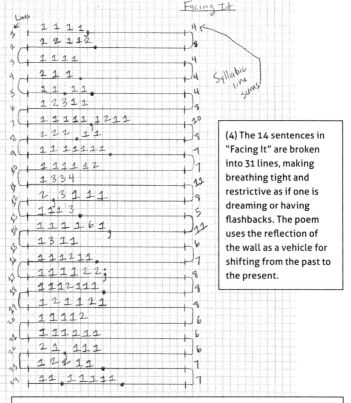

(3) The 31-line poem caught my ear. I was listening for a particular music in the language that felt familiar. Music that made a home in the ear and created meaning and tone.

(4) The 14 sentences in "Facing It" are broken into 31 lines, making breathing tight and restrictive as if one is dreaming or having flashbacks. The poem uses the reflection of the wall as a vehicle for shifting from the past to the present.

(5) The poem's syllabic line sum increases as we begin to flashback. As it increases, breathing becomes more difficult flashing from present to past every four lines. The first flash occurs in line 10. The line is monosyllabic until the last word, "inside." When we are taken to the Vietnam Veterans Memorial, the syllabic pattern increases, 1-3-2-4 until line 14. Then we are brought back to the present to read 58,022, which is the longest syllable in the poem.

(6) The poem breaks the pattern of scene changing in line 14. The poem establishes a new way of moving from the past to the present and a new speed at which we move. In lines 15–18, we telescope into the long list of names to focus on one name, "Andrew Johnson." Keeping with the original pattern of flashing scenes every four lines in line 19, we move further within the names to imagine the names shimmering "on a woman's blouse." The syllabic count increases with the line, making the breath do the same.

(7) In lines 22–31, the flashing continues. The poem's syllabic count increases in lines 24–31. We go from the completely monosyllabic line of 24. Then we increase the syllabic count slightly in lines 25–27. From lines 29–31, the poem has increased the syllabic sums significantly in a poem of one-word syllables.

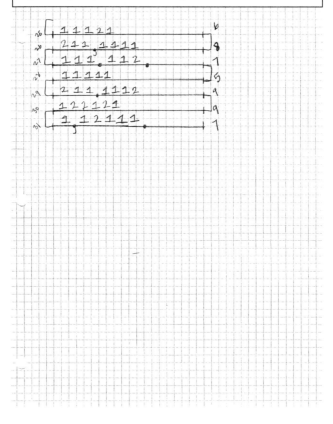

Beauty, Victory, and Survival in the Poetry of Yusef Komunyakaa

"It's truth we're after," Komunyakaa says in "Safe Subjects," a poem from his first book *Copacetic*. But it won't be an easy truth.

> Redemptive as a straight razor
> against the jugular vein—
> unacknowledged & unforgiven.
> It's truth we're after here,
> hurting for, out in the streets
> where my brothers kill each other . . .

For Komunyakaa that truth is not a matter of conveying literal or narrative subjects. In fact, in his first books, his poems retreat from language in terms of these functions—and I do not mean retreat in the sense of giving up. I mean retreat as an act of resistance, as one retreats in military strategy. In a world in which African American identity, in particular African American male identity, is constantly threatened, language and the poem itself become a last defense, the ultimate weapon of the ego against dissolution. For Komunyakaa language avenges pain, brings back what is lost, masks suffering, denies it and heals it. In Komunyakaa's poetry, language is the expression of an embattled ego determined by whatever means necessary to survive.

Rarely does Komunyakaa use the word "I" in his earlier books. In most poems he speaks in the voice of another person or merges with nature. ". . . I am the space / my body believes in," he says in "Unnatural State of the Unicorn." The disappearance of the poet is often embodied by sexual union with another. "[T]here's a stillness in us / like the tip of a magenta mountain," he says in "Woman, I Got the Blues." There's a timeless quality, a placeless quality to these poems. It's no time and it's now. It's no where and everywhere. The most permanent thing about the voice is the language it leaves behind—images so real they are like ripe fruit in the mouth.

The poems in *Dien Cai Dau*, Komunyakaa's sixth book, published in 1988, are held together by the excruciating tension between memory and forgetting. In the first poem, "Camouflaging the Chimera," soldiers prepare themselves for combat. "We tied branches to our helmets. / We painted our faces & rifles / with mud from a riverbank . . ." Later in the poem he says, "We aimed at dark-hearted songbirds." This reference to the gentleness of the adversaries and to their darkness may be indicative of the mixed feelings he faces in this conflict against people of color, and the sense that he is doing the dirty work of the oppressor of them both. The tone of the poem is dreamlike, as if he is watching all this happen. The men are anonymous, faceless. There is a sense of compulsion—the men are doing what they have to do and they don't stop, ". . . we waited / till the moon touched metal, / till something almost broke / inside us." They are so still "the river ran / through [their] bones." At the end of the poem, while they wait to ambush the enemy, each man is lost in his own private vision, "we held our breath / . . . as a world revolved / under each man's eyelid." Is the war a dream? Is the poem itself a dream? The title of the book, *Dien Cai Dau*, is a Vietnamese expression for American GIs meaning "crazy in the head." This is a book about seeing and not seeing, about not being there in order to be there. It presents the paradoxes of a psyche, of an art, that is compelled to examine itself, and yet determined to control reality in a way that makes it able to be survived. What may be termed pathological in one situation may be in fact a necessary and healthy response to an untenable reality. So we are introduced to the havoc that war wreaks on the psyche, and to the creation of states of consciousness, which keep horror at bay—denial, sleep, dream, hallucination, drug-induced states of unconsciousness, even insanity.

In *Magic City*, his eighth book, he writes about his childhood among people in Bogalusa, Louisiana, a rural Black Southern community isolated by racism, and driven by compelling economic, physical, and spiritual needs. These are among Komunyakaa's most lyrical and beautiful works. They have a straightforward lyricism, as if anger has been released and opened the door to the bittersweet pleasures of the past. The poems are closer to the real world, its matter, heaviness and sorrow, its cry and moan of sex. "But I know things / I don't supposed to know," he says in "Venus's-flytraps." Adults appear in the glorious way a child first sees the people that he or she admires and loves. There is a richness and vitality that is unforgettable. The time frame for these poems is from about age five to about fourteen or fifteen, from boyhood to sexual initiation, that protected period when a boy learns to be a man. "Soon we'd be / Responsible for the chambered / Rapture honeycombed in flesh," he says in "Boys in Dresses." The poet combines a child's vision and passion, an adult's understanding and wisdom, and a poet's eye. "Don't mess with me / 'Cause I have my Lone Ranger / Six-shooter. I can hurt / You with questions / Like silver bullets." There is always a driving question—what is the nature of good and evil. Martin Luther King distinguished between primary evil and secondary evil by saying that primary evil is the evil that causes other evils to happen. If so, certainly the community he evokes in these poems—even in their acts of violence—are innocent.

Komunyakaa's language makes memory visceral. For me his metaphors don't illustrate reality—for example, he says "her breasts rose like swamp orchids," or "everything breaks for green cover like a hundred red birds released from a wooden box." It seems the reverse is true, that reality's purpose is to illustrate art. This is the art of consciousness, which is a celebration of the sheer made thing itself. In *Thieves of Paradise*, Komunyakaa's most brilliant and provocative poems, the poet synthesizes the varied voices he has used in the past. As in the past, he is intent on forming poems rooted in song and mythology, and one is aware of the long tradition of black magic, voodoo, and conjure. However, this voice speaks from a sacred place, as if Komunyakaa, with knowledge of our personal, social, and spiritual history, has gone through a transformative experience. It is as if we are reading a sacred text, one that has found a personal resolution that contains forgiveness, compassion, and joy.

Quite simply, Komunyakaa is one of the most extraordinary poets writing today. He takes on the most complex moral issues, the most harrowingly ugly subjects of our American life. His voice, whether it embodies the specific experiences of a Black man, a soldier in Vietnam, or a child in Bogalusa, Louisiana, is universal. It shows us in ever-deeper ways what it is to be human.

The Calamity of Unknowing

In August of 2016, from the Strand bookstore, I bought a copy of Yusef Komunyakaa's *The Emperor of the Water Clocks*. This was one of the books I'd take to North Africa, where I'd been living for seven years. The title intrigued me. And this poet was one I ardently admired and sought new work from upon publication. Reading the collection on the airplane, and then for a second time in a café in Morocco, and then a third time in a different Moroccan café, I kept stopping to re-read the poem, "A Night in Tunisia." The title refers to the country of Tunisia, but more obviously, Dizzy Gillespie's 1942 composition, now jazz standard. The song itself, sublime. Moving the listener through color, space, emotion, time. But I'm interested in Komunyakaa's speaker. Namely, the speaker's position as an outsider, the speaker beginning with two questions both regarding duration, the experience of hearing a song and the death of its maker: "How long have I listened / to this blues & how long / had Dizzy Gillespie been dead?" The speaker is asking for knowledge of which he has some inclination, some vague idea of but longs to know more, longs for precision, longs for fullness, something more complete. The speaker moves through memories of his life, explicitly that of his youth: reading, traveling, pondering. These experiences of gathering knowledge are fueled by a "longing" for it. He's specifically thinking about the country, Tunisia, which he's visited often, loves, sees as beautiful, perhaps quaint, peacefully alive in its quaintness. But then, there is a change, "a lifetime before" . . . the country erupts. ". . . Tunisia burned . . ."

Of course, the speaker is referring to Mohamed Bouazizi, the fruit and vegetable vendor who set himself on fire, December 17, 2010, to protest corruption and injustice. Bouazizi's act of defiance initiated dissent: often violent, often frenzied throughout the nation and region. The speaker, even after visiting the country often, still didn't know it. He couldn't see or hear the rumble of regular people, their whispers while trying to make a life in that place of "naked feeling," in that place where quotidian existences are often unfair, grim, unbearable. Komunyakaa is asserting one of the most problematic realities of humanness, our inability to fully know something or someone. We don't know even having experienced, seen, a place, or person. We remain outside of that place, outside of that person. We can't fully know it or them.

I traveled to Tunisia to visit friends and see Sidi Bouzid, the town where Bouazizi burned himself, the town where the Tunisian Revolution, the Jasmine Revolution, and the Arab Spring were ignited. There, sitting at a table outside of Café Tunis; there, sipping a short glass of mint tea for several hours, I re-read the book then re-read and re-read that poem as Tunisians strolled home from the markets, restaurants, theaters, work, or school. I kept thinking of Komunyakaa's speaker and the complication of his wanting, needing, believing he'd had knowledge of that place. But then realizing he didn't, and mourning that which he thought he knew, what he'd understood. And not only that, but the violence, the upheaval, the literal destruction of that "known" beloved place and some of its people, "tear gas & machine-gun fire / & my head in my hands / an hour."

I think about this knowledge of the unknown and this idea of positioning often, as I'm someone, as well, whose work is informed by what I learn and often observe elsewhere. What does it mean to know yet not know? What does it mean to feel close to something or someone, yet realize one is not—or not as—close? Or what does it mean to know there is more, there is always more to know? Yes, what one sees, what one experiences is the thing, but not everything. Komunyakaa places the reader and the speaker in that awkward space. The questions for me are, what will we do there, and what will this space make?

MELISSA C. JOHNSON

Yusef Komunyakaa's *Dien Cai Dau*
Vietnam as Femme Fatale

In Yusef Komunyakaa's 1988 poetry collection, *Dien Cai Dau*,[1] a Black soldier narrates his experiences in and observations about the war and reflects on the aftermath of the war on Vietnam, on the Vietnamese, and on American veterans and their families. Through the narrative voice of the Black soldier, Komunyakaa draws attention to the racial politics of the Vietnamese war and its aftermath, in the form of racism against Black soldiers, the Vietnamese, and Amerasian children. As Don Ringnalda notes, the collection is unusual for Vietnam War poetry in that it includes a large cast of characters other than White soldiers, "civilians, bar girls, *bui doi* (sic) Amerasian, Red Cross workers, prisoners, an army nurse, the boat people, and himself [the narrator] as an underrepresented member of African American people."[2] The Vietnamese prostitutes, rape victims, soldiers, and casualties, and the American Red Cross workers, USO entertainers, and lovers back home who people these poems merge into the landscape[3] of Vietnam, sexualizing the Vietnam War experience by depicting Vietnam and the Vietnamese as both a feminine and racial other, seductive, silent, and deadly—a *femme fatale* who can only be known or conquered through conjugal knowledge or sexual subjugation.[4]

Throughout *Dien Cai Dau*, Vietnamese men and women are associated with nature, with birds, and with sensual fabrics like silk, as well as with weapons, explosives, and death. In "Camouflaging the Chimera," the first poem in the collection, the Viet Cong soldiers are described as "dark-hearted songbirds" (line 14) and "like black silk / wrestling iron through grass" (lines 24–25). "Hanoi Hannah" is "a bleeding flower" (line 34) whose "knife-edge song cuts / deep as a sniper's bullet" (lines 25–26). The rape victim in "Re-creating the Scene," "floats on [their rapists'] rage / like a torn water flower" (lines 17–18). The prostitutes in "The Edge" "have an unmerciful memory," "know a slow dying," and "scatter like birds" (lines 3, 13, and 18). Through these repeated images in the descriptions of Vietnamese men and women, they become associated collectively with the natural, particularly birds and flowers, and with death, a metonymic chain expressing the feminine, and particularly the *femme fatale* of the essentializing Western literary tradition.[5]

Images of embracing the Vietnamese, both the women and the male soldiers, are woven throughout the collection, serving both to eroticize the conflict, in terms of both heterosexual and homosexual desire, and to further feminize the Vietnamese. In "Sappers," Viet Cong commandos

             fall
& rise again like torchbearers,
with their naked bodies
greased so moonlight dances
off their skin. They run
with explosives strapped
around their waists,
& try to fling themselves
into our arms.
(lines 9–17)

On one hand, as Susan Conley has observed, these images express empathy with the enemy,[6] as in "Starlight Scope Myopia," where the speaker describes the men he sees through the starlight scope in a manner which makes clear his desire to protect them from the American soldiers, and to help them in their labor: "This one, old, bowlegged, / You feel you could reach out / & take him into your arms" (lines 35–37). On the other hand, that empathy can only be expressed through the language and gestures of sexual desire, desire in which the speaker/observer is in a putative position of power, by virtue of race and gender privilege, a privilege complicated by his own subordinated racial position in terms of Black/White race categories, as well as his empathy with the subject position of the Vietnamese.[7] The issue is further complicated by the use of the Vietnamese women's bodies as substitutes or stand-ins for either the bodies of American women, lovers in "the world," or Vietnamese men, who the speaker "embraces" through the bodies of the women—limiting the physical expression of his desires, and of his belief in the common humanity of the Vietnamese, to heterosexual relations.[8]

One poem which particularly highlights these complex intersections of systems of race, gender, and sexuality is "Tu Do Street." In this poem, the color line is transferred from the United States' Jim Crow South to Vietnam. This relocation calls into question defining racial difference[9] along a Black/White axis through the introduction of a third racial category, the Vietnamese, who are seen as a subordinate race by both Black and White people.[10] Komunyakaa complicates "race" and racial difference through the role of the Vietnamese, particularly the women, in maintaining and subverting the traditional Black/White color line, a geographic, economic, and political barrier based on a racist power hierarchy.[11] The color line in Vietnam exists outside the enforced integration of the armed services, in the areas where soldiers go when off-duty, and even here is subverted in "off-limits" areas such as brothels. In these off-limits areas, hierarchies of power along race lines are undermined, while gender hierarchies are reinforced and homosexual desire is displaced. The bodies of the Vietnamese women become a site for questioning racial difference, transgressing the color line, and affirming male and American superiority.

A major trope of the poem is the intangibility and impermanence of the color line, equated with the absence of a traditional front line in the war in Vietnam, which was characterized by guerrilla warfare. The arbitrary and incorporeal nature of the color line is figured as a line in the dust, and as sound:

> Music divides the evening.
> I close my eyes & can see
> men drawing lines in the dust.
> America pushes through the membrane
> of mist & smoke, & I'm a small boy
> again in Bogalusa. *White Only*
> signs & Hank Snow. But tonight
> (lines 1–7)

The speaker of the poem is reminded of his childhood in a Louisiana town by the music he hears as he enters Tu Do Street in Saigon for a little R and R. The competing sounds of Hank Williams, and the unnamed music emanating from the "turf" of the Black GIs, mark the "color line," which bisects the street. The speaker's realization that the color line exists, even among the integrated troops in Vietnam, is presented as a metaphorical rape—"America pushes through the membrane of mist & smoke." As he is confronted with the replication of the racial politics of America and particularly of the American South among the American troops in Vietnam, a line drawn in the dust and demarcated by music, the speaker loses power and agency—becoming a "small boy again."

The end of line seven, "But tonight," suggests that the experience in Tu Do street will differ from the speaker's remembered experiences of racial segregation, and as the poem progresses we see that the experience does differ. The difference is that the experience of racism is filtered through the Vietnamese women who work at the bar the speaker enters.

> I walk into a place where bar girls
> fade like tropical birds. When
> I order a beer, the mama-san
> behind the counter acts as if she
> can't understand, while her eyes
> skirt each white face, as Hank Williams
> calls from the psychedelic jukebox.
> (lines 8–14)

The bar girls are depicted as exotic creatures—like tropical birds—emphasizing their female and racial otherness as well as their ability to disappear into the jungle, much like the Viet Cong, and their lack of individual identities. They are merely Vietnamese bar girls, numerous and interchangeable.[12] The bar girls are equated, here and later in lines 23–25, with the enemy: "Back in the bush at Dak To / & Khe Sanh, we fought / the brothers of these women / we now run to hold in our arms." This correlation of the bar girls with the enemy can be understood in three ways. Primarily, during the Vietnam War, it was exceedingly difficult for American troops to distinguish the enemy from the general populace, and thus these women could be "brothers" to the Viet Cong, either politically or fraternally. This is memorably pointed out by Michael Herr in *Dispatches*: ". . . the VC got work inside all the camps as shoeshine boys and laundresses and honey-dippers, they'd starch your fatigues and burn your shit and then go home and mortar your area."[13]

Secondly, the speaker's desire to embrace the enemy, seen particularly in "Starlight Scope Myopia," a desire that could be seen as homosexual, is here displaced onto the women. And finally, in this particular bar, the bar girls interact only with White troops and thus take a position along the color line, thus siding with the White racist "enemy." In fact, it is the Vietnamese women who enforce the color line by refusing the Black speaker service, but they do so at the instigation of the White troops. The mama-san avoids the Black soldier's face, "skirting" the White soldiers' faces as she looks in their direction to see if they are watching her transaction with the Black soldier. By looking in the direction of the White soldiers as she pretends not to understand his request for a beer, the mama-san informs the Black speaker that she refuses service because of the White soldiers' presence and that only White soldiers will receive service, both drinks and "skirts" in the form of the bar girls. The "Whites-only" status of this bar is communicated to the speaker both through the mama-san's actions and through the Hank Williams song playing on the jukebox. Thus the women of this particular bar are identified as the "enemy" both for their own race, Vietnamese, and their racial prejudice toward the Black speaker.

The speaker's awareness of the origins of the mama-san's racially prejudiced behavior is seen in the lines that follow:

> We have played Judas where
> only machine-gun fire brings us
> together. Down the street
> black GIs hold to their turf also.
> (lines 15–18)

The American troops have betrayed one another by transporting the idea of racial difference and the racism of the color line into Vietnam and thus undermining the unity of the American troops. The "we" here can be seen to refer both to the American troops—both Black and White—and to the troops and the Vietnamese women. The poem suggests that the troops are brought together across race lines only in battle and because they have a common enemy, the Vietnamese, and a common desire to survive. In their "leisure" time, they betray the solidarity of battle through segregation. The troops and the women are brought together through the war itself—"only machine-gun fire brings us / together"—and they betray one another as well. This betrayal is not a central focus of this particular poem but other poems in the collection, such as "One More Loss to Count," "Saigon Bar Girls, 1975," "Hanoi Hannah," "Toys in a Field," and "Re-creating the Scene," deal with these betrayals by and of Vietnamese women, who are raped, lied to, impregnated, and abandoned by the American troops, and who, in turn, attempt to undermine the Black soldier's loyalty to America by fanning the flames of Black/White racial tensions in order to win the war. These racial tensions are temporarily resolved in "Tu Do Street" through the sharing of Vietnamese women's bodies by Black and White soldiers. However, throughout the collection the American troops continue to play Judas to the Vietnamese women.

After encountering the racial segregation of Tu Do Street, the speaker leaves the street for the "off-limits" area located in the alleys surrounding it, looking "for a softness behind these voices / wounded by their beauty and war" (21–22). The voices are the voices of the Vietnamese women, who are of the same race as the Viet Cong, and who have joined the racial "war" against African Americans by barring the speaker from the White bar. They are also the voices of the White country singers, Hank Williams and Hank Snow, whose music is synonymous with the color line and the "war" between the races in the speaker's mind. The speaker finds softness with the Vietnamese women in the form of sex with Vietnamese prostitutes, but these women have no voices and no names. They are shadowy figures who serve as a conduit between the Black and White troops:

> There's more than a nation
> inside us, as black & white
> soldiers touch the same lovers
> minutes apart, tasting
> other's breath,
> (lines 27–31)

Through the bodies of Vietnamese women, the Black and White troops share a Judas kiss across racial lines, a kiss which marks as well as blurs racial difference. They achieve unity, become a united nation, only through warfare against and sexual intercourse with the race of people they are at war with. The "us" in line 28 is as multivalent as the "we" of line 15, referring not only to the American troops of both races, but to the American troops and the Vietnamese women. Inside and among the troops, there are race identifications and ideologies which are at odds with the idea of nation. Through their shared sexual possession of the Vietnamese women, the Black and White troops achieve unity, an eroticized sharing of breath, and of a subordinated other, temporarily bridging the color line. The women and the troops, both Black and White, share a human connection which refutes the racist ideology expressed through America's involvement in Vietnam, an ideology signified by the "off-limits" sign posted to keep troops from miscegenation. The customary American taboos of miscegenation are inapplicable to this situation, however, because the Vietnamese women are seen as subordinate to both Blacks and Whites.

Abdul R. JanMohamed's idea of "racialized sexuality," a development on Foucault's theories of sexuality, is interestingly applicable here. Although JanMohamed deals only with Black/White sexuality, particularly the origins of racialized sexuality in slavery, his observation that since the master's sexual desire for the slave "implicitly admits the slave's humanity, it undermines the foundation of the [racial] border—the supposed inhumanity of the Black other, her putative ontological alterity" can be expanded to elucidate the situation in this poem.[14] Through their desire for the Vietnamese women, the soldiers refute the official ideology of the lesser humanity of the Vietnamese. Through their shared sexual desire for the same women, the Black and White soldiers reveal a common humanity which unifies them as male Americans.[15] The soldiers also share a lack of knowledge about this unity, which is known only to the Vietnamese prostitute and the speaker of the poem.

In the final three lines of the poem, the temporary unity of the troops is seen as a form of damnation:

Without knowing these rooms
run into each other like tunnels
leading to the underworld.

The prostitutes are once again equated with the enemy; their rooms are connected like the intricate underground tunnel systems of the Viet Cong. The soldiers can enter the rooms from different ends of segregated Tu Do Street, without realizing that they are sharing the same women, without realizing that they have crossed the color line, and at the same time drawn another one to take its place. This crossing is a form of damnation and of transgression, associated with the underworld, the mythological realm of the dead, and the sphere of criminal activity not sanctioned by society. On the bodies of the Vietnamese women, the Black and White troops write and erase the racist ideology signified in America's Black/White color line, as well as the racist ideology of the racial inferiority of the Vietnamese used to indoctrinate American troops in Vietnam. Even in sharing the same women by enacting gender and race privilege, the American troops discover that "There's more than a nation" inside them. Racism cannot be cured by further acts of oppression.

This truth is brought home to the speaker/narrator in the poems that examine the aftermath of the Vietnam conflict, particularly *"Dui Boi, Dust of Life,"* a poem which deals with the narrator/speaker's first meeting with his Amerasian son. In this poem, the child, like the men and women of Vietnam throughout the collection, is associated with nature, particularly birds and flowers:

You followed me, blameless
as a blackbird in Hue
singing from gutted jade.
Son, you were born with dust
on your eyelids, but you bloomed up
in a trench where stones were
stacked to hold you down.
(lines 16–22)

In addition to feminizing the Amerasian boy through the use of the same imagery used throughout the collection to describe both Vietnamese men and women, the poet directly addresses the figurative emasculation of the Vietnamese as a "racialized" other, and the sometimes-literal emasculation of the despised Amerasian children in the lines, "Come here, son, let's see / if they castrated you" (lines 8–9). This unwanted child, the "dust" or detritus of life, a mixture of two subordinated races, who was "born disappearing" (line 15) because no one wanted to see him, echoes the burning girl from "'You and I Are Disappearing,'" a memory that won't fade, a reality that can't be denied. Like the abandoned machinery of war in "Toys in a Field," upon which Vietnamese and Amerasian children play, this child's presence reminds the speaker that Vietnam, both its landscape and its people, as well as his own life, have been radically changed by the experience of the Vietnam War, but that racism has not altered or disappeared. Although the Black speaker has achieved a temporary equality with White male soldiers in the subordination of the Vietnamese bar girls, that equality disappears when the war ends. In "To Have Danced with Death," "The black sergeant first class" (line 1) who emerges from the plane, minus a leg, finds himself in a racially divided country:

> He half smiled when
> the double doors opened for him
>
> Like a wordless mouth taking back promises.
> The room of blue eyes averted his.
> (lines 14–17)

The promise of racial equality for the Black soldiers that was found in the subordination of the Vietnamese vanishes when they return to America.

At the end of the collection the image of Vietnam as a *femme fatale* has undergone a revision. In "Saigon Bar Girls, 1975," the girls of "Tu Do Street" have gained names and individual stories, and they forgo seduction to return to villages dressed in "peasant clothes / the color of soil" (lines 3–4). The mother of the Amerasian boy, both Vietnam and his biological mother, is described as "a half-broken / shield" (lines 11–12) that the speaker held against himself, revealing both his own reliance on a conception of Vietnam and the Vietnamese as a sexualized feminine presence, a *femme fatale*, and the destructive and reductive nature of this conception.

NOTES

1. The title translates as "crazy" or "crazy in the head." Susan Conley, "About Yusef Komunyakaa: A Profile," *Ploughshares* 72 (Spring 1997): 2. See also Don Ringnalda, "Rejecting 'Sweet Geometry': Komunyakaa's *Duende*," *Journal of American Culture* 16, no. 3 (1993): 23.

2. Ringnalda, "Rejecting," 25.

3. Interestingly, in an interview with Muna Asali, Komunyakaa has said

about his experience in Vietnam: "I did not fear the land. I realized that there was a kind of beauty in the overall landscape. And many times that is what we have, beauty and violence side by side. We have been taught to see that as a contradiction, but, to me, contradiction is a sort of discourse." Muna Asali, "An Interview with Yusef Komunyakaa," *New England Review* 16, no. 1 (1994): 142–43. I hope to delineate one thread of that contradictory discourse as it is articulated in *Dien Cai Dau*, through the imagery of the *femme fatale*.

4. Adi Wimmer's article "Vietnam as the Feminine 'Other' in the Rhetoric of Vietnam War Poetry" argues that "both American poets of the 1960s and Vietnam Veteran poets after the Vietnam war articulate their protest and sorrow in terms of constructing an *implied feminine Other* as an *alternative* to a discredited masculine self" (emphasis in original text), thus putting a much more positive spin on the feminization of Vietnam. Wimmer does qualify her argument with "even though their attempts are not always convincing and satisfactory" (101) and points out that these feminine representations tend to stereotype and sometimes exhibit a "veiled misogyny" (107–08). Wimmer deals only with the representations of women and the country itself in American poetry, does not address race, and only briefly mentions Komunyakaa's work.

5. For treatment of the *femme fatale* figure in literature and art, see Virginia Allen's *The Femme Fatale: Erotic Icon* and Patrick Bade's *Femme Fatale: Images of Evil and Fascinating Women*.

6. Conley, "About Yusef Komunyakaa," 2.

7. This empathy is seen most clearly in "Prisoners," where the speaker resists the impulse to bow to Vietnamese prisoners, "thin-framed as box kites / of sticks and black silk" (6–7).

8. Although I do not mean to imply here that Komunyakaa is gay, it would be difficult and reductionist to ignore the homoerotic overtones of the descriptions of the male Vietnamese soldiers, as well as the similar imagery used to describe these soldiers and the Vietnamese prostitutes. This imagery should not lead to conclusions about the sexuality of the author, but it certainly sheds light on the ways in which dominant cultures feminize subordinate cultures.

9. By referring to "racial difference" I do not mean essential or biological differences between the "races," but refer rather to those differences of morphology and phenotype that are and have been used to designate or categorize persons as belonging to specific races. The term also encompasses the differences in social, economic, and political power accruing to those of privileged and marginalized "races."

10. As Angela Davis notes in chapter 11 of *Women, Race and Class*, "Rape, Racism and the Myth of the Black Rapist," during the Vietnam War, "it was drummed into the heads of U.S. soldiers that they were fighting an inferior race." Angela Davis, *Women Race and Class* (New York: Vintage, 1981), 179.

11. In addition to the racism directed toward the Black soldier in this poem

by the Vietnamese women in the bar, several other poems in the collection deal with the Vietnamese response to the American color line. In "Hanoi Hannah," Hannah directly addresses Black soldiers, informing them of Martin Luther King's death and asking, "Soul Brothers, what you dying for?" (27). In "The One-Legged Stool," a Black captive is isolated from his White companions and told by his captors that they are making racist remarks about him; they also tell him about King's death. In "Report from the Skull's Diorama," "a platoon of black GIs" find leaflets saying "*VC didn't kill / Dr. Martin Luther King*" (7 and 21–22). This psychological warfare tactic reveals not only that the Vietnamese knew their enemy, but also that the irony of a subordinated people fighting another subordinated people does not escape them or the author/speaker.

12. As JanMohamed observes, systems arising from or promoting racial oppression, such as colonialist literature and racialized sexuality, function "by first reducing the colonized or racialized subject to a generic being that can be exchanged for any other 'native' or racialized subject." In this instance, the speaker enacts his race privilege by seeing the bar girls as indiscreet. Abdul R. JanMohamed, "Sexuality on/of the Racial Border: Foucault, Wright and the Articulation of 'Racialized Sexuality'" in *Discourse of Sexuality: From Aristotle to Aids*, ed. Donna C. Stanton (Ann Arbor: University of Michigan Press, 1992), 106.

13. Michael Herr, *Dispatches* (New York: Avon Books, 1978), 13–14.

14. JanMohamed, "Sexuality," 104.

15. Alvin Aubert in his article, "Yusef Komunyakkaa: The Unified Vision—Canonization and Humanity," argues that the line "There's more than a nation inside us" indicates the shared humanity of the Black and White soldiers. While this analysis explains part of the poem, it is also an oversimplification, concerned only with making Aubert's overall argument about Komunyakaa's "resistance, textualized formalistically as well as thematically in his poems, to those forces in the hegemonous counterculture aimed at excluding him as an African American from the ranks of humanity." What Aubert ignores is that the "we" could just as easily mean the Vietnamese women and *all* the soldiers, as the White and Black soldiers, or as my reading argues, both at the same time. Alvin Albert, "Yusef Komunyakaa: The Unified Vision—Canonization and Humanity," *African American Review* 27, no. 1 (1993): 119.

WORKS CITED

Allen, Virginia. *The Femme Fatale: Erotic Icon*. Troy, NY: Winston Publishing Co., 1983.

Asali, Muna. "An Interview with Yusef Komunyakaa." *New England Review* 16, no. 1 (1994): 141–47.

Aubert, Alvin. "Yusef Komunyakaa: The Unified Vision—Canonization and Humanity." *African American Review* 27, no. 1 (1993): 119–23.

Bade, Patrick. *Femme Fatale: Images of Evil and Fascinating Women.* New York: Mayflower Books, 1979.

Conley, Susan. "About Yusef Komunyakaa: A Profile" *Ploughshares* 72 (Spring 1997). www.pshares.org/issues/spring-1997/about-yusef-komunyakaa -profile.

Davis, Angela. *Women, Race and Class.* New York: Vintage, 1981.

Herr, Michael. *Dispatches.* New York: Avon Books, 1978.

JanMohamed, Abdul R. "Sexuality on/of the Racial Border: Foucault, Wright and the Articulation of 'Racialized Sexuality.'" In *Discourse of Sexuality: From Aristotle to Aids,* edited by Donna C. Stanton, 94–115. Ann Arbor: University of Michigan Press, 1992.

Komunyakaa, Yusef. *Dien Cai Dau.* Hanover, NH: Wesleyan University Press, 1988.

Ringnalda, Don. "Rejecting 'Sweet Geometry': Komunyakaa's *Duende.*" *Journal of American Culture* 16, no. 3 (1993): 21–28.

Wimmer, Adi. "Vietnam as the Feminine 'Other' in the Rhetoric of Vietnam War Poetry." In *The Insular Dream: Obsession and Resistance,* edited by Kristiaan Versluys, 99–109. Amsterdam: VU University Press, 1995.

The Poet as Shape Shifter:

Yusef Komunyakaa's "Ode to the Chameleon"

In "Ode to the Chameleon," Yusef Komunyakaa's twenty-three-line poem from his book *The Chameleon Couch*, the poet calls the lizard a "little shape shifter," thereby hinting at the transformation that will occur in such a brief and compact space. Komunyakaa employs indirection, accumulation, and intense music to create lyric intensity and layers of meaning. Like all great poems, this one keeps evolving, giving more with each reading, revelations that take us on a journey through history while never seeming to leave the small twig on which the chameleon "is no more than an eyeblink."

Komunyakaa opens the poem with a focus on the chameleon, a magical creature who dares "the human eye / to see deeper." Enacting the poet's way of knowing the world through a cascade of metaphor—"you are a glimpse / of a rainbow, your eyes an iota / of amber"—Komunyakaa unfolds a complex and mysterious point of view. As the poem progresses, the context in which the silent chameleon sits keeps expanding until it encompasses a huge span of history, the chameleon-poet changing before our eyes, always there but disappearing into the background, waiting for us to see what is right before us. Layer by layer, what has always been there comes into view, though we were blind and impatient, not always caring to linger long enough to take in and to get to know our world or ourselves. Here, the everyday is both miraculous and terrifying, and poetry rides the paradox, poetry is the paradox, absorbing and employing beauty and horror, never resolving, always changing and deepening our experience.

Ode to the Chameleon

Little shape shifter, lingering
there on your quotidian twig
of indifference, you are a glimpse
of a rainbow, your eyes an iota

of amber. If nature is mind,
it knows you are always
true, daring the human eye
to see deeper. You are envy
& solace approaching green,
no more than an eyeblink
in a corner of the Old World.
You are a tilt of the head
& vantage point, neither this
nor that, clearly prehistoric
& futuristic, & then you are
gone. In your little theater
of osmosis, you're almost
a piece of tropical work woven
from the alchemist's skin habit.
Called into the hanging garden,
you sit there, almost unseen
as dusky shadows climb
the blooming Judas tree.

There is so much skill in "Ode," and so much of what Komunyakaa calls *alchemy*. Look at how the poem shifts from line to line. It begins with the chameleon on its "quotidian twig," an image the underlying musicality of which would seem rich enough in itself, never mind how the image will continue to resonate throughout the poem. Then the line turns and the ordinary twig becomes a "twig / of indifference," which brings a level of truth and accuracy to the image, for the twig is both ordinary and indifferent, qualities the human eye usually ignores, qualities the human doesn't want to embody or accept in itself. The chameleon is perfectly at home on such a twig, even though, as the description immediately tells us, the chameleon itself is not ordinary, but quite beautiful, "with its glimpse of rainbow" and its tiny amber eye. And in fact, chameleons' eyes are quite distinct, among other things each eye can rotate separately, meaning they can focus on two things at once. Komunyakaa always brings an understated erudition to his poems; here it is in the knowledge of a specific creature, a creature that can notice layers of history and human waste, while being in the moment, sitting on a twig and watching.

Try speaking this poem quickly—you cannot because the repetition of sounds, as in all the short i's of "little" "shifter" "lingering" "twig" "quotidian" "indifference" and "glimpse," or the *sh* sounds of "shape" and "shifter," combined with the length of the words, makes us read more slowly, makes us stop a bit to think, just as the chameleon makes us look hard in order to find it. There's no rush here despite the brevity of the poem; the musical patterns give pleasure and the poem reveals itself gradually, deliberately, and yet with constant surprise. "If nature is mind" is the kind of confident statement this poet makes, as we slide over it half wondering, *is nature mind? Is nature intelligent? Intentional? Does it see and hear? Does it know itself?* But Komunyakaa won't linger long on philosophy—the shape shifter is "always / true, daring the human eye" and here the line break pulls the reader another layer down into the poem, "to see deeper." Now the poet begins the series of paradoxes that the mysterious chameleon must embody: *envy & solace, neither this nor that, prehistoric & futuristic,* a creature spanning dimensions of time and yet it is "no more than an eyeblink / in a corner of the Old World." The eyeblink refers both to the actual eye of the animal, as well as to how easily it can disappear from sight, but we won't truly understand till the end of the poem just what he means by "Old World." The paradoxes the poem implies are also a feature of the chameleon's ability to see more than one thing at a time—to hold two disparate things in its vision.

Komunyakaa has introduced to the reader so many qualities that the chameleon/poet/poem must embody—for this is a poem about a strange animal as well as it is about creation, about art and human treachery, and it also is an Ode, a celebration of those mysteries. As the poem turns yet again, the metaphors become riskier, more dramatic. The chameleon is in its "little theater," and watch the leap of the line break and the surprise of what follows: "theater / of osmosis," a surprising phrase which calls to mind the magical changes chameleons embody in ways that are chemical and biological, but ultimately mysterious, little dramas in nature. Such changes, he suggests, are at the tipping point of our understanding in that they are natural and yet seemingly unnatural: "tropical work woven / from the alchemist's skin habit." Who is the alchemist—nature? Some deity working its tricks? To keep up, the reader must leap from metaphor to metaphor, held together by the notion of change. The word *skin* speaks of the lizard's changes in color, yet it is eerily human as well. So much has gone on in those few lines that the poem has become a little theater itself. The language is tight; it sings and gives us little room to stop for breath as the poet moves from image to image, idea to idea.

But where is this all leading? "Called into the hanging garden," we are called into the final drama of the poem, a mere four lines, and our vision now steps back a bit and we are not just looking at the twig where the chameleon sits, we suddenly have a more panoramic view, as if we are on that twig, seeing through the eyes of the chameleon. Now the creature is almost unseen and yet we feel it watching. Watching what? The "dusky shadows climb / the blooming Judas tree"? What is this hanging garden?

At first it's just a beautiful garden with hanging vines and flowers. But that's not quite right. There is a blooming Judas tree with its purple blossoms, the tree on which Judas is said to have hanged himself, and suddenly we are literally in the *hanging* garden where the chameleon watches the human tragedy unfold; the chameleon, the shape shifter, is a witness to history. It reaches back to the *Old World*, to the time of Jesus, and yet it speaks to us in the moment, helping the reader to become a surprised onlooker.

Such is the power of the artist-chameleon who must take any shape or form, however humble, to tell the story of human waste and grief, of death in the middle of a blossoming tree where the narrative has taken one more terrible turn. This is a long story, and the poet can only give us, as he says, *an eyeblink*. But what a layered and full blink it is. The Judas tree holds other resonance, other horrors. It not only invokes the ancient story, a history-changing event, it also invokes a lynching, a historical violence much closer to home for the poet and for the contemporary reader. Do we see it? Or look away? Are we watching from the distance, or are we immersed in the horror? Will we see the echoes of violence, not only those of deep history, but our own history, or will we choose to see only the beauty of that strange place?

For the poem to take such a turn, and to take it so successfully and gracefully, with such a light touch so that the deeper meaning does not at first come through, is characteristic of Komunyakaa's work. The beauty of the scene is undercut by the violence and self-destruction implicit in the tree's name. The "Ode" becomes an ode not to a simple animal that we readers can admire and romanticize—it becomes an ode to the hidden intelligence of nature, to the secret witnessing by a creature that is seemingly invisible or insignificant—though it is also "prehistoric

/ & futuristic." The poem gives and gives, it enacts the complexity of seeing, of witness, as well as the complex relationship between humans and the rest of creation, twisting the reader's expectations and fantasies about nature before we realize what is happening. We can read the poem on a simpler level, where we are the witnesses stepping out of the poem and watching the chameleon disappear into the scenery, or we can read it more deeply and completely by following each clue as the poet leads us toward horror: Judas hanging in the midst of beauty, with only the hidden and vulnerable creatures looking on—or the American horror of lynching, a history we have hardly begun to reckon with.

Who is the deceiver and who is deceived? Judas or Jesus? The chameleon? Or we who fail to see? Nature is mind, the poet says, but we humans think we are outside nature and that we, not nature, are mind; we think we are separate, that nature is blank and we must impose ourselves upon it. But here, it is the other way around. We are blank, unseeing, and the truth must be gently imposed on us.

The complexity of the poem comes to us not just in its argument or images, but also in the musical patterns, the internal and slant rhymes, the repeated sounds. When Komunyakaa makes his list of paradoxes, his metaphors for the little shape shifter, he ties that wild list together sonically, as in the words *this, prehistoric, futuristic, little, osmosis, alchemist's skin.* This sound pattern carries us through till the poem turns in the last four lines, and as the tragedy unfolds, the music grows more hushed, with less staccato and more open vowels, and finally a regular iambic meter that brings closure and unease as the shadows rise and we are given the final piece of this puzzle. The almost-rhyme of *unseen* and *tree* also adds to that unease because that hint of sonic accordance at the end of the poem is false and frightening: the chameleon disappears, as chameleons do, while a man comes into view, hanging in a blossoming tree.

And so we have seen the chameleon close up, telescopically, and we have stepped away to see the larger picture, the fuller scene that puts an end to any romantic fascination we might have been cultivating about nature, or our relationship to nature. Yet the mystery of the creature remains a binding force in the poem. As the creature disappears into the background there is also a time shift, and the immediacy of the poem is shaken. The poet adds his historical moment, or more accurately, his moments, that stretch from the present into the deep past as time collapses. And although right through to the end Komuyakaa uses the present tense—"Called into the hanging garden, / you sit there"—it takes only the brief mention of the Judas tree to give deeper meaning to the word *hanging*, and to place ourselves within the despair of human history.

This poet, even in celebration, and this is still an ode, whatever else it is, a poem of celebration, even love, for the created world and for a particular creature of that world, this poet won't let us forget that for all the beauty and mystery of creation, there is also relentless violence. Zoom in or out, be in the moment or fall into history—it is all necessary. The poet and the poem must be able to sustain paradox and uncertainty, wonder and unspeakable suffering, and presiding over it all is a humble reptile, close by, even if camouflaged, quietly attending the suffering.

Thank You for the Eyes in Your Head

Yusef Komunyakaa will be seen historically as one of the top American poets of the late twentieth century. In their lifetimes, poets get measured by collections. But over the long haul, their entire careers get boiled down to their best five poems. Put Yusef at a poker table, with the top late-twentieth-century poets; if he's holding any combination of "My Father's Love Letters," "Thanks," "Facing It," "Venus's-flytraps," "You and I Are Disappearing," and "Anodyne," I like his chances. This is not an Allen Ginsberg situation, where only a handful of poems truly shine. Yusef has written with lucidity and vigor for decades, amassing a serious body of work.

Yusef is the best war poet America has produced. And one of the top jazz poets (even if we can't agree on what that term actually means). But his gifts don't suddenly abandon him when he ventures beyond specific content. He's not a poet whose best poems are exclusively rooted in a single subject, or location. He is naturally gifted: precise lyricism, exquisite diction, great metaphorical gifts coupled with taut storytelling. And he's been blessed/cursed with intense experiences: an autobiographical terrain for his prodigious gifts to be challenged by and to navigate.

It's undeniable that Yusef has been at the pinnacle of the American poetry world for decades. But how did he get here? What was the trajectory of his ascent? And what was the atmosphere of the era he traveled through?

I first became aware of Yusef's work as a twenty-two-year-old in Thomas Lux's poetry workshop at Sarah Lawrence College in 1989. Tom described him as an up-and-coming poet who deserved more recognition than he was getting, who'd served in Vietnam. Tom said the work was *undervalued*, and I thought (mistakenly) the first two books had been published on an obscure press, but they were, in fact, published by Wesleyan. The poems were certainly fresh and alive, but what jumped out most of all was the title: *I Apologize for the Eyes in my Head*. It made my brain quiver. A straightforward statement on the surface, but why must one apologize for the eyes in their head? Usually one apologizes for an action, not a physical fact of their humanity. Or was the title insinuating that the author had seen too much, that the author was apologizing for all that they had seen, perceived?

Fast forward three years to 1992. Veterans Day. I dragged two fellow MFA students from George Mason University, in Northern Virginia, down to American University in DC to see Yusef read. A packed house. One large, rectangular room with a low ceiling. No elevated stage. Twenty to thirty rows of folding chairs. An introduction by Henry Taylor. No longer was Yusef *undervalued*. An electric current in the room. Yusef inhabited the moment. Everyone entranced. Mesmerized by his words.

Three years later, 1995. Yusef had just won the Pulitzer and was reading at George Mason, now my alma mater. I was working for Writers-Corps, a poets-in-the-community project in DC. Kenny Carroll (my boss), DJ Renegade, and I, with a few other poets, drove thirty minutes west on I-66 to see Yusef: on stage, elevated, a large theater, a microphone, a lectern, hundreds of people. Us in the third row. It felt historic. Again Yusef inhabited the moment, delivered. I don't want to say we were going to Mecca. But we were going to see only the second Black American poet who won the Pulitzer in poetry. Through the lens of 2022, it seems impossible to imagine that Gwendolyn Brooks won the Pulitzer in 1950, and then there was a forty-four year wait until Yusef. (It would be another twelve years of White poets winning, until Natasha Trethewey claimed the award in 2007, which did feel like the opening of a door—not just in terms of race, but also generationally.)

The racial exclusivity of the American poetry world in the late nineties cannot be overstated. It was like Birmingham in the 1950s. The poetry world was so White (and male) that in 1998 the Chancellors of the Academy of American Poets were twelve White people (mostly male) and zero poets of color. Chancellors Carolyn Kizer and Maxine Kumin both resigned. Months before that, Fred Viebahn, the husband of Rita Dove, had written the Chancellors:

> *Did the "Whites Only" question ever come up among the chancellors? If no, how self-centered and otherworldly can twelve poets be in one room? If yes, what kind of inane, pseudo-intellectual Jim Crow arguments were brought forth to keep this bastion of rarefied wordsmiths free from the "dark forces"? It can't be that there were no qualified minority poets, can it?*

Fast forward to 2003. I was driving into Manhattan with two Black poets in their thirties who had just read at Sarah Lawrence, where I'd been hired as a professor. One of them said, "Terrance [Hayes] is going to be the next Yusef." The other poet nodded. What this quick exchange revealed was: even in the early 2000s, the poetry world was so White that the prevailing mindset among talented, younger Black poets was: 1.) Yusef occupied a position of utmost respect, and 2.) there could only be one Black poet to eventually replace him.

In 2016, I got to interview Yusef on stage for an hour at the Sarah Lawrence Summer Seminar. And in 2019, I got to sit alone with Yusef for an hour at a book table in a secluded area of the Brooklyn Book Festival. Poetic heaven. The man has an aura, an intangible quality, like he's a transient being, moving between the shared world and some other realm. A voice like no other. Mystique about his origins. Uncertainty about the year he was born. A grandfather who reached the United States as a stowaway from Trinidad. The mystique adds to the overall experience, but Yusef's poems levitate off the page because of their language and imagery. He is a product of his era, the 1980s and '90s. He did not revolutionize the writing style of his generation, but he did write some of the best poems in the predominant mode of that era: lucid, autobiographical, first-person, lyric-narrative poems, that feature tight diction and internal rhyme and strong figurative language.

Let's look at his poem "Venus's-flytraps" in closer detail. This poem could have been written in the past tense: a grown man looking back on being five-years old. But Yusef sets it in the present tense and *becomes* his five-year-old self, which intensifies the poem, heightens the sense of urgency. The poem does the dual job of being authentic in the voice of a five-year-old speaker, but also simultaneously talking to a grown-up poetry audience. The poem begins:

I am five,
    Wading out into deep
        Sunny grass,
Unmindful of snakes
    & yellowjackets, out
        To the yellow flowers
Quivering in sluggish heat.
    Don't mess with me

'Cause I have my Lone Ranger
　Six-shooter. I can hurt
　　You with questions
　　　Like silver bullets.

Good, realistic, tactile details early on establish the setting: "sunny grass,"
"yellow jackets," "yellow flowers." There's exquisite insinuation: the grass
must be several feet high since the speaker has to "wade out" into it like
a body of water. Initially the poem feels bucolic, idyllic. Yes, there are
snakes—injecting a hint of danger—but overall the mood is playful. The
speaker addresses the reader "don't mess with me / 'Cause I have my Lone
Ranger six shooter," suggesting this is just an ordinary kid, playing out in
nature, imagining he is in a Western movie, with his toy gun.

"I can hurt / You with questions / Like silver bullets" is a curious de-
viation from what an ordinary kid might say. An ordinary kid would
stay in the pretend world of pretend hurt with the pretend silver bullets
in the pretend gun. But here the speaker is going to hurt the "you" (the
reader, or any grown-up) with questions. What does it mean to hurt with
questions? This is not an ordinary kid statement. This speaker is preco-
cious, on a higher level. The poem continues:

The tall flowers in my dreams are
　Big as the First State Bank,
　　& they eat all the people
Except the ones I love.
　They have women's names,
　　With mouths like where
Babies come from. I am five.
　I'll dance for you
　　If you close your eyes. No
Peeping through your fingers.
　I don't supposed to be
　　This close to the tracks.

The simile, "The tall flowers in my dreams are / Big as the First State
Bank," takes us into the mind of the child—nature is alive in his subcon-
scious—but it also lets us know more about the setting: a small town,
where the tallest building is the First State Bank, the tallest reference

point the child has. When the child narrator speaks of the flowers eating people, it feels sly. The form of the poem, with the cascading indents, mimics the narrator's dance between playfulness and seriousness.

An effective line break divides the child's offer to dance from a condition that the offer is predicated upon. The child speaker is being coy and hip to the tricks grown-ups are inclined to employ. This sweet moment of humor disarms us as readers. Right after this moment of innocence, the poem turns, or perhaps begins to sink, into heavier territory. The child-speaker switches from his most playful tone—"No / Peeping through your fingers" (a light-hearted admonishment)—to a confession: "I don't supposed to be / This close to the tracks." Suddenly rules are brought into the world of the poem. Some grown-up, who has not appeared in the poem yet, has created a boundary that the child is not obeying. The line brings us back to location. The child has wandered through the tall grass and now is standing next to the train tracks. How close is the child to the tracks? Ten feet? Five? And where are his parents or guardians? Wandering in tall grass is one thing. Wandering next to the train tracks is something else. How old is this kid again? Five?

The poem plummets down several levels with the ensuing lines:

One afternoon I saw
   What a train did to a cow.
      Sometimes I stand so close
I can see the eyes
   Of men hiding in boxcars.
      Sometimes they wave
& holler for me to get back. I laugh
   When trains make the dogs
      Howl. Their ears hurt.

This is no longer a happy-child-in-nature poem. The child has seen a cow get obliterated by a train. Instead of being graphic, the author dials it back and delivers something more oblique: "What a train did to a cow." The child stands so close that he "can see the eyes / Of men hiding in boxcars." These are not employees of the railroad company. These are illegal passengers.

We wonder in earnest where the kid's parents are, but then something surprising happens. The illegal passengers on the train, who could be seen as potentially dangerous, essentially parent the child-narrator, hollering for him to get back.

The child-narrator has been extremely perceptive up to this point. Observing. Drinking details in. Processing. But here we see an action—the child laughs "When trains make the dogs / Howl. Their ears hurt." Here the mystery is: why is the child laughing at something that is not typically funny. Also worth noting: the enjambment of the word "laughs" results in the reader initially seeing it as a response to the men hollering for him to get back. The poem continues and leaps associatively in very mature ways:

> I also know bees
>   Can't live without flowers.
>   I wonder why Daddy
> Calls Mama honey.
>   All the bees in the world
>   Live in little white houses
> Except the ones in these flowers.
>   All sticky & sweet inside.
>   I wonder what death tastes like.

The line starts "I also know"; the speaker is not only perceptive, but has the gift of converting those observations into knowledge. The parents appear, but only in the context of the speaker's mind. The speaker makes an association between honey from the natural world (what bees eat) and honey from the metaphorical/emotional world (what the Daddy calls Mama, perhaps in a moment of intimacy). What is most gripping here is the final line: "I wonder what death tastes like." The speaker was just musing on the natural world and lovemaking. And then he asks: "I wonder what death tastes like." What?! A five-year-old asks this!

We wonder if he's jumping back to the cow. (Readers of Komunyakaa know that in his work sexual love and death sometimes brush against each other in unexpected ways: death and the origins of life almost touching. A variation of Lorca's idea of *duende*?) But, regardless of the reason, this line is unexpected and establishes the speaker as a highly unique being. This poem happens long before the Vietnam War, but, even at five years old, the speaker has a heightened awareness of, or sensitivity to, death. The ensuing lines:

Sometimes I toss the butterflies
   Back into the air.
      I wish I knew why
The music in my head
   Makes me scared.
      But I know things
I don't supposed to know.

I love the implication of "Sometimes I toss the butterflies / Back into the air." It begs the question: what happens when the butterflies don't get tossed back into the air? Are they merely released, or are they crushed to death in the speaker's five-year-old fist? The next line leaps: "I wish I knew why the music in my head / Makes me scared." It's interesting to look at this line through the lens of Yusef's experience in Vietnam. This suggests Yusef was haunted long before Vietnam. It's not the music of the external world; it's the music of his unique interior that is making him scared. This deepens the sense of mythology that surrounds Yusef, like a kind of halo.

And then the kicker "I know things / I don't supposed to know." This child has learned too much for a five-year-old. It makes us wonder: what else does he know? The intensity level of the poem is heightening here. The ensuing lines dial down that intensity:

   I could start walking
      & never stop.
These yellow flowers
   Go on forever
      Almost to Detroit.
Almost to the sea.

"I could start walking / & never stop" is a very intense statement. It's an urge to escape. We don't know the source of the child's discomfort yet. We just know that at five, this child has seen too much, learned too much, and contemplates running away to a place of spiritual freedom. What cuts the intensity, for me anyway, is the yellow flowers going on for: 1) Forever. 2) Almost to Detroit. 3) Almost to the sea. We see the limitations of the speaker's knowledge. The speaker is mature and aware and perceptive, but maybe hasn't studied geography yet. In the logic of the speaker's mind, there is forever, and then beyond forever is Detroit, and just beyond Detroit is the sea. There's an innocence to that. We know that the sea is not in the direction of Detroit. It's almost a relief to have this child speaker (who reminds me a little of the boy from the movie *The Sixth Sense*) be revealed to be just a kid again.

The last five lines are absolutely devastating and open the door to the poem being considered a second-generation confessional poem; the speaker is sharing private glimpses of family trauma.

> My mama says I'm a mistake.
> That I made her a bad girl.
> My playhouse is underneath
> Our house, & I hear people
> Telling each other secrets.

Those first two lines slap the reader in the face. Yusef, the writer, had us focusing on flowers and Detroit and geography and *Wham!* The child-speaker hears something that no child should ever hear. And we wonder: did the mother say this to the child directly? The subsequent lines clarify. The speaker has been accruing this horrible knowledge not out in nature, but in his secret hideout: underneath the house. We imagine houses in Louisiana flood zones, elevated on stilts, and the speaker underneath, hearing way too much. Suddenly the five-year-old is incredibly powerful (the keeper of everyone's secrets and able to connect all the dots), and yet it is incredibly sad—no child should have such information. The final lines lower the temperature in the reader's body several degrees.

In the end, we can only be thankful for the eyes in Yusef's head, and the factory in his heart, able to convert such painful experience into song.

Dear Yusef Komunyakaa:

On *Neon Vernacular* and the Half-Life
of Double Consciousness

Dear Yusef,

It's been twenty-five years since *Neon Vernacular* won the Pulitzer Prize. I hope you did something to mark the anniversary. My stained and fly-leafed copy, when I tipped it from the shelf, dragged with it a magician's scarf of memories like the first time I met you in 1997. Major Jackson let me tag along to the campus dining hall for lunch with you when you were in Camden to give a reading. I was terrified and kept my mouth full of chicken tenders, distracted by the repeating click, swish, and thump of the juice machine behind us. I hoped you wouldn't notice my lack of mental presence or that I could think of nothing to say. Even now, more than twenty years later, whenever I see you I suffer a brain fart so incapacitating I can manage talk no bigger than teaching schedules and pub dates. But I have questions. I've had questions about *Neon Vernacular* that I've wanted to ask since the eighth or ninth time I put myself under the spell of that "New and Selected" poetry collection of yours. Questions about the poetic imagination read through the ideological prism of what you might agree is the patrimony of American poets: race. Questions also about patterns and themes I see (or imagine?) in your work, starting with early poems selected from your first book in 1977, tracing through poems from the subsequent six books, and finally, to the twelve "new" poems—but who's obsessively counting—in *Neon Vernacular.* This might get personal, and we know you can be, well, reserved. Which is to say, there are many reasons why you might not respond. If I don't hear from you, I won't overthink why. I'll just let it resonate like a koan or like the ending of one of your poems.

For years, I was content to curl around the feet of your poems without reaching after explanations for how you conceived them or how you made their subtext seismic. The majority of your poems are autobiographical, which I once took to be idiosyncratic and anecdotal rather than architectural and deliberate. I shrugged off your process as beyond anyone's comprehension, a thing charmed by Erzulie or won haggling at some crossroads, and just felt what the poems made me feel. The more I read you, however, the more frustrated with my own work I became, and I wanted to hold you responsible for that frustration. Empathetic reading bred contempt. Thinking of James Baldwin taking down his hero Richard Wright, and Baldwin's less notorious but no less scandalous takedown of Langston Hughes, I began devising an elegant ambush. Turns out I saw more in (or could project more onto) your work that way, having removed myself from the scene, so to speak. I searched for ways into your poems as myself rather than as some idealized Black man from Bogalusa, the son of an illiterate carpenter (you don't talk about your mom much), whom I've superimposed like Forrest Gump on already cinematic fantasies of the Civil Rights Movement and the Vietnam War, a process that was no more empathetic than the kind of speculation you describe in "Starlight Scope Myopia." Viewing the enemy through an infrared scope, you describe guessing at the inner lives of Viet Cong soldiers as they work in the night loading an oxcart. "What are they saying," you write. "Are they talking about women / or calling the Americans / beaucoup *dien cai dau*?" (Vietnamese for "crazy"). My empathetic reading made me feel closer to you, but that trick of the lens required nothing of my imagination. When I stood on my own in relation to the text, however, I began to appreciate more fully how special *Neon Vernacular* is within your oeuvre. With its sharp imagery and bluesy swagger, it continues to discipline the ears of American poets today, but I don't think we talk about what makes *Neon Vernacular* a turning point in African American poetics: its unique engagement, intentional or not, with the challenges of double consciousness.

Readers, presumably White, often praise your work for showing *what it means to be a Black man in [insert generic spatio-temporal context]*. I don't think you fancy yourself a racial ambassador in that way. In interviews you've disapproved of criticism that renders Black writing a "service literature" made to compensate for gaps and omissions in the literary record (a challenge you later take on in 2004 with *Pleasure Dome*). Neither are you interested—I'm inferring here—in decrying racism outright, because to do so would require you to exhume America's racist imagination from inside your own, a process which, unless you're writing didactic poetry that simplifies the world to good and evil, threatens to poison the mind. Simply negating or ignoring that racist imagination altogether would risk making the poems irrelevant in a society obsessed with race. This leaves a very narrow space in which to dance. How does one derive an aesthetic from self-alienation without resorting to postmodern clichés or to writing, to paraphrase Baldwin, "everybody's protest poem"?

How do I know your aesthetic is grounded in this deeply psychological phenomenon, the drama of double consciousness? It's in the poems. "Introduce me first as a man," you write in "Unnatural State of the Unicorn." The directive doesn't come from nowhere. It's in response, perhaps, to someone introducing you as a role model or as a representative of your race. The poem argues against measuring a life by the outward appearance of success. "I have no birthright to prove." It is striking how, as a comment on racial identity, a context you may not even have intended for this poem, it refuses the kind of collectivist dogma espoused by your contemporaries in the Black Arts movement. The poem concludes existentially, "I am this space / my body believes in." It is precisely this solipsism, this refusal to internalize the judgement and narratives of others, that gives your poems virtue and, ironically, nobility. This does not mean your work is free of racial conflict. You removed it from the public sphere and placed it under your own jurisdiction.

Langston Hughes reviewed James Baldwin's *Notes of a Native Son* in 1958 for the *New York Times*. The review was polite but disdainful. In it, Hughes wrote, "Baldwin's viewpoints are half American, half Afro-American, incompletely fused." The math doesn't compute for me; it sounds too much like Hughes is calling Baldwin three-fourths of an American, but his conclusion that Baldwin's divided identity is "a hurdle which Baldwin himself realizes he still has to surmount" makes sense. When Baldwin reviewed Hughes's *Selected Poems* a year later for the same publication, he was less polite but insightful, writing, "Hughes is an American Negro poet and has no choice but to be acutely aware of it. He is not the first American Negro to find the war between his social and artistic responsibilities all but irreconcilable." We could parse the nuances between Hughes's critique and Baldwin's rejoinder, but they both amount to diagnoses of double consciousness. Do you consider how you reckon with this Du Boisian notion that Black people in particular, though not exclusively, have a social habit of viewing ourselves through the eyes of Whites?

Double consciousness, put simply, is an alienated self-awareness. "This sense of always looking at one's self through the eyes of others," as Du Bois defines it in *The Souls of Black Folk*, abstracts the inner lives of African Americans and divides the imagination against itself. But as a poet, I can't *actually* look at myself through the eyes of others. Whatever others are present in my head at the moment of composition, their presence is my own. Their voices are my own. I am the one who imagines, based on my experience and cultural knowledge, what others are seeing and reading when they see and read me and my work. This is not to discount the very real existence of #BBQBecky and her ilk, sometimes armed and in uniform, but to suggest that double consciousness is an inside job.

In poems, double consciousness is often symbolized by various forms of masking. Another one of Du Bois's great contributions to our understanding of racial dynamics is his figure of the veil. Du Bois refers to the veil so often and so variously that there is room for debate as to what the veil actually represents. Some people think the veil represents the way race in America can prevent a White person from seeing African Americans as individuals, while simultaneously undermining a Black person's ability to see herself outside the context of a White gaze. I'm interested in the veil less as a diagnosis for why some White people react to me with fear and suspicion, and more as a common, but by no means universal, feature of the Black imagination. As a poet, I'm interested in the veil as a figure for the ways racism in America threatens the autonomy of the Black poet's imaginative gaze. As you put it in the poem "Jungle Surrender," "The real interrogator is a voice within." The object as I understand it is to get whole, to free my imagination from the racist gaze, and all similar corrosive forces, internalized. I want to write poems from my whole self without anything covering my face or obstructing my vision.

Sight, figuratively and literally, has long been a vexed faculty for African Americans. As early as the seventeenth century, priests and scholars justified slavery by claiming Black folks were the descendants of Ham. As you know, Ham saw his father Noah passed out drunk and naked, and for that Noah cursed him and all his descendants to be a race of servants. Ham's sin of witness is allegorical of the very real prohibitions against African American visual agency that have existed throughout our country's history. Black people were denied the right to testify in court, and denied the enlightenment of literacy. Black people were subject to various prohibitions against looking a White person in the eye. Of course, there was the capital offense of reckless eyeballing, a charge leveled against the fourteen-year-old Emmett Till, and for which he lost his life.

This history comes to mind when I read poems in *Neon Vernacular*, especially those taken from the collection *I Apologize for the Eyes in My Head*. Between poems like "Touch-up Man" and "When in Rome—Apologia," there is inscribed an autobiography of the veil. All filter and feigned reserve, you're a photographer "lean[ing] over the enlarger, / in the light table's chromatic glare" where you're "doctoring photographs" in "Touch-up Man," while "When in Rome—Apologia" is set among well-dressed diners in a restaurant. With an ironic formality you beg forgiveness "for the attention // I've given your wife." Removed from the original point of witness you exert power over the image captured in the photograph. Without the mediating device of a camera (or a poem), your vision is a source of guilt, however ironic.

The poem "I Apologize," comprised of a series of disclaimers, begins, "My mind wasn't even there. / Mirage, sir. I didn't see / what I thought I saw." It's hard not to think of our current president's efforts to blind the nation with his Orwellian tactics. It's hard not to link your performative guilt to a history of oppression.

Paul Laurence Dunbar preferred to write in standard English, but the publishing world of the late nineteenth century, by and large, didn't want those poems. In effect, Dunbar was coerced into writing in a dialect that White readers idealized as authentic Black speech. Although Dunbar's dialect poems are rich fodder for exposition and analysis, it is fitting that we remember him mostly by poems like "We Wear the Mask," written in the dominant American dialect and highlighting the symbol of double consciousness stiffened into relief.

If un-masking by demystifying the mask is one response to double consciousness, another effective response is what Gwendolyn Brooks called "verse journalism." One could adopt an improvisational aesthetic or turn to the revolutionary subjectivity of surrealism as in the manner of Bob Kaufman, Aimé Césaire, and César Vallejo. You seem to be experimenting with all of these modes in *Neon Vernacular*.

Literary critic Keith Leonard points out that jazz is not a metaphor for your aesthetic, but rather its paradigm. Jazz is the architecture of faith you elaborate as you glide from one image to the next, trusting some miracle of physics will emerge to contain your epic loneliness. Take the scene from a poem like "Work," which begins, "I won't look at her," an assertion that becomes a refrain. While you are mowing the lawn of an "antebellum house," a White woman installs herself poolside to sunbathe in the nude. That you two are the only people on the premises makes this a dangerous, nay, a life-threatening situation. You focus on the rhythm of work and Johnny Mathis coming from her radio. Or "Salt," where, noticing as a White woman at a lunch counter "Grabs her purse / & pulls at the hem / Of her skirt," you describe the way you can "feel her / Strain not to see me." You privilege your feelings over her actions. When, in "February in Sydney," a White woman on the street notices you emerging from a theater and she "grabs her red purse / & hugs it to her like a heart attack," you reach for the anesthetizing veil of Dexter Gordon's saxophone playing "April in Paris," which comes to rest "behind [your] eyelids" as you "try to feel how it is / to scream for help through a horn."

Jazz is the subject *and* its medium of expression. It is an ethos and a refuge from the corrosive White gaze. You are not only reporting on the scene as a journalistic witness, you expand the scene by privileging your subjective experience within it. Compare "February in Sydney" to Countee Cullen's poem "Incident," for example, in which, on a visit to Baltimore as a child, another little boy calls the speaker the N-word. We are left to infer the speaker's emotional response from the closing lines, "of all the things that happened there / That's all that I remember." Whereas the offending boy continues to dominate Cullen's imagination (as far as the poem tells us), you turn inward at the racial confrontation to assess the interior landscape with the emotional logic—more so than the music itself—of jazz.

Jazz, with its Zen-like insistence on being in the moment, is one of the few contexts in which we can imagine such a thing as Black masculinity. Masculinity in America is as enduringly coded as White as it is coded male. Attempts to perform masculinity by anyone non-White and/or male are destined to be interpreted as aberrant, perverse, or criminal. There is a bright thread that runs from *Neon Vernacular* directly to recent works like Claudia Rankine's *Citizen*, which has been celebrated for revealing the mechanics of microaggression. While Rankine reveals the rationale informing microaggression, you were one of the first American poets to reveal the psychology. We internalize the damage of racism—oppressor and oppressed—and finding solutions to double consciousness is not only salutary on an individual level but has the potential to prefigure a world in which racism is at least recognized as the self-defeating folly (all hate is self-hate) it is. By not participating in the self-erasure of double consciousness, you make that imbalance evident and all the more palpable. This not only offers us a more complex, fully populated understanding of history and social dynamics in America, you situate us more firmly within our own narratives of self. War creates its own surreality. And war, your poems demonstrate, is the great equalizer. War carries us beyond the reach of hierarchy and the empty promises of ideology to a place where we can imagine social equality rather than making spectacles of each other's pain. Adorno claimed there could be no lyric poetry after Auschwitz. Lyric poetry requires optimism and perhaps a naïve faith that poetry reflective of the culture that produced Auschwitz can do anything other than affirm brutality. What's needed is a paradigm shift. But by its existence, the blues suggests that one acclimates to horror and the absence of civility when one is faced with long exposure to them.

ED PAVLIĆ

"Modern Man in the Pepperpot"
The Black Musical Substructure of Yusef
Komunyakaa's Poetic Thought

I. Introduction: Komunyakaa's Musical Modernism

Bringing African American traditions into dialog with modernist aesthetics, Yusef Komunyakaa's poems resonate with blues lyricism illuminating crucial aspects of Black sense-making and survival in a world
which reduces poetry and people to marginal commodities. The Black
musical substructure of Komunyakaa's poetic thought supports his
works' resistance to reified understandings—especially racially determined understandings—of American selfhood. Avoiding approaches
that would dismiss the "self" as an essentialist fantasy, Komunyakaa's
poems and prose sculpt a musical model of selfhood that claims a fluid,
durable, and authoritative presence in the world. Generating moments
of what I term "existential surprise," Komunyakaa's musical modernism advances an alternative version of American selfhood tough and
malleable enough to resist the choices of color-blindness and blindness-
to-color that structure many of our creative/intellectual/personal conversations (*Blue Notes*, 25).[1] In poems and lyrical prose, Komunyakaa
shows how such choices function as part of a "mechanism of control"
that keeps Americans from engaging with the full complexity of their
lives. When Komunyakaa advises that we "place ourselves in the hands
of who we are," he's, in fact, drawing upon a conception of selfhood
being created in his work, one informed simultaneously by the history
of modern aesthetics and Black musical composition and performance.

Meditating on limitations in his early, unpublished poems in his
essay "Poetry and Inquiry," Komunyakaa expresses his wish that he'd
had "a closer relationship to the basic elements of the blues tradition
and the fundamentals of the modernist aesthetic." Rather than specific
techniques, writers, and performers, Komunyakaa clearly conceives
these intersecting musical and poetic traditions in structural as well as
contextual, aesthetic as well as experiential, terms: "Perhaps [such dual

awareness] would have given me a scaffold that would have supported the ideas that ushered me into manhood." Taking shape in relation to patterns in Black musical composition and performance, Komunyakaa's work eludes the restrictions of racial, rational, ego-driven forms of modern and contemporary experience, often through deploying surrealistic images that bear a close relationship with three interrelated aspects of the Black musical tradition: blues, jazz, and gospel impulses (*Blue Notes*, 25).[2]

Building explicitly on the critical insights of James Baldwin and Ralph Ellison (and as clarified by Craig Werner), I will engage blues, jazz, and gospel as experiential and aesthetic impulses (rather than musical forms or genres) to provide a guide to Komunyakaa's investigations of identity in terms deeper, more fluid, and more complex than racially determined (or race-neutral) concepts of American selfhood allow. Komunyakaa's thought sketches an interlocking repertoire of musical selves: a blues self situated at a crossroads of internal and external (subjective/objective) perspectives on experience and informed by a crafted, lyrical awareness capable of "surprising" itself with existentially resonant truths; a jazz self at once fearfully expansive and securely rooted in an imagined sense of vernacular origins in which ideals are never singular and identity is always a plural quantity; and a gospel self-conscious of its dialogic relationships to community (extending explicitly to cultural origins in West Africa) and informed by a sense of proportion owing to pragmatic political realities (directly related to historical struggles for human rights). The blues, jazz, and gospel impulses, then, provide a discourse which illuminates and informs the repertoire of selves which interact throughout Komunyakaa's interviews, essays, and poems.

II. Blue Intrusions: Lyricism, Existential Surprise, and "The Uses of Pain"

Komunyakaa's approach to the blues is part of an ongoing response to the ancestral presence of James Baldwin and Ralph Ellison. In his essay "Richard Wright's Blues," Ralph Ellison defined the blues impulse as "an impulse to keep the painful details and episodes of a brutal experience alive in one's aching consciousness, to finger its jagged grain, and to transcend it, not by the consolation of philosophy but by squeezing from it a near-tragic, near-comic lyricism" (*Collected Essays*, 129). Ellison's conception of the blues makes the energy of experience new, keeps "the painful details . . . alive," via lyricism (129). As a form, Ellison writes, "the blues is an autobiographical chronicle of personal catastrophe expressed lyrically" (129). In *Blue Notes*, Komunyakaa notes, "In my poetry I desire surprises. Of course, those surprises can hurt" (81).

Similarly, in "Uses of the Blues," a 1964 essay for *Playboy*, James Baldwin wrote that the blues comes from an impulse at the core of (and is itself a constituent element in) experience itself. Baldwin explicitly leaves behind discussions of generic boundaries: "The title, 'Uses of the Blues,' does not refer to music: I don't know anything about music. It does refer to the experience of life, of the state of being, out of which the blues come . . . I'm using them as a metaphor—I might have titled this, for example, *The Uses of Anguish* or *The Uses of Pain*" ("Uses of the Blues," 131). But, as Baldwin knew, the blues aren't reducible to the experience itself, they're not received passively (as in "I've got the blues"); the blues are active. They depend upon formal expertise and, simply put, a level of toughness, guts. Baldwin writes: "I want to talk about the blues not only because they speak of this particular experience of life and this state of being, but because they contain the toughness that manages to make this experience articulate. I am engaged, then, in a discussion of craft or, to use a very dangerous word, art" (131). For Baldwin, the blues carry an existential mandate emanating from beneath the intellectual and cultural buttresses of the modern self. They, therefore, offer a way to "walk away from the TV set, the Cadillac, and go into the chaos out of which and only out of which we can create ourselves as human beings" (241). Craft prevents illusions and delusions that create the manifold dissociations of American life. To craft and art, Baldwin could have easily added work and labor to the short list of evaporating ingredients in a functional American self. As Baldwin sees it, a person "who has somehow managed to get to, let us say, the age of forty, and a great many of us do, without ever having been touched, broken, disturbed, frightened" is a dangerous character. Aware that no one actually eludes these elements of experience, Baldwin argues that American culture prompts people to avoid internalizing them, to avoid creating, as it were, a blues sense of self and world.

One of the strengths of Komunyakaa's poetry is his Baldwinian awareness of how contemporary American culture seems predicated on the wish to avoid allowing such disturbances to the surface in the consciousness. Avoidance, and, if lightning does strike, closure. In "Sonny's Blues," Baldwin provides the contrafact to the cultural mandate for an even-keel, abstract sense of life in America. To the narrator's very American question of what to do with the scars of experience if we can't always avoid and/or forget them, Baldwin's Sonny responds that the effort is to "keep from drowning in it, to keep on top of it, and to make it seem—well, like *you*" (*Going to Meet the Man*, 132). This amounts to the deeply un-American tautology: one's lived life should bear some resemblance to the life one lives. Living experience. For Baldwin, the blues operate on tandem logical premises: first, "you can't know anything about life and suppose you can get through it clean" ("Uses of the Blues," 241); second, that the "most monstrous people are those who think they are going to" do just that (241). These observations identify key impasses between the blues self and the myths that undergird and guard the American self.

Commenting upon the sheer tonal energy beneath the blues lyricism in "Jazz and Poetry: A Conversation," Komunyakaa echoes Baldwin and Ellison observing how the "music became an argument with the odds, a nonverbal articulation of our pathos. In this sense, even the blues dirge is an affirmation—the theft of possibility" (646). Of the presence created by such energy, Komunyakaa concludes that these "words made flesh" (646).

The energies of blues affirmation contend with pain from the flawed match between humans and the social world. Meditating on the ever-presence of these tensions in "Crossroads," Komunyakaa discusses the artistic endeavor to grapple with "the awkward reality of our contemporary lives and imaginations" (*Ploughshares*, 6). At their crucial best, blues truths come as dispatches to the self from experiences stored in locations of consciousness beyond conscious awareness. As John Engels notes in "A Cruel Happiness," "the kind of knowledge" conveyed by Komunyakaa's work "intrudes from beneath and beyond the boundaries of biography" (169). In the blues, such intrusions of energy and insight from beyond one's conscious awareness mark moments of "existential surprise." In "Poetry and Inquiry," Komunyakaa discusses the fundamental role of blues energies in the creative process. He warns that "many times people try to pull away from the center of their lives, but that is where the energy exists. We don't have to impose superficial subject matter in order to write" (*Blue Notes*, 27). Of lyrical surprises and the energies of affirmation, Komunyakaa told Tony Barnstone that the "surprise is very important . . . That's the joy in the imagination, and it has a lot to do with possibility" (*Blue Notes*, 125).

Komunyakaa's understandings of the connection between blues lyricism and existential surprise echoes Baldwin's comment on the shifting nature of this lyrical dimension of personal experience: "this passionate detachment, this inwardness coupled with outwardness" enables the existential surprises to occur ("Uses of the Blues," 132). In "Sermons and Blues," a 1959 review of *Selected Poems* of Langston Hughes, Baldwin wrote that "the poetic trick, so to speak, is to be within the experience and outside it at the same time" (*Collected Essays*, 614). In a 1973 interview, Baldwin credited Billie Holiday's split position with part of her authority as a lyricist and as a witness: "Billie Holiday was a poet. She gave you back your experience. She refined it and you recognized it for the first time because she was in and out of it and she made it possible for you to bear it" (*Conversations*, 155). For Baldwin, the politics (that is to say, the inter- and intra-personal importance) of the blues follows directly: "if you can bear it, then you could begin to change it" (155). In order for it to be borne, however, experience must be excavated via the inside/outside processes of occupying misaligned and simultaneous vantage points. In his essay "Crossroads," Komunyakaa achieves his most succinct phrasing of this creative kind of improvised presence vis-à-vis experience. Of such positions, he writes that there "is an accrued bravery here. It is this cultural dualism, this ability to be two places at once, to be a shape changer, that strengthens the creative quest" (*Ploughshares*, 6). The crossroads becomes a state in which the self opens itself to the existential surprises that result from the lyrical intrusions of the blues.

Existentially surprising lyrics communicate much more than they appear to say when printed on the page. In "Remembering Jimmy," Ellison writes of singer Jimmy Rushing: "when we listen to his handling of lyrics we become aware of that quality which makes for the mysteriousness of the blues: their ability to imply far more than they state outright" (*Collected Essays*, 276). In a passage from *The Blue Devils of Nada* (in a section quoted by Komunyakaa), Albert Murray writes that the blues come out of chaos and futility but meet it with an organic, artistic rigor: "the very existence of the blues tradition is irrefutable evidence that those who evolved it respond to the vicissitudes of the human condition not with hysterics and desperation but through the wisdom of poetry informed by pragmatic insight" (*Blue Notes*, 34). Komunyakaa links the existential surprise of blues lyricism directly to writing: "poetry [that] helped me articulate the anguish. It surprised me. In that sense, we can't map out the journey because our lives become the map. And what we see isn't always beautiful." (*Blue Notes*, 81).

Accenting the romantic, mystical dimensions of modernist lyricism in "Forces that Move the Spirit," Komunyakaa links the blues to Lorca's cante jondo (as Ellison had) and principle of "duende." In "Rejecting 'Sweet Geometry,'" Don Ringnalda paraphrases Lorca's definition of duende as "the pre-rational wild spirit of death, darkness, and blood" (26). From his conception, the relationship of duende to intrusive, blues insights becomes clear. For Komunyakaa, the blues is a rural, lyrical tradition born of the "brute force and almost obscene beauty of its peasantry, and how the music and songs are closer to prayers than anything else— and earthy atticism" (*Blue Notes*, 12). Born in 1947, a native of small-town Louisiana, Komunyakaa has often discussed his origins in close proximity to rural, peasant life. Even in Vietnam during the war, he contends, his early life close to nature and the soil allowed him to "identify with the peasants and their rituals" (*Blue Notes*, 81). This sense of direct contact is part of the reason the blues forms the center of his wide-ranging poetic repertoire: "The blues are existential. They're also Black and basic. And it is this down-to-earthness that I hope informs the main tenor of my poetry—a language that deals with the atrabilious nature of our existence as well as the emotional weight of its beauty" (*Blue Notes*, 12). Echoing Ellison's initial phrasing, Komunyakaa affirms that "often the blues singer can get us closer to the truth than the philosopher. This is the function of my poetry" (*Blue Notes*, 13).

Beyond questions of personal/existential grounding, Komunyakaa acknowledges the social and political dimensions of the blues. In "Jazz and Poetry: A Conversation," William Matthews discussed the "extreme difficulty [of describing 'the life of the emotions'] and the great spiritual cost of not trying to describe it" (647). Discussing the blues logic of Robert Hayden's poem "American Journal" in "Journey into 'American Journal,'" Komunyakaa positions blues awareness against the fear of ambiguity and pain, a fear that has "driven most Americans into the psychological melting pot" (*Blue Notes*, 11). Echoing Baldwin's comment about bearing experience before one can change it, in Komunyakaa's understanding the blues stakes are high: Americans "are redeemable only if they can name their crimes and insanities" (*Blue Notes*, 10). Naming one's crimes and insanities begins as a blues task. But it doesn't end there.

III. The Jazz Impulse and the Plural Ideal:
Trading Fours with William Matthews

The names, however, shift. Things become new things. New things need new names. The jazz impulse maps this important sense of shift and gives it a(n always provisional) name. Komunyakaa's poetic thought plays along, adding its distinctive perspective to the pre-existing voices in the tradition. If the blues impulse is Black—and American—culture's existential discourse, jazz provides a laboratory for exploring difference and change: a continual tonal workshop on the relationship between identity and non-identity played out with one foot in the blues (in what we can know of experience) and the other foot in any and every cultural, spiritual, intellectual discourse available. The jazz impulse attends the constant movement and adjustment of the blues lyric to the texture of experience, the signifier to the signified. It listens for the new lyric coming into being from inside the old. The useful, living dimensions of pain are in constant motion, always new each time, always only partially involved with the faculties of consciousness that attempt to insulate us from various levels of what's going on. Craft is always coming apart at the seams. In "Shape and Tonal Equilibrium," Komunyakaa describes how jazz offers a model of "extended possibility" and concludes directly: "Jazz offers something else" (*Blue Notes*, 7). Existential from bar one, the shifting blues "this" often becomes political when the discourse alters or destroys understandings of phenomena previously thought to be stable, defined, named. Komunyakaa notes that "anything related to jazz has always been somewhat of a threat" (*Blue Notes*, 7).

The threatening nature of such shifts link personal and political dimensions of experience; the link itself is part of the risk. During performances, when Charles Mingus called out "Get into yourself!" to the members of his jazz workshop, he meant the immediate self, tonight ("You'd be Playing . . ." Hentoff, 55). It's not for nothing that one of Mingus's greatest albums was titled, *Mingus, Right Now!* For his part, Mingus also understood how the blues-jazz continuum had to reach deeper than the racially limited sense of American biography:

It's not only a question of color anymore. It's getting to be deeper than that . . . People are getting so fragmented, and part of that is that fewer and fewer people are making a real effort anymore to find out exactly who they are and to build on that knowledge. Most people are forced to do things they don't want to most of the time, and so they get to the point where they feel they no longer have any choice about anything important, including who they are. (Hentoff, 55)

Like Baldwin and Komunyakaa, Mingus understood the crisis of self-hood in expansive terms that explicitly include the absence of meaningful work.

In spite and also because of all the ways they need each other, a real tension exists between the blues and jazz impulses. Without attention to these complexities, the blues basics can become their own kind of deadly confusion. In "The Modern World," Komunyakaa's observer notes mute movements beneath people's conscious lives. In the end, the unattended shift gets deadly, Komunyakaa warns, "you load the gun / when you think you're unloading it" (*Pleasure Dome*, 362). The best way to ensure losing the blues self back into mute chaos is to enlist the same certainties for too long. Names change. Consider the lines from Komunyakaa's "Audacity of the Lower Gods": "The audacity of the lower gods— / whatever we name we own" (*Pleasure Dome*, 161). The matter isn't abstract. The poem continues: "*Diversiloba*, we say, unfolding poison oak" (161). Preferring jazz's proffered "something else," the poem's persona concludes:

I'd rather let the flowers
keep doing what they do best.
Unblessing every petal,
letting go a year's worth of white
death notes, busily unnaming themselves.
(161)

The line break at "white" gestures toward the racial politics inherent in American naming and the jazz impulse's obsession with changes in structures whereby things and even people are named, and even owned. Possibly, this is the most concise restatement possible of what the jazz impulse is all about: the thing newly unnamed.

Misunderstanding the way the jazz impulse works its unique form of "joy" from the blues act of naming experience can cause problems interpreting Komunyakaa's poems that might lead to misunderstandings characteristic of the open-ended selfhood his work creates. In one instructive case, Vince Gotera interprets the string of images in Komunyakaa's minor masterpiece "You and I Are Disappearing" as a list of abortive attempts to fix a vision, a semi-successful series of failures. In "Killer Imagination," Gotera writes:

> The speaker here is at a loss to describe this scene fittingly. . . The speaker, again and again, tries to find a metaphor that will convey both the beauty and horror. And he comes enticingly, asymptotically close without finding the ideal phrase. Finally, the speaker simply has to stop. (369)

The singular notion of "the ideal phrase" runs counter to the core of the jazz impulse as it plays with naming and unnaming. This approach has a genealogy in musical performance (an approach which caused similar problems for jazz critics). Many critics, for instance, consider Miles Davis's first solo in the *Kind of Blue* version of "So What" one of the best single utterances in jazz. Miles Davis, invoking the spirit of the song's title, never played it that way again. The solos (by Miles and the other players in two or three different groups) in various versions of "So What" offer a seminar in the jazz impulse. I think there's a good argument that *all* the solos by Miles combine to form a *plural ideal*: over Bill Evans in "So What" from *Kind of Blue*; over Wynton Kelly on *Live at the Blackhawk*; or over Herbie Hancock on *Live at the Plugged Nickel*. In turn, I'd argue that each, rather than none, of the images in "You and I Are Disappearing" can be considered ideal in jazz/blues impulse terms: the plural ideal.

The connection between jazz and "You and I Are Disappearing" (as well as with many of Komunyakaa's poems, most of which don't mention music explicitly) is more than theoretical. In an interview with Robert Kelly and William Matthews, "Jazz and Poetry: A Conversation," Komunyakaa singled out "You and I Are Disappearing" as one of his most jazz-inspired poems and associated it explicitly with the right hand of pianist Thelonious Monk. Komunyakaa's association of "You and I Are Disappearing" with jazz provides key insights into the connection between the musical tradition and the substructure of his poetic thought:

"You and I Are Disappearing" . . . has a rhythm that came out of listening to Thelonious Monk . . . repetition with slight variations, playing with pauses and silences, an un-spoken call and response. Monk knew how to be his own Amen Corner. (656)

Despite the crucial motion in the poem from one register of experience and reference to another (chemical, personal, physical, spiritual, political, economic, biblical), without the jazz impulse (and its relationship to the blues) as a basis for interpretation, the repetition can be mistaken for faltering, a futile groping toward "the ideal phrase." This misconstrues the ideal as singular. A sensibility informed by jazz knows it's not. Of his own approach, Komunyakaa said: "if you listen to Monk, you hear all of his repetition constantly, and I tried to capture that repetition . . . in the very short space of 'You and I Are Disappearing'" ("Jazz and Poetry," 660). Gotera's reading concludes that the poem's speaker, as if throwing in the towel, "Finally . . . simply has to stop." Far from a surrender, Komunyakaa characterizes the close of the poem as a victory directly inherited from Monk:

I love his jagged tonality, how he was able to leave a piece unresolved—a door left ajar that invited you in as a participant. I want to write poems like that . . . That poem pretty much ended itself when Thelonious ended the record . . . a kind of completion that happens that you cannot plot. ("Jazz and Poetry," 656–60)

Sounding the final note about the relationships of the blues/jazz continuum to the notion of the plural ideal, Komunyakaa states that his "creative universe is always in flux" ("Jazz and Poetry," 661). In "The Charlie Christian Story," Ralph Ellison wrote that "the jazzman must lose his identity even as he finds it" (267).

Reflecting his self-conscious modernism, Ellison's version of the jazz impulse features the twin quests to attain and thwart one's individuality. Discussing jazz's pursuit of the next version of the thing in *A Change Is Gonna Come*, Craig Werner adds a social and historical underlay to the jazz impulse's conceptual, psychological, and aesthetic suspicion of the way things are. Echoing Komunyakaa's comment about the perceived "threat" of jazz, Werner writes: "[p]art of the reason jazz comes from the African American tradition has to do with what conventions [such as rationalizations like segregation] have meant to Black folks. Stay in your place, over on the other side of the tracks. Enjoy the back of the bus" (133). Adding the political edge to the historical roots, he writes: "[j]azz does its best to blow that kind of complacency away. Which is why jazz sounds revolutionary even when it doesn't pay too much attention to next week's election or anybody's party line" (133).

Komunyakaa credits jazz with his sense of himself as, in Ellison's words, "an individual, a member of the collectivity, and as a link in the chain of tradition" (*Collected Essays*, 267). In "Jazz and Poetry," Robert Kelly asked Komunyakaa and William Matthews about the importance of jazz to their work. The conversation itself becomes something of a laboratory of identity and difference as the two writers' thoughts weave shared material into a performance of convergence and divergence. Responding to Kelly's questions, Komunyakaa and Matthews trade fours, offering statements and counter-statements toward capturing a shared— but resolutely non-identical—version of an intricate subject matter.

The two poets begin the conversation moving in nearly antithetical directions. As an aural signature of identity, Komunyakaa observes that music kept Black people "closer to the essence of themselves" and that jazz helped him, personally, to: "get to a place I thought I had forgotten . . . a closer spiritual connection to the land and the place I come from" ("Jazz and Poetry," 645). Komunyakaa described writing "Venus's-flytraps," a poem about his childhood surrounded by secrets: "I wanted to write a poem that dealt with childhood, so I put on Louis Armstrong. . . what I was hearing were the secrets coming out of Louis Armstrong's trumpet, and I tried to let the music take me back . . . The music becomes a place in which to recapture, to reexperience certain things" (647–49). In personal and cultural terms, for Komunyakaa, jazz offered "a process of reclaiming," which, in terms of Ellison's version of jazz, is to say *creating*, identity. Identity and difference. Lost and found. In response to the issue of jazz and identity, Matthews begins, "Yusef's comments seem to me very astute, and I endorse them almost entirely," and then proceeds in the opposite direction (646). In contrast to Komunyakaa's sense of jazz rootedness, Matthews's version of jazz offered people like him "ways to describe their relationship to rootlessness" (646). He reminds us that a city like New York has become an "ultimate haven for homeless people" (646). People, like almost all of the mid-century jazz players themselves, often come to cities "because [they] have no emotional or social home" where they come from (646). Instead of jazz ushering him closer to a lost connection to home, a journey back, Matthews describes a journey out and away: "the crucial years . . . I spent as a weird white be-bop groupie hanging around the Village and trying to figure out what I was listening to and why I loved it so much" (650). Via drastically different tonal paths, the two perspectives come together when Matthews and Komunyakaa describe a role for jazz as a connection to elusive emotional (as opposed to geographic, historical) realities. Komunyakaa relates how "jazz works . . . as a way for me to discover the emotional mystery behind things" (645). Matthews echoes: "The music I heard then helped me forge an introduction to my emotional life and not to be terrified of it" (650).

If their thoughts revolve in different directions, Matthews and Komunyakaa agree that jazz presents unparalleled opportunities for working with the existential surprise of the blues. Komunyakaa discusses the role of jazz in a writer's disparate, eclectic quest: "I write about whatever captures my imagination. Anything that touches me significantly: philosophy, psychology, nature, cultural concerns, folklore, world history, sex, science, from the gut-level to the arcane, whatever. Yes, for me, jazz moves underneath many of these topics . . . a necessary balm" (649). For Matthews, jazz allowed him to connect the various registers in American language. Trapped in his bookish beginnings, Matthews reports:

> If it weren't for what I learned listening to jazz, the gap between the two kinds of English would have seemed vast to me, but it didn't because jazz gave me permission to begin composing a poetic language based on the rhythm of the speaking voice; the voice rationalizing to itself, jiving other people, trying to seduce a comparative stranger, explaining why a paper is not ready on time, doing puns and jokes and imitations—in sum, doing the real emotional business of daily life, full of weird quirks and odd lilts. (651)

Through thoroughly compatible observations about the power of jazz's composite potentials, Matthews and Komunyakaa arrive, again, at antithetical positions. Komunyakaa concludes: jazz "worked for me as a way of reestablishing a kind of trust. A trust in what I had known earlier" (652). It springs Matthews out. Claiming he "learned to read Whitman by listening to Don Cherry play his pocket trumpet," Matthews allows: "For me . . . improvisation meant not staying trapped in the [elevated, literary] dialect of my upbringing and education, meant moving out and experiencing as a ventriloquist the lives of my fellow citizens. That's what it means to be American, I thought" (652).

The conversation between Matthews and Komunyakaa works much like a jazz performance, in which alternate routes arrive at mutual points of departure and mutual routes deliver travelers to very different destinations. The tension and harmonies all contribute to the sense of the conversation as an improvised duet, a cooperative meditation. Komunyakaa's journey back, it bore its own powerful sense of otherness and difference. His somewhat romantic statements about "reestablishing a kind of trust," in a neatly dovetailed personal/cultural sense of rootedness, leave room for a level of chaos and rootlessness crucial to jazz extensions of the existential surprise of the blues lyric. The comfortable prose surface of Komunyakaa's journey back through the sound of jazz might obscure an awareness of a multileveled sense of African American homelessness encoded in his poems. Such dual levels of meaning are at home in the jazz impulse. The journey back is incomplete(d) by jazz design. Lost even as found. On the final page of the pocket-sized edition of *February in Sydney*, under the heading "Six Facts About the Author," Komunyakaa acknowledges that "he was born in Bogalusa, Louisiana . . . a good place to be a long ways from" (32). Earlier in *February in Sydney*, Komunyakaa quotes his then-father-in-law Gerry Sayer, "The difference between the difference is the difference" (19). Of homelessness and modern nothingness, lost and fragmented legacies, Komunyakaa comments that "the African American has had to survive by his sheer nerve and wit, often it seems as if we have been forced to create everything out of nothing" ("Jazz and Poetry," 645). Propelled by the high stakes of this sense of difference and nothingness, the music became an "argument with the odds. . . serious business in the . . . community" (646).

Echoing Baldwin's in/out poetic crossroads, in many ways, then, even—possibly especially—for so-called insiders on their way back to where they come from (and often from where they escaped at all costs), jazz is an outsider's music. As Werner suggests, jazz is about "the parts that don't fit: the dreams, desires, unanswered questions" (*A Change Is Gonna Come*, 133). Jazz offers the insight available from the outside of conventional, accepted phrasings. Call it "outsight." Reliance on familiar phrasings could get a musician fired by bandleaders like Miles Davis and Charles Mingus (it could get you *worse* than fired by Mingus!).

Historically, Komunyakaa notes, writers like "Langston Hughes, Helene Johnson, and Zora Neale Hurston, turned to jazz to escape 'the Harlem Renaissance'—the cultural straightjacket—the whole movement defined by European standards" (649). But if jazz complicates the inside of things, its blues base reminds that—in at least one dimension of life—there's nowhere to run either. As Teddy Pendergrass sang, "everywhere you go, there you are."

In the title poem in *February in Sydney*, having traveled all the way down under only to encounter racism outside a theater that reminds him of racism back home, Komunyakaa's persona confides: "An old anger drips in my throat" (30). Reeling from the encounter and recalling Dexter Gordon's "April in Paris," he couples the blues pain and jazz quest that constantly mixes surprising intrusions with improvisations:

> Tremelo. Dexter Gordon comes back to rest
> behind my eyelids. A loneliness
> lingers like a silver needle
> under my black skin
> as I try to feel how it is
> to scream for help through a horn.
> (31)

Echoing Baldwin's Sonny's impulse to "make it seem—well, like *you*," (132) Komunyakaa's jazz changes work in concert with the ever-complex, basic blues of the quest to "feel how it is."

Closer to Komunyakaa's own journey back, "Venus's-flytraps" images the dangerous, ambiguous interior/exterior dimensions of existential surprise lurking in mood, memory, and music. The five-year-old persona recollected through Komunyakaa's trust in Louis Armstrong's trumpet sits outside the action: "My playhouse is underneath / Our house, & I hear people / Telling each other secrets" ("Jazz and Poetry," 649). This young man snatches self-awareness by insinuating himself into the silences of the adult world. Mistakes and mysteries are handed down: "I wonder why Daddy / calls Mama honey" (648). Sweet. Until the line breaks occurs to us and we hear the five-year-old who wonders, "why Daddy?" Skipping ahead through *Magic City* (the book in which "Venus's-flytraps" is the first poem), and stopping on "My Father's Love Letters," we can infer something about the violence that prompts this particular five-year-old's "why." One begins to wonder how much of this trumpet (and by whom) is really to be trusted? By this inside/outside vantage, surrounded by the culture of the rural American South in the 1950s—banned books and deadly intra- and inter-racial sexual taboos—the persona arrives in the precarious position of awareness: "But I know things / I don't supposed to know" (648). Caught between the blues impulse for immediate impact ("to feel how it is") and the jazz impulse to pursue the next unanswered question, a series of mysteries usher the young boy outward toward his sense of the ultimate: "I wonder what death tastes like" (648). The sense impression (taste) and the children's vernacular fact that the word "tastes" occupies two (instead of one) syllables in the line keep even the ultimate otherness (death) within reach of the sense of the immediate crucial to the blues. Duende. Komunyakaa knows that following the jazz impulse into nothingness beyond comfortable/cultural familiarity "is a scary venture, but if it felt safe, it might become static or contrived" (*Blue Notes*, 29).

Infusing the blues with jazz explorations and changes becomes a way of engaging fear itself. Commenting on performing with one of his electric bands in 1974, Miles Davis told a *Chicago Tribune* reporter: "You can't know how terrifying it is to be in the middle of all of that. It's endless sound. Music is a curse" (Szwed, *So What*, 339). In comments that foreground the contradiction in the essay's title, "Control is the Mainspring," Komunyakaa discussed the first stages of his writing poems about Vietnam. Describing the feeling of "riding a wave of images . . . coming forth at such a panic-ridden haste," he confesses: "Something was happening to me, and I was afraid" (*Blue Notes*, 14). That's why jazz is a virtuoso's music. Jazz pits instrumental skill, craft, against the rising existential tide of tension, fear, desire, anger (held in open-ended, unresolved ways); the blues set loose by the jazz impulse. In the near-perfectly crafted "Venus's-flytraps," the five-year-old, underground, jazz outsider wonders about the quest for answers and the ever-changing music emanating from his own insides: "I wish I knew why / the music in my head / makes me scared" (648). Throughout all Komunyakaa's best work the blues immediacies are always connected to an uncertainty principle at the core of jazz. If blues surprises can hurt, jazz openings can be scary.

The key to jazz's affective changes is expansion. The blues push deeper, jazz expands the perimeter. In "Jazz and Poetry," Komunyakaa recalls that jazz "helped to expand my creative universe" (650). The expansions were internal and external, personal and communal, intellectual and geographical. External, geographical: it was to a jazz score, Komunyakaa argues, that Black artists chipped away at the eastern horizon of nothingness as they began "to rediscover that which was ours, redefining ourselves with Africa as an emotional backdrop" (653). Internal, psychological: "I just love the sound. The music helped me free up my mind for more vivid extrusions. Jazz was just a part of my life, a continuous score to the images inside my head" (649).

Apart from an ambiguous (at times verging upon nihilistic) fascination with change, disruption, and expansion, jazz players and poets often foreground the hope that the loosed identities and play of ambiguity can lead to improved democratic, humanistic circumstances. At a roundtable discussion about politics and poetry in 1999, Komunyakaa used a quotation from Muriel Rukeyser to evince a faith in the democratic potential of the shifts at the core of the jazz impulse. Quoting Rukeyser, he said:

> We need a background that will let us find ourselves and our poems, let us move in discovery. The tension between the parts of such a society is health: the tension between the individual and the whole society is health. This state arrives when freedom is a moving goal, when we go beyond the forms to an organic structure which we in conscience claim and use. (*American Poetry Review*, 22)

Here, the jazz sensibility begins to point beyond its own strict discipline of identity and non-identity, of difference. Of this sense of balance, in "Shape and Tonal Equilibrium," Komunyakaa writes: "Being in motion—improvisation, becoming—this is the mode of our creativity. The accent is on the positive even when the negative pervades" (4). There's a horizon and a social vision implicit in Rukeyser's language and an overlaying vision implicit in Komunyakaa's regard for her words. The notion of freedom as a "moving goal" is historically accurate, of course. In *The Story of American Freedom*, Eric Foner cautions against understandings of American freedom in terms of "fixed definition[s]," "predetermined concept[s]," or by "narrative[s] of linear progress" (xiv). Instead, he views American history as an improvisational story of how "different ideas of freedom have been conceived and implemented, and how the clash between dominant and dissenting views has constantly reshaped the idea's meaning" (xv). The tension at the pulsing heart of a jazz impulse approach to freedom may be healthy and progressive, but it also has the potential for chaos, madness, and disillusionment. The tension can spin awry. Atom bombs dropped. Pre-emptive wars waged. Millions of Americans (many of them children) medicated against "how it feels" to be in the world, against hearing the music in their heads. Against such evidence, however, something in Black American culture usually agrees with the impulse that to be on the move is the way (often it's the only way) to be. Or, if not now, it will be. But, what and how? When the blues impulse "feels how it is" and the jazz impulse turns it wrong-side-out and upside-down, and finally, having blown the walls away, steps through into a new space, the tension *can* still feel like it leads toward healthier, higher ground. One just has to, as it is said, "keep the feeling," and believe a little bit. Step out on it. But out on what?

IV. The Gospel Impulse: The Dialogic Image, Africa, and the Pragmatic Amen

The truth is that it's not really a question of "on what" but of "with whom?" If the energy of the blues impulse comes from the existential surprise of anguish transformed into an individual's lyrical joy, and the jazz impulse plays the bridges between one thing and its always-altering selves, the feeling of abiding "health" that characterizes the gospel impulse comes from the communication of the ever-renewing surprise on the move *between* people. Whether expressed in ritual, prayer, two step, slow drag, or sexual healing—in "Jesus Gave Me Water," "Take Me to the River," "What's Going On," or "In Between the Sheets"—the gospel impulse always involves the *interactive* nature of human energy and presence. In *A Change Is Gonna Come*, Werner explains, "the gospel impulse helps people experience themselves *in relation to* rather than *on their own*. Gospel makes the feeling of human separateness, which is what the blues are all about, bearable" (28). Theoretically, the gospel impulse takes the battered and bruised existentialism of the blues (in which the self becomes in some way other to the world) and the hall-of-mirrors-like, virtuosic self-reflexivity of jazz (in which the self becomes other to itself), and situates *both* in an engaged sense of spiritual community, an intense sense of connection with other people. Donny Hathaway sings

"Hang on to the world as it spins around." Multiple worlds. Worlds inside worlds. We don't do that alone.

As Baldwin did, Komunyakaa understands his own work, at least in part, as an act of witnessing. Witnessing has its formal dimensions. For Komunyakaa, because it relies on nonverbal (tonal, rhythmic) dimensions of language in ways similar to instrumental music, the poetic image itself has an important role to play in connecting people to each other. In a 1999 interview with Ernest Suarez, Komunyakaa stresses the ways that statements (as opposed to images) in poetry can bear false witness. Consequently, he confesses that he is "not so much interested in making a statement . . . I think many political poems fall short because they're filled with empty antics and gestures" (20). Instead, Komunyakaa approaches images in poems in terms of blues confrontation and gospel connection. Images, he observes, provoke "a question in the reader or the listener; that's the confrontation" (20). The mutual nature of the issue emerges as confrontation becomes connection:

> The reader or the listener entering the poem [becomes] a cocreator of meaning. I don't want the poem to talk to the reader or the listener, but to establish a dialogue. Sometimes there's a dialogue within the privacy of one's psyche when we're not told what to think, or how to think, but imagistically guided toward feelings that are already within our grasp. (20–21)

Together with a skeptical attitude toward direct statements that strip language of its nonverbal resonance in the interest of expedient communication, Komunyakaa expresses a faith in the poetics of the image to join otherwise (at least apparently) disconnected sensibilities. This dimension of communication runs beneath controlled, rigid grammars and meanings fundamental to rational, conceptual identities. Egos. Komunyakaa continues: "One doesn't necessarily have to know what it means, but he or she does have to feel something. It's like music. There can be an immense clarity though sheer feeling . . . that inspires the willing reader to go the distance and become emotionally or psychologically involved in the possibilities" (21). Like an improvised version of the West African tonal languages that inform Black culture, Komunyakaa seeks "a narrative of tone, or tonal narrative that may focus on a central story, but it allows encountering others within it" (17).

The connection between privacy and mutual fluency involves a blues/jazz substructure beneath the gospel impulse. The impulses interlock and Komunyakaa's regard for the dialogic power of poetic images echoes Miles Davis's account of the importance of tone over words, especially song titles, in his playing on ballads. Like Komunyakaa, Davis understands that a crucial part of a conversation takes place within (as well as between) people. Davis commented:

> You know when a singer sings, he gives you a map of what to think when he sings a ballad with a title. But when we play we don't bother your thoughts [for one, by introducing songs by their titles]. You use your own thoughts. What you think is yours. When you hear someone singing a ballad you have to think what he means. He gives you the route. But when you hear—I hate to say jazz—jazz musicians, jazz musicians give you the privacy of your own head. (Szwed, 183)

Many critics and listeners construed Miles's approach as disregard or even disrespect for the audience. Similarly, some critics and reviewers (see Alvin Aubert and Toi Derricotte) have interpreted the difficulty inherent in Komunyakaa's poems as a retreat from connection to an audience. Maybe so. Of Komunyakaa's book *Magic City*, Calvin Bedient asks "Is this perhaps a poetry against epistemology?" ("Short Reviews," 168). Critics have missed the impulse to mutuality and read Komunyakaa's work as an attempt to forego connections to an audience. But, couched in the gospel impulse understood in mutual terms (and in opposition to a decadent mainstream world), Komunyakaa's approach, echoed by Miles Davis above, evinces a deep concern for the artistic medium and the listener/reader.

In a letter to Sol Stein in 1956, James Baldwin anticipated Komunyakaa's and Davis's distrust of lyrics and titles and the fake inter-personal fluency that cheapens and falsifies communication. Baldwin asserts a radical conception of consensus-domination that relates directly to the battle between the world of false cultural witness and the personal, private interiors crucial to the imagistic call and response suggested by Komunyakaa's mode of musical/poetic witnessing. Warning that domination doesn't always involve tanks and barbed wire, Baldwin considers the insidious dangers lurking in "the kind of domination which is achieved when the same idea becomes real in many lives" (*Native Sons*, 98). Immersed in a 1960s still hungover with these forces of the 1950s, in *The Dead Lecturer*, LeRoi Jones suggests the reason for his dense, expressionistic approach to poetry. In "Footnote To A Pretentious Book," he writes: "There is no one to entrust with / meaning" (81). The dialogic image works with at least one foot beneath verbal meaning. Sub-fluent.

In Komunyakaa's approach, the subversive nature of a reader's and writer's co-participation in meaning eludes the hegemonic forces infecting more direct means of so-called communication. The power of Komunyakaa's conception (which might well be called "imagistic resistance") accrues via linking the (gospel) sharing of the (blues) burden directly to the jazz-informed notion of changing, expanding, blurring identities: "Imagery makes the meaning elastic, amorphous as an organism attempting to deny or defy its design" (*Blue Notes*, 21). Identity surprised by itself (blues), lost as found (jazz), but now shared as well. Even with the difficulties of communication via such an imagistic approach, and the fact that he has "never purposefully written a poem for a select group of people," Komunyakaa finds that his work at times does communicate directly: "There are certain poems I can read to young black men and women and automatically they grasp the poetry" (*Blue Notes*, 29).

In his imagistic elegy for Thelonious Monk, "It's Always Night," Komunyakaa witnesses how Monk used silence as *shared* space: "silence shaped as tonal artifact, is what Monk captured . . . An exactitude defined by what's left out" (*Caliban*, 52). The counterintuitive logic of the piece spins the gospel in a way exactly antithetical to the aims of evangelists and missionaries searching for converts. It's interesting, here, to think about Monk's own time spent working as piano player for a traveling evangelist. More, Komunyakaa doesn't seek a counter-domination either. Truly mutual, if a bit esoteric, the ties that bind this kind of community must remain partially unstated. Instead, they're imaged, inscribed by the author and reconstituted by the reader. Embedded in the fluidity and unpredictability of the exchange is a flexible faith in the jazz impulse. In his early poem, "Instructions for Building Straw Huts," Komunyakaa imagines poetry as a shared structure. The first step in building the structure invokes a contradictory baptism (if not a baptism in contradiction): "First you must have / unbelievable faith in water (*Pleasure Dome*, 99). As in Miles's or Monk's instrumental music, an image's meaning in a poem depends upon what people bring with them and "requires an active listener—someone who doesn't have to be told the whole story" (22). Old visions of new wholes, there's a dream-like, surrealistic quality to Monk's gospel of syncopated, shared silence. Things bend into shape, hover beyond the border, punch into being, and snap off to elsewhere just before their shadow can catch up. Komunyakaa writes, there's "an emotional elasticity to Monk's world" (22). In a near-verbatim reiteration of Freud's insights into the non-rational structure of the unconscious, Komunyakaa dispels stereotypes by foreswearing allegiance to predictable associations and stereotyped images of familiarity. At this depth of connection, as in Freud's analysis of dream imagery, Komunyakaa explains how, in Monk's compositions, "Things that seem at odds with each other fit side by side" (22). In relation to a segregated nation, the democratic force of this erstwhile-subconscious structure becomes clear. Like joy and pain in the gospel vision, Monk's "musical theory can be found in his title 'Ugly Beauty.'" Komunyakaa's gospel operates in a similar fashion as he creates "an open-endedness that invites the reader to enter not merely to read the poem as an outsider but to experience it from within. . . a connection fused by interactive minds" (*Blue Notes*, 30). That he considers the mutual possibilities redemptive (if contradictory) is clear when he states: "to me, contradiction is a sort of discourse . . . sometimes . . . the merger of opposites can save us from ourselves" (*Blue Notes*, 78–79). The poems suggest that people so constituted can do something good for each other. Like Baldwin wrote to his brother David: "Hell is *not* other people."

However avant-garde this may sound, for Komunyakaa, the idea of the poetic witness emanates directly from his thoughts about the African American church. Within "black churches, there's a choral response, a call and response; the minister stands there rendering a syncopated oration to 'amen' that comes in chorus or individually from the congregation: 'Amen, tell it like it is'" (Suarez, 20). In Komunyakaa's apprehension, an artist like Monk, possibly during his work in revivals, internalized exactly this dynamic: "Monk knew how to be his own Amen Corner" ("Jazz and Poetry," 656). By this statement, Komunyakaa implies a similar internalization on his own part. Werner emphasizes the ancestral meaning of call and response, noting that the gospel impulse draws directly on "values brought to the new world by the men and women uprooted from West African cultures" (*A Change*, 28). Komunyakaa's images engage a familial, cultural, and artistic sense of ancestry in a call-and-response conversation that, like those in the churches (or in Miles Davis's untitled ballads, for that matter), creates a "kind of dialogue [that] echoes all the way back to Africa" (Suarez, 20). Reminding us that the gospel images come with their own communally enacted joy, Komunyakaa writes that "attempting to encapsulate action and stasis through imagery propels release—this is celebration" (Suarez, 20).

NOTES

1. I first employed this term in relation to Komunyakaa's work in the essay "Open the Unusual Door: Visions from the Dark Window in Yusef Komunyakaa's Early Poems," *Callaloo* 28, no. 3 (2005): 780–796.

2. What I'm after here, and by turns throughout the essay, is Komunyakaa's way of engaging a racialized sense of self without accepting the limitations imposed by various discourses used to describe a racialized self. Racialized labels for people such as "Black" or "African American," in fact, rarely appear in Komunyakaa's poems, though he most certainly doesn't attempt to universalize or "avoid" themes and topics of racial nuance and particularity. Akin possibly to the contradictory sense Langston Hughes gestured to as "racial individuality" in his 1926 essay for *The Nation*, "The Negro Artist and the Racial Mountain," this shifting space in which Komunyakaa's poetic thought operates is difficult to describe in American prose, which tends to break down on the fulcrum of race-neutral ("blindness-to-color") or race-essential ("color-blindness"). In his "Introduction" to his 1961 book of essays, *Nobody Knows My Name: More Notes of a Native Son*, James Baldwin attends this veiled complexity warning his readers that "The question of color takes up much space in these pages, but the question of color, especially in this country, operates to hide the graver questions of the self" (*Collected Essays*, 136). Komunyakaa's poems and poetic thought approach questions of race/self in terms much like Baldwin described here.

Drawing upon phrasings from Ralph Ellison's *Shadow and Act* and upon insights from a wide range of musical and literary artists, the vocabulary of musical impulses as a device for understanding literary art and culture takes shape most notably in Craig Werner's books *Playing the Changes* and *A Change Is Gonna Come*. Craig Werner presents the blues as a "philosophy of life, a three-step process that can be used by painters, dancers, as well as musicians" (*A Change Is Gonna Come*, 69). The process, as Werner understands it, begins when a figure finds a lyrical voice to articulate and order the chaos of experience. It closes with the expression of this lyrical understanding as a joyful act of "reaffirming your existence" (69). Werner distinguishes reaffirmation from transcendence; in the blues "[a]ll you can do is reach down inside the pain, finger the jagged grain, and tell your story . . . You never really get away, transcend" (70). Other musical impulses keep track of dimensions of experience that accompany the blues core. The "gospel impulse" (see pages 173–78, in this essay) explores the shared and therefore somewhat more joyous extensions of the blues self. Historically, the gospel impulse ties a vision of transcendence ("crossing over" into higher ground) to a resolutely earth-based, historically engaged, and tactically deployed vision of political, social change. The "jazz impulse" (see pages 163–73, in this essay) accompanies the other two impulses with an insistence that all phrasings and understandings be understood as in process, in flux, not just subject to—but an active agent of—change.

In addition to the work of Ellison, James Baldwin, and Werner foregrounded in this essay, a range of critical work informs my sense of the role of music in literary art and thought (also developed at some length in my book *Crossroads Modernism*): Le Roi Jones's *Blues People* and Amiri Baraka's *Black Magic*; Richard Powell's edited volume, *The Blues Aesthetic*; Albert Murray's *Stomping the Blues*; Gayl Jones's *Liberating Voices*; Shirley Anne Williams's *Give Birth to Brightness*; Stephen Henderson's *Understanding the New Black Poetry*; Nathaniel Mackey's *Discrepant Engagement* and *Paracritical Hinge*; Jurgen Grandt's *Kind of Blue*; Sascha Feinstein's *Jazz Poetry*; Rob Wallace's *Improvisation in the Making of American Literary Modernism*; Meta DuEwa Jones's *The Muse is Music*; and Tony Bolden's *Afro Blue*.

WORKS CITED

Aubert, Alvin. "Yusef Komunyakaa: The Unified Vision—Canonization and Humanity." *African American Review* 27, no. 1 (1993): 119–23.

Baldwin, James. "Sermons and Blues." In *Collected Essays*, edited by Toni Morrison, 614–15. New York: Library of America, 1998.

——. "The Uses of the Blues—A Soliloquy." *Playboy* (1964): 131–32, 240–41.

——. *Conversations with James Baldwin*. Edited by Fred L. Standley and Louis H. Pratt. Jackson: University Press of Mississippi, 1989.

Bedient, Calvin. "Short Reviews." *Poetry* 162 (1993): 167–70.

Derricotte, Toi. "The Tension Between Memory and Forgetting in the Poetry of Yusef Komunyakaa." *The Kenyon Review* XV, no. 4 (1993): 217–22.

Ellison, Ralph. *The Collected Essays of Ralph Ellison*. New York: Modern Library, 1995.

Engels, John. "A Cruel Happiness." *New England Review* 16, no. 1 (1994): 163–69.

Feinstein, Sascha. "Survival Masks: An Interview with Yusef Komunyakaa." *Brilliant Corners: A Journal of Jazz and Literature* 2, no. 1 (1997): 53–79.

Foner, Eric. *The Story of American Freedom*. New York: W. W. Norton, 1998.

Gotera, Vicente. "Depending on the Light: Yusef Komunyakaa's *Dien Cai Dau*." In *Critical Essays on Literature and Film of the Vietnam War*, edited by Owen Gilman and Lorrie Smith, 282–300. Garland, NY: Garland Press, 1990.

——. "Killer Imagination." *Callaloo* 13, no. 2 (1990): 364–71.

Hughes, Langston. "The Negro Artist and the Racial Mountain." In *The Norton Anthology of African American Literature*, edited by Henry Louis Gates Jr. and Nellie Y. McKay, 1267–71. New York: W. W. Norton, 1997.

Hentoff, Nat. "You'd be Playing and He'd Yell 'Get into Yourself.'" *The Progressive* (August 1981): 52–53.

Komunyakaa, Yusef, and William Matthews. "Jazz and Poetry: A Conversation." *The Georgia Review* 46, no. 4 (1992): 645–61.

Komunyakaa, Yusef. "It's Always Night." *Caliban* 4 (1986): 52.

——. *February in Sydney*. Unionville, IN: Matchbooks, 1989.

——. "Crossroads." *Ploughshares* (1997): 5–6.

——. "'How Poetry Helps People Live Their Lives.'" *The American Poetry Review* (September/October 1999): 21–22.

——. *Blue Notes: Essays, Interviews, and Commentaries.* Ann Arbor: University of Michigan Press, 2000.

——. *Pleasure Dome: New and Collected Poems.* Middletown, CT: Wesleyan University Press, 2001.

Suarez, Ernest. "An Interview with Yusef Komunyakaa. *Five Points* 4, no. 1 (1999): 15–28.

Szwed, John. *So What: The Life of Miles Davis.* New York: Simon & Schuster, 2002.

Werner, Craig. *Playing the Changes: From Afro-Modernism to the Jazz Impulse.* Urbana: University of Illinois Press, 1994.

——. *A Change Is Gonna Come: Race, Music, & the Soul of America.* New York: Plume, 1998.

Yusef Komunyakaa's Scenes of Vietnam and Louisiana

The Forever Crisis of Racial Terror in *Dien Cai Dau* (1988)

1. "Shared *Historical* Time"

Yusef Komunyakaa's *Dien Cai Dau* (1988) comes out of lived experiences and the re-living of one experience embedded in a thousand other experiences of racial violence, testifying to the eternal weariness or perennial, preternatural crises common to Americans of color, at home and in uniform abroad. The most compelling aspect of the poetry collection is Komunyakaa's evocation of "shared *historical* time"[1] that unpacks how quotidian, how present, how rupturing the two converging scenes are: the imperialist, racialized violence evident in the Vietnam War and in the Jim Crow American South of the poet's birthplace, rural Louisiana. Indeed, Louisiana and Vietnam share in common aspects of climate and lush, leafy terrain, as well as horrendous histories of oppression, colonialism, and US-sanctioned violence; critics have noted the impact of New Orleans on the poet, including the city's "sense of deep time"[2] and its music.

Readers of Komunyakaa's poems in our current political moment will also navigate a "shared *historical* time" as they connect the American legacies of slavery, segregation, violence, and imperialism with the current pandemic of anti-Black racism in every aspect of American life.

As a former combat journalist who served in the Vietnam War, Komunyakaa mediates images, personae, and trauma from the Vietnam War through the scarred landscape of his hometown of Bogalusa, Louisiana. Komunyakaa's Vietnam War poems reorder various harrowing moments in Vietnam and Louisiana; through this fractured representation of time, the poet constructs a narrative present-tense in each poetic scene, episode, or encounter. The poems collectively testify to the horrors of everyday existence for people of color, whether that's in a war or in the warzone of daily life. Following Lauren Berlant's insight that trauma might be understood not as a shattering single event but as an ongoing "systemic crisis,"[3] I contend that Komunyakaa's war poems reveal, across time, space, and location, the many ways in which White "supremacist space is crisis space embedded in the ordinary."[4] In Komunyakaa's poetry collection, "the crisis of the present" in Vietnam converges with "multiple crises of presence"[5] in the American South and nested in the social construction of race, which has always been tied to racism and domination. The poems accrue emotional poignancy and moral imperative through Komunyakaa's poetic strategies of representation such as 1) the flashbacks from Vietnam to Louisiana which resituate American racism, violence, and imperialism, and 2) the use of simile and nature imagery to tranquilize and disperse terror into a disquieting beauty that engages the reader by way of defamiliarization. This essay closely reads two poems from *Dien Cai Dau*, "The Three-Legged Stool" and "You and I Are Disappearing" to explore representations of the forever crisis of racialized violence. Ultimately, Komunyakaa's poems testify to the perpetual crisis of systemic racism, which since the Black Lives Matter protests in the summer of 2020 has reached newfound visibility in our current era.

2. On "The Three-Legged Stool"

Throughout the poetry collection, Komunyakaa recounts the ever-present White supremacy and hatred that is embedded in American nationalism and history. Indeed, the violence and horror of the Vietnam War brings Komunyakaa back to memories of Jim Crow: "& I'm a small boy / again in Bogalusa. *White Only* / signs."[6] In another poem, Komunyakaa questions not only the horrors that three White southerners, raising a Confederate flag, commit in raping a Vietnamese woman, but the injustices of a predominantly White military, military court, military paper, and media that allow the rape and murder of a brown woman to go unpunished.[7]

James Willie Brown Jr., the given name of Komunyakaa, was one of the mere 5 percent of African Americans serving in Vietnam as combat correspondents producing the military newspaper, *The Southern Cross*. Due to institutionalized racism, men of color didn't have the same opportunities to evade the draft, given the realities of an all-White drafting board and poverty that prevented a full-time-student status, which would exempt one from military service. For example, a Black man attending community college or attending college on a part-time status due to finances couldn't evade the draft; thus, draft evasion was yet another privilege afforded to White middle-class individuals. A majority of Black soldiers were drafted, and these soldiers were killed in higher numbers than were Whites, such that civil rights leaders intimated (or just said) that the Vietnam War was the genocide of American Blacks. Behind the scenes of the Vietnam War protest were African Americans who faced enormous discrimination in every aspect of life, from education and politics to housing and transportation; civil rights activist Stokely Carmichael captures the ironic position of Black men drafted to perpetuate the handiwork of omnipresent White oppressors at home and abroad: "Why should black folk fight a war against yellow folk so that white folks can keep a land they stole from red folk? . . . We're not going to Vietnam. Ain't no Vietcong ever called me nigger."[8] Although Komunyakaa avoided the front lines as a war journalist, he says in "Begotten," "I'm the son of poor Mildred and illiterate J.W.,"[9] reflecting larger societal issues that circumscribed many poor Southern Black men to military-sanctioned death. In Vietnam, the front lines were called "Soulville" because of the disproportionate Black death rate. In 1966, statistics proved that Black men eligible for the military made up 12 percent of the population, but the death rate of Black soldiers was at 21 percent.[10] By the end of the war, the death rate was 13.1 percent; the death rate for paratroopers and elite combat units for Black men rose to 25 percent in 1968.[11] For African American veteran writers, there could be no protest of the Vietnam War without an exposé of imperialism and racism that ran amok in the American South and across the globe.

Thadious M. Davis coined the term "southscapes" to reflect the complex relationships Black authors from the Deep South have not only with their environment and the social injustices visible or invisible within that environment, but also their relationships to the Global South through imaginative restructuring of regional boundaries and borders that might "initiat[e] the flow of ideas and empowerment of actions"[12] that confronts segregation and racial terror. Davis uses the term "southscapes" to probe the way "black writers from the Deep South use their spatial location to . . . assert geographical claims and transgress regulatory boundaries that counter racial exclusion as a practice of power and privilege."[13] Along similar lines, David Cross Turner notes the ways in which the "national imaginary" posits the "South . . . as synonymous with 'racial trauma.'"[14] Turner argues that Komunyakaa's poetry refuses fatalistic repetitions of racial trauma through art, but, instead, seeks to "bring the buried into the light, manifesting a need to make trauma meaningful for the survivors and for others through poetry's intersubjective potential"; in so doing, Komunyakaa offers readers a "responsible engagement with the traumatic past."[15]

In the prose poem "The Three-Legged Stool," Komunyakaa most clearly aligns the imprisonment in two countries; through adopting a persona of a Black prisoner of war, the poet reveals how Black men are imprisoned in the American South and in Vietnam. The poem's speaker isn't just a prisoner of war in Vietnam; he is a prisoner of war in his own country. The "prison of [his] skin"—or, rather, the imprisoning racial construction of his skin—is both "a source of strength" and "a struggle" across time and place.[16] Indeed, imprisonment is a forever crisis of existence for a Black American man, rather than a stint of time spent in a POW camp. The soldier refuses to break down, and keeps digging deep to reveal his resilience, born from years of enduring racism in the American South. Unrelenting imprisonment has developed coping strategies in the speaker, who survives because he can visualize justice, he can laugh, and he can recount all the ways he's endured oppression already.

The VC guard attacks the psyche of a Black POW by reminding him that MLK Jr. is dead and that the White POWs are betraying the Black POWs in segregated cells. Viet Cong soldiers who torture a Black POW capitalize on racial tensions in the American military to further alienate the POW, for whom the VC and Southern Whites are fellow torturers in several different spaces and times. The sprawling prose of this poem, against the standard taut, lyrical line of most Komunyakaa poems, suggests the fertile landscapes of the POW's psychic interior, that, though tormented, cannot and will not capitulate with the torturer's demands. Emerging from physical and psychological torture is the figure of a Black POW who carves out a name for himself and a will to survive. Through survivalist constructions of Black masculinity, the POW embodies the insistence, pride, tirelessness, and creative spirit of one man who refuses to be castrated or forgot by his country— this iteration of Black masculinity bespeaks someone who doesn't wait on someone else to give respect, but takes it. The daring, the audacity of the speaker is what fuels the poem, juxtaposing the layered moments of oppression in two countries with the hard-won language of resistance, agency, and autonomy.

The survivalist mantra of the Black POW, who is separated from the White prisoners, and tortured by the VC into a sleepless, starved semblance of existence, nonetheless bespeaks wholeness, dignity, and mental wellbeing. Hardened by racial terror in the Deep South, the Black POW tells Charlie, "I know how to walk out of a nightmare backwards. I can survive. When you kicked me awake, then back into a stupor, did I break? Maybe I slipped back a few feet deeper in the darkness, but I didn't break."[17] The dramatic monologue crests when the speaker takes the offensive, explaining the sudden breakout into "roaring laugher," telling the VC what was so funny: "You know what I was thinking? I was thinking a hundred ways I could bury you. Charlie, you can kill me, you can turn me into an animal, you can make me wish I was never born, but you can't break me. I won't cooperate."[18] It's as if the POW isn't fazed by the bamboo shoved under his fingernails; the rainwater dripping steadily on his head for weeks; the month of interrogation, loss of sleep, starvation; and the existential isolation from all the other POWs. The reason being: he is from the American South, and he is Black. It's understood that this Vietnamese prison camp is not a place, but a reality he lives with daily—back home. And he's still alive. The strength the POW draws from recalls previous generations of African Americans who despite subjugation and enslavement and disenfranchisement refused the psychic chains of a slavery mindset. The statement, "I refuse to cooperate" shines light on the power of personal and collective identity against tyranny (in the contexts of slavery, war, imprisonment, colonization, or so-called democracy): the power of not letting anyone else define you but you. So significant is one's internal monologue to reclaiming dignity and empowerment, particularly for groups that have been marginalized, that this message of unwavering confidence is crystallized in songs such as Nas's "I Can" from God's Son (2003). Thus, Komunyakaa's poem, in the form of an internal monologue, resonates with the mental toughness, wit, word play, and hope that we might associate with late '90s and early 2000s hip-hop.

But what is the meaning of survival in Vietnam, for a Black soldier who would only be imprisoned again upon return to the soil of the American South? The speaker tells the VC: "All I have to go back to are faces just like yours at the door."[19] What does it matter, if the Black POW comes home in his uniform, expecting respect from White America? The US army uniform, the symbol of brotherhood, patriotism, and nationality, is deconstructed as a symbol of White supremacy. The Black soldier aspires to look so good in his uniform as to subvert the racist assumptions by White Americans that a Black man is inferior, less American, less human. The uniform becomes the language with which this Black prisoner of war can articulate his dissent from American myths of combat brotherhood and interracial unity:

> They [White American men] used to look at me in my uniform like I didn't belong in it. *(Struts around in a circle.)* I'd be sharper than sharp. My jump boots spit-shined till my face was lost in them. You could cut your fingers on the creases in my khakis. My brass, my ribbons, they would make their blood boil. They'd turn away, cursing through their teeth.[20]

Komunyakaa's poem exposes how the Black POW in Nam is emblematic of Black civilians in Louisiana, Mississippi, and Alabama. From Bogalusa, Louisiana, a hotbed of Klan activity, born into the end of the Jim Crow era, and the descendent of Trinidad stowaways forced to lose their name, Komunyakaa acknowledges and also resists certain imprints of history. For instance, the poet rejected his given name, "Brown," because it bespoke "a planation owner's breath."[21] William M. Ramsey surmises: "Given Komunyakaa's familial and southern experience, both of which greatly sensitized him to violence and cruelty, he perceived American foreign policy through the lens of historical racial oppression and personal pain."[22] The Vietnam War poems defamiliarize the reader from their expectations by suffusing the war narrative with flashbacks and flashforwards to a more comprehensive look at how Southern Black men are continually, perpetually fighting to reclaim their dignity, and doing so. What they are often fighting against are the myriad projections and stereotypes that are cast onto them in the forever crisis of racism, including social death, actual death, and social control.[23] Similar to W. E. B. Du Bois's concept of double consciousness, David Marriott draws on Frantz Fanon to argue that the "black man [is] irrevocably and unforgettably at war with himself" as "black self-consciousness is already occupied by a foreign force,"[24] which is that foreign, othering

White racist force of projections, stereotypes, and media images continuing to breathe life to the lies of Black inferiority and criminality.

"The Three-Legged Stool," and the book more broadly, shed light on our current moment and the ongoing need for activism and anti-racism work. In a recent essay, Erica S. Lawson asserts, "Trump's rise to power unleashed a state of racial, xenophobic, and misogynistic hatred across the country. In particular, his political authority has lent legitimacy to anti-Black racism, evident in the behaviors of White nationalists who feel empowered."[25] Breonna Taylor was murdered by police who entered her apartment without cause or warrant (the officer was subsequently acquitted of murder); George Floyd was killed, by a White police officer who wouldn't stop kneeling on his neck for the whole eight minutes and forty-six seconds it took to kill Floyd. (Sadly, it was broadly seen as a triumph that Floyd's killer was held to account.) A Black woman, Sandra Bland, who didn't put out her cigarette in her own car at the demand of a White policeman, was wrongfully jailed and then "mysteriously" deemed dead by suicide. In his poem "Bullet Points," Pulitzer-prize-winning poet Jericho Brown makes the sobering point that if he, as a Black man, is dead anywhere near the police, don't call it suicide, but homicide. Claudia Rankine's poetry collection, *Citizen*, which elegizes victims of police brutality, and points to the effects of both police brutality and daily microaggressions on people of color, has gone through multiple reprintings to include more and more names.

On January 6, 2021, Americans witnessed the Confederate flags that White supremacist insurrectionists brandished in the US Capitol, as they sought to seize power for Trump and, through this insurrection, decry the election results and the democratic process. In the summer protests of 2020, the Black Lives Matter movement drew international attention to the ongoing work of anti-Black racism as a social issue of deep urgency. Ta-Nehisi Coates, in his *Between the World and Me*, captures how the problem of anti-Black violence, and fatal violence at that, has never really been given the proper attention it needs, or even the proper language:

All our phrasing—race relations, racial chasm, racial justice, racial profiling, white privilege, even white supremacy—serves to obscure that racism is a visceral experience, that it dislodges brains, blocks airways, rips muscle, extracts organs, cracks bones, breaks teeth . . . [it] all lands with great violence upon the body.[26]

This is why Komunyakaa's poem, which speaks from a POW camp in Vietnam, fleshes out so well the physical and psychological violence that racism enacts upon the body—that the Black body is always in survival mode. Coates goes on to say how personal this is, that he has always known, felt, that, as his father before him did, his "body was in constant jeopardy."[27]

3. On "You and I Are Disappearing"

Komunyakaa's poem "You and I Are Disappearing" places in the present tense a moment that indeed stops time: the witnessing of a Vietnamese girl screaming in agony as she suffers, burns in the aftermath of a napalm bomb that an American plane dropped. The poem centers on the image of a young Vietnamese girl depicted screaming, running naked, skin aflame with napalm. The girl, though unnamed, evokes and mirrors the Vietnamese child-victim, Kim Phuc, famously photographed while running, her clothes burnt off by napalm, on a road. Her mouth is open in one of the loudest silences ever to be captured on camera; the vulnerability of the child in this context is juxtaposed with the power of the image as an anti-war emblem. The photograph entitled "The Terror of War" secured a Pulitzer for AP photographer Nick Ut in 1972. Komunyakaa doesn't name the girl in his poem, refusing to reduce her to a poster child, and refusing to position himself in the ethically dubious role of journalists and photographers who earn prizes for capturing the horrors of a vulnerable child-victim, and often without consent. The incident, infamously captured by Ut, was a recurring scene during the Vietnam War.

Komunyakaa's poem subjects readers to the disquieting experience of internalizing one such scene: as a combat journalist, the poet encounters a napalmed girl, a child, and does nothing in the moment. He bears witness, stays present, and in his title, insists on this moment—this eternal present that evokes so clearly the cost of American imperialism, war, violence, and hatred of the "other." The title, "You and I Are Disappearing" is the cry of protest, not only of the Vietnam War, but of the dehumanizing forces of racism and imperialism: "you and I" is a concept and should be a basic given of existence—our shared humanity and our own specific individual identity. If a napalmed child is burning and no one cares to oppose the forces of hatred, the self of every actor is disappearing. In this specific case, the American soldiers labeled Vietnamese people "gooks," and from there it was easy for them to rape the women, blow up villages, burn the skin of children, and in the end, destroy around two million Vietnamese lives, and all for an unknown cause with no strategy or exit plan, except that vague imperialist, arrogant, White-supremacist calling of "spreading Democracy." But note the present tense, not only of the poem's narrative, but its title. We continue to live under this threat of our humanity disappearing.

In the poem "You and I Are Disappearing," the string of similes and nature imagery that bears witness is evasive, at times poeticizing suffering, yet all the while performing the emotional labor of defamiliarizing the narratives of racism. The disquieting beauty of nature imagery and of poetic simile fill the reader with a new enraged awe, which has as one of its aims the kind of self-reflection and racial consciousness that might lead to radical change.

The poet claims "the cry I bring down from the hills / belongs to a girl / still burning / inside my head."[28] How is the cry—that which the girl supposedly owns—"inside" the poet's psyche? The poet's internal drama is the frame of the poem: the scene is that which the poet has absorbed in seeing the girl burn. The girl does not cry out. The only allusion to her cry is in the opening lines, where the poet has internalized her cries. The poet opens the scene with a bold claim that the girl's cries have merged with his own cries, and the similes in the poem similarly emblazon the cries, tiered like a "red pagoda" (the title of another poem), into the reader's consciousness. We learn throughout the book that the poet's cries of pain, of protest, testify to the brutal racism of the American South; thus, the poet has more in common with the Vietnamese child-victim than he does with the White American soldiers who are his so-called "brothers," but who wield Confederate flags, bomb and burn children, and rape village women.

The poem invokes a disturbing feeling of terror and helplessness, as the reader is subjected to simile after simile about how the girl burns. Similes that denote her burning include the following: she burns like "a piece of paper"; "foxfire"; "a thigh-shaped valley"; "a skirt of flames"; "a sack of dry ice"; "oil on water"; "a cattail torch dipped in gasoline"; "the fat tip of a banker's cigar"; "quicksilver"; "a tiger under a rainbow"; "a shot glass of vodka"; "a field of poppies"; and "a burning bush."[29] Paradoxically, the descriptions of burning attenuate the pain of the girl, while at the same time creating distracting, tantalizing imagery to signify the girl's pain through natural and material objects with juxtaposing moods: the fanciful imagery of tiger, rainbow, skirt, foxfire, valley, paper, bush, and the violent, eerie imagery of flames, sack, oil, vodka, cigar, banker, and burning bush. The pain and shock of the napalm bomb is so all-encompassing that the metaphoric burning nearly eclipses the girl at the center of the poem.

The anaphora of "She burns like," repeated seven times,[30] extends the narrative moment into the kind of terrifying nowness—a flashback so real it enacts the present. The poem is in present progressive tense, lives-treaming in the poet-soldier's PTSD nightmare loops. The only interruptions in the poem signal the way in which the moment is not interrupted. The first references the speaker's inability to act: "We stand with our hands / hanging at our sides / while she burns."[31] The speaker is complicit, yet helpless. The other interruption elaborates upon the way in which the speaker is breathing in the child's burning skin: "She rises like dragonsmoke / to my nostrils."[32] The wistful imagery of dragonsmoke reveals how the young child's innocence evaporates within the context of horror.

The poem is unbearable. That is the point. Like the poet, we as readers become witnesses of a child-victim who did not ask to be burned, seared with the racist, sexist legacies of American democracy. The nondescript, mediated cries of the girl in the poem suggest the ways in which "pain is not only itself resistant to language but also actively destroys language, deconstructing it into the pre-language of cries and groans."[33] For anyone who "hears those cries" becomes a "witness [of] the shattering of language."[34] The poet-speaker doesn't repair the "shatter[ed] language" of the girl's cries, but rather embraces the deconstruction of language by flinging simile after simile at the reader: simile as a form of burning, of self-immolating, of being seared inside and outside. Each simile in the poem is like another layer of clothing, of cells, burning through to the body. The poem is heat. The similes enact the ways in which pain is so personal, so totalizing, so overwhelming that it denotes "the complete absence of referential content" such that individuals speak of pain via a "dense sea of artifacts and symbols."[35] In Komunyakaa's attempt to articulate suffering, to paint the picture of another's suffering to one who is not even present, perhaps all that is evident is the emotional labor of the poem, the PTSD of the poet as he ponders and feels the effects of

American violence in his own body. I wonder if Komunyakaa had this moment in mind when he wrote that, decades after having traveled the world: "I'm still ashamed / of memories that make me American / as music made of harmony & malice."[36]

The poem embodies an unending, traumatic cry of a victim of war, a child, who is eternally vulnerable in the poem that stops time and keeps the reader inside the scream, one that the soldier-speaker still hears. Komunyakaa's poem argues that the burning girl's cry is "still burning inside my head" from "daybreak" to "dusk" to "nightfall"[37] in an eternal, cyclical moment. To name the girl Kim Phuc here would be to negate all of the other village children who were victimized by the war, and to locate the injustices of the American military into a seemingly happy ending whereby a photographer saves the girl, wins a Pulitzer, and reunites with her decades later. The girl is nameless, eternal, stuck in the ongoing present of White supremacy and imperialism. There is an equally significant "I" in the poem: the speaker who hears, carries the cry of the suffering girl; the implication is that the speaker identifies with the girl, as he too has been a victim and a survivor.

The highly publicized image of a child as a victim of war, for good or ill, becomes a powerful litmus test of a society's ethics, and yet is always a controversial touchstone. For example, the narrative of the photograph of Emmett Till's body, or of Kim Phuc's nude, napalmed flesh, suggest the way in which trauma is personal and global, private and political. In Komunyakaa's poem "History Lessons," the lynched body is internalized as a message about the precarity of life for Southern young Black men in particular, and for the mothers left in their wake only to prophecy first, as in, *"Son you ain't gonna live long,"* and mourn later.[38] The shocking nature of Till's disfigured, defaced corpse and the shocking nature of the nudity and vulnerability of Phuc's body became rallying cries for justice, change, and peace; significantly, Till was brutally murdered, whereas Phuc was not, although both children became global iconography, evidence, symbol, fate, terror: brutalized innocence first, individuals second. The well-known photographs of Till and of Phuc awakened public consciousness, speaking to the collective responsibility infamously captured in Martin Luther King Jr.'s dictum, "Injustice anywhere is a threat to justice everywhere."[39] King argues for the moral imperative to defend justice on the basis of shared, interconnected fates: "We are caught in an inescapable network of mutuality, tied in a single garment of destiny.

Whatever affects one directly, affects all indirectly."[40] The concept of "affect' in King's oft-quoted statement is crucial, particularly in the way the two "affects" are contrasted, yet brought together. The uncomfortable empathy in Komunyakaa's poem is aspirational, because, like the poet who stands there and watches the girl burn, the reader too is frozen, stuck. Is watching a form of complicity, or is it a necessary act of witnessing and self-reflection?

If there is a nefarious criminal in "You and I Are Disappearing," beyond the amorphous guilty world that is American racism, greed, and oppression, it is noticeably buried in the metaphor of "the fat tip / of the banker's cigar / silent as quicksilver."[41] The motif of Vietnam as the rich White man's war or Whitey's war resonates in the lines that associate White male privilege with lies and a legacy of rich, White oppressors— from slaveholding presidents to Southern segregationists to the Nixon Administration profiting from war and inequality. The ways in which the banker's burning embers are "out of touch" with the common people is directly connected to the napalmed girl, as if the cigar detonated into napalm, eviscerating villages and human beings into cries at the barriers of speech—the invisible cigar behind the decisions to drop bombs on innocent people in the name of business-as-usual politics and profit.

The poem will not move on. That is the point. Komunyakaa's poem, "You and I Are Disappearing" is un-Google-able and wholly unrelated to a single news story or archive. It is not based on a single traumatic moment, but rather a forever crisis, one that we see not only in the burned bodies of children in the Vietnam War, but also in the lynched bodies hanging as what Billie Holiday would call "the strange fruit" (1939) of Southern trees.

4. Coda

We see the same forever crisis today in the cellphone videos of dying and dead Black bodies, human lives which were killed, dehumanized, by racist police. In the summer of 2020, George Floyd's daughter said, "Daddy changed the world," which similarly asks us all, as responsible, humane citizens, to consider not only the present moment, but the forever crisis of racism, and the very visceral ways it has taken human life.

David Marriott discusses the racist stereotypes that American and European culture have used to define Black masculinity: "imbecilic, oversexed, criminal, murderous, feckless, rapacious"[42] and that such a legacy from slavery is a continuous factor for Black men. Furthermore, these stereotypes were created by Whites as a defining juxtaposition to their own social construction of Whiteness; this act of othering explicitly reflected and reflects domination over people of color. As Toni Morrison puts it, "Descriptions of cultural, racial, and physical differences that note 'Otherness' but remain free of categories of worth or rank are difficult to come by,"[43] thus articulating that racism always exists in the matrix of power and domination. Through racialized othering, White men have sought to project onto Black men their worst fears of themselves; thus, the historic White concerns and policing of the Black body, through absurd, nonsense racial science that associates Blackness with hypersexuality and criminality tell us about Whiteness. The history of the police force and that of overseers and fugitive slave predators clearly overlap. What is it that White men have been hunting, in the bodies of Black men, for so long? Why, for instance, have White men repeatedly lynched Black men, castrated them, then sewed their penises into their mouths, and burned them? All the while, like at a picnic, the White women and children gather at the spectacle of the Black body. A disturbing feature of photographs of lynchings in the South concern the party White people were having, some White faces (smiling) even pushing in to be sure to make it in the photograph. For centuries, Whites have been projecting criminality, barbarity, and dangerous sexuality onto Black bodies, and we see this clearly in the way White policemen have hunted innocent Black men and boys in public spaces, even a child, Tamir Rice, on a playground. James Baldwin clearly discussed what he believed to be part of the root of racism: "The white man's unadmitted—and apparently to him, unspeakable—private fears and longings are projected onto the Negro."[44]

Applying Komunyakaa's poems to our current moment might reveal the possibilities of poetry to speak out against oppression, to create new solidarities and empathy, to birth new ways of talking about history, racism, and identity, and to recognize the long, troubled history and nowness of racism in this country. Komunyakaa's poems offer a protest against myriad forms of oppression. A call to return to those more hopeful, aspirational ways of knowing than the American tendencies to oppress, label, possess, and destroy. Readers of the poems become complicit, awakened, and sensitized in what Lauren Berlant has called "affective eavesdropping," which is "located in traditions of silent protest" and "aims broadly to remobilize and redirect the normative noise that binds the affective public of the political to normative politics," as it denies "speech as cushion" so that "affect shapes the event."[45] Berlant points to an array of "portable and improvised memorializing from dramatic self-immolation to the silent vigil."[46] Komunyakaa's poems across the collection center conflagrations that evoke affect rather than language, pointing to the unspeakable yet perfectly articulate cry of protest: a child on fire, an anti-war message unto itself ("You and I Are Disappearing"). Or a monk whose self-immolation and utter stillness in the flames surely burns itself across political, moral, social conscience ("The 2527th Birthday of the Buddha"), and whose protest begs the unanswered question of the centuries: "Could his eyes burn the devil out of men?"[47]

Across other poems in the collection, the poet absorbs the destruction of Vietnamese villages and families—the rape of a Vietnamese woman, the self-immolation of a monk, the pain of a napalmed child, and the plights of Vietnamese refugees—and pens these stories with empathy, guilt, concern, terror, and, at times, unsettling beauty. Such cross-hatchings of disparate experiences are not without complications concerning the limits of empathy and witness, the complicated nature of positionality by which two minoritized individuals aren't automatically brother and sister. In one of the few uses of "I" in the book (that is not in persona), the speaker bears witness to seek justice, and says, "I inform the *Overseas Weekly*," advocating for a Vietnamese victim of gang rape.[48] The poem, entitled "Recreating the Scene," exposes the brutality of three Southern White American soldiers who rape a Vietnamese woman with her infant there, and either kill or bribe her into silence, all while their Confederate flags flap on the radio antenna. The speaker's masculinity presents in the form of a protector of Vietnamese girls and women in several important poems, yet the poet's efforts to protest a White military court or to rally others are ineffectual due to the emasculation that White supremacy subjects Black men to. The absurdity of trying to defend the rights of others while having no power to advocate for oneself, let alone another victim, resurfaces.

Komunyakaa recovers the most unexpected version of so-called combat brotherhood: he approaches a fallen Vietnamese soldier, shot down by someone in his platoon (or perhaps he shot the man at a distance?).

The poet sees the photograph of the soldier's lover in the dying man's hand: "I pulled the crumbled photograph / from his fingers. / There's no other way / to say this: I fell in love."[49] As if he were a brother-in-arms, Komunyakaa turned the man's body over "so he wouldn't be kissing the ground."[50] Seeing the photograph of the lover, the poet-soldier empathizes with the "enemy." Becomes him. The very thing his own country refuses to acknowledge in himself: his specific individuality and dignity. Using his poetic skills to slow down time, to linger in the moment, to extend the moment, Komunyakaa creates unexpected kinship with various Vietnamese individuals during the war, from the napalmed child to a fallen Vietnamese soldier, thus embodying an "urgency to reinvent, from the scene of survival, new idioms of the political, and of belonging itself."[51]

This re-imagining is especially powerful in light of the failures of the American Dream, foreign policy, and so-called democracy. Komunyakaa's Vietnam poems defy conceptions of combat brotherhood and racial unity, myths surrounding the desegregated military, and exposes how the story of one Black POW in Vietnam is yet another iteration of the American nightmares experienced by many, many Black men in Louisiana, Mississippi, and Alabama. Even as Komunyakaa draws attention to the Vietnam War Memorial as a black mirror of public and political and personal reckoning in his most infamous war poem from *Dien Cai Dau*, and arguably his most widely anthologized and well-known poem, "Facing It," the rest of the collection supplies the multiple, layered antecedents for "it." The book asks us all to face the personal and collective trauma of anti-Black violence and all forms of oppression, particularly against people of color. Komunyakaa's *Dien Cai Dau* holds endless capacity for moral and social awakening, for breaking immense political silencing around racism, war, and dehumanization. Having taught this work in composition and creative writing classrooms, I've seen the book's power to resist the history-book version of human experience like the lonely testifying voice of mere victim who can be inadvertently blamed; the timeline-based history featuring powerful White men, neat periods, and bombastic events; and a tendency to view oppression always in tandem with brisk, one-liner narratives of progress, resilience, self-reliance, or the covering of exceptionalism, which can also be an erasure of suffering. I remember a student commenting after reading Komunyakaa's *Dien Cai Dau*, "I don't like war poems at all, but these are different, and not really just about Vietnam." The poems which never shut doors but leave them slightly "ajar"[52] invite deeper reading in deep time.

NOTES

1. Lauren Berlant, *Cruel Optimism* (Durham, NC: Duke University Press, 2011), 15.

2. Keith Cartwright, *Sacral Grooves, Limbo Gateways: Travels in Deep Southern Time, Circus Caribbean Space, Afro-Creole Authority* (Athens: University of Georgia Press, 2013), 126.

3. Berlant, 10.

4. Berlant, 88.

5. Berlant, 59.

6. Yusef Komunyakaa, "Tu Do Street," *Pleasure Dome: New and Collected Poems* (Middletown, CT: Wesleyan University Press, 2001), 210.

7. Komunyakaa, "Re-creating the Scene," *Pleasure Dome,* 202–3.

8. Qtd. by James E. Westheider, *The African American Experience in Vietnam: Brothers in Arms* (Lanham, MD: Rowman & Littlefield, 2008), 25.

9. Yusef Komunyakaa, *The Chameleon Couch* (New York: Farrar, Straus, and Giroux, 2011), 89.

10. Herman Graham III, *The Brothers' Vietnam War: Black Power, Manhood, and the Military Experience* (Gainesville: University Press of Florida, 2003), 21.

11. Graham, 21.

12. Thadious M. Davis, *Southscapes: Geographies of Race, Region, and Literature* (Chapel Hill: University of North Carolina Press, 2011), 4.

13. Davis, 4.

14. Daniel Cross Turner, *Southern Crossings: Poetry, Memory, and the Transcultural South* (Knoxville: University of Tennessee Press, 2013), 121.

15. Turner, 146.

16. Yusef Komunyakaa, "An Interview," in *Blue Notes: Essays, Interviews, and Commentaries,* ed. Radiclani Clytus (Ann Arbor: University of Michigan Press, 2000), 77.

17. Komunyakaa, "The One-Legged Stool," *Pleasure Dome,* 219.

18. Komunyakaa, *Pleasure Dome,* 220.

19. Komunyakaa, *Pleasure Dome,* 220.

20. Komunyakaa, *Pleasure Dome,* 220.

21. Komunyakaa, "Mismatched Shoes," *Pleasure Dome,* 292.

22. William A. Ramsey, "Knowing Their Place: Three Black Writers and the Postmodern South," *The Southern Literary Journal* 37, no. 2 (Spring 2005): 125.

23. For more discussion, see Victor M. Rios, *Punished: Policing the Lives of Black and Latino Boys* (New York: New York University Press, 2011).

24. David Marriott, *On Black Men* (New York: Columbia University Press, 2000), 66–67.

25. Erica S. Lawson, "Bereaved Black Mothers and Maternal Activism," *Feminist Studies* 44, no. 3 (2018): 734.

26. Ta-Nehisi Coates, *Between the World and Me* (New York: Penguin Random House, 2015), 10.

27. Coates, 18.

28. Komunyakaa, *Pleasure Dome*, 200.

29. Komunyakaa, *Pleasure Dome*, 200–201.

30. Komunyakaa, *Pleasure Dome*, 200–201.

31. Komunyakaa, *Pleasure Dome*, 201.

32. Komunyakaa, *Pleasure Dome*, 201.

33. Elaine Scarry, *The Body in Pain: The Making and Unmaking of the World* (Oxford, UK: Oxford University Press, 1985), 172.

34. Scarry, 173.

35. Scarry, 162.

36. Komunyakaa, *The Chameleon Couch*, 11.

37. Komunyakaa, *Pleasure Dome*, 200–201.

38. Komunyakaa, "History Lessons," *Pleasure Dome*, 282–84.

39. Martin Luther King Jr., "Letter from a Birmingham Jail," in *The Essential Writings and Speeches of Martin Luther King Jr.*, ed. James M. Washington (San Francisco: Harper Collins, 1986), 290.

40. King, 290.

41. Komunuyakaa, "You and I Are Disappearing," *Pleasure Dome*, 201.

42. Marriott, *On Black Men*, Foreword, viii.

43. Toni Morrison, *The Origin of Others* (Boston: Harvard University Press, 2017), 3.

44. James Baldwin, "The Fire Next Time" (1963) in *The Collected Essays* (New York: Library of America, 1998), 341.

45. Berlant, *Cruel Optimism*, 228.

46. Berlant, 228.

47. Komunyakaa, "The 2527th Birthday of the Buddha," *Pleasure Dome*, 201.

48. Komunyakaa, "Re-creating the Scene," *Pleasure Dome*, 203.

49. Komunyakaa, "We Never Know," *Pleasure Dome*, 207.

50. Komunyakaa, 207.

51. Berlant, *Cruel Optimism*, 262.

52. Komunyakaa, "Jazz and Poetry: A Conversation: Yusef Komunyakaa, William Matthews, and Robert Kelly," *Georgia Review* 46, no. 4 (Winter 1992), 656.

"Facing It"
Of Soldiers, Patriotism, and Literary Resistance

I have always been haunted by Yusef Komunyakaa's poem "Facing It," the last poem in his 1988 collection *Dien Cai Dau*. Personal loss radiates outward in the poem from the narrator's point of view along several distinct narrative threads: a confrontation with self, a depiction of a soldier's survivor's guilt, and the poignant story of a mother who kissed her boy goodbye, only to have him return home from the battlefield in a box.

My generation learned about the Vietnam War from Hollywood movies like *Apocalypse Now* (1979) and *Full Metal Jacket* (1987) until Tim O'Brien's *The Things They Carried* (1990) became the default classroom text about the war. I visited the Vietnam War Memorial sometime after reading Komunyakaa's poem, and at that point understood just how clearly his free verse caught the play of living bodies behind names superimposed on polished granite. The title "Facing It" involves the psychic return to war that is part of the baggage that comes with memorializing a traumatic event, especially when the memorial is situated on the National Mall, the site of what to many represented the Washington, DC power structure that guiltlessly endorsed the fighting of the Vietnam War.

I admire the way the narrator situates himself as subject in the opening lines:

> My black face fades
> hiding inside the black granite.
> I said I wouldn't,
> Dammit: No tears.
> I'm stone. I'm flesh.

This treatment of Blackness in the first two lines is seemingly passive. On the surface, the narrator makes note of the fact that his skin reflects a certain way to the play of light on polished black stone. This perspective is secondary, though, to the emotion of not seeing his name there alongside the others who didn't make it.

In a split second, the narrator is forced to consider what making it really means, because despite being present, "My clouded reflection eyes me / like a bird of prey." Even as he seeks to make his peace with the war, he feels that he is still being hunted: "I go down the 58,022 names, / half-expecting to find / my own in letters like smoke."

According to the Poetry Foundation website, Komunyakaa served in the Vietnam War as a press correspondent from 1969 to 1970. The African American soldier as subject and narrator in Komunyakaa's poem is symbolically important to me. During my formal education of American history, I always believed my own family dwelt outside the national armed forces narrative. I knew nothing of our familial legacy relative to military service. The best I could do was recall watching Sunday afternoon television with my father and his preference for old black-and-white World War II movies. These films rarely contained African American soldiers, so my perspective of the Black soldier as narrator was nonexistent. Years later, however, I would learn that three men in my family fought in WWII. Two were my father's brothers, and one was his uncle. His uncle actually lost his life in the war, while one of his brothers died in an accident while home on furlough. Learning about these particular histories put a new spin on my father's interest in WWII films. I now believe he was looking for firsthand knowledge of the war to bring him closer to the soldiers who had perished in his family during his youth. Like film, literature can satisfy this need for firsthand battle tales.

This early dearth of knowledge about the military men in my family may have made me more attuned to the Black soldier's story when I encountered it in literature. The lines "I touch the name Andrew Johnson; / I see the booby trap's white flash" for me immediately recall the tragic vision of the African American soldier Shadrack and his WWI experience in Toni Morrison's novel *Sula* (1973). Morrison evokes the luck-of-the-draw circumstances of the battlefield in three swift sentences:

He ran, bayonet fixed, deep in the great sweep of men flying across this field. Wincing at the pain in his foot, he turned his head a little to the right and saw the face of a soldier near him fly off. Before he could register shock, the rest of the soldier's head disappeared under the inverted soup bowl of his helmet.

The brilliance of Morrison's writing is that her language makes readers recoil in horror equal to that of the fictional witness of such a violent battlefield death. What better logic could she have used to help civilians understand warfare than to place them in the middle of the action. Morrison drags readers deeper into the soldier's psyche by examining Shadrack's reckoning with PTSD after being wounded and before his subsequent release from a military hospital:

> Like moonlight stealing under a window shade an idea insinuated itself: his earlier desire to see his own face. He looked for a mirror; there was none. Finally, keeping his hands carefully behind his back he made his way to the toilet bowl and peeped in. The water was unevenly lit by the sun so he could make nothing out. Returning to his cot he took the blanket and covered his head, rendering the water dark enough to see his reflection. There in the toilet water he saw a grave black face. A black so definite, so unequivocal, it astonished him. He had been harboring a skittish apprehension that he was not real.

I cannot escape Morrison's orchestration of a scene where the soldier, released from battle, must now find himself anew and reckon with the present. Komunyakaa depicts this same need to reground oneself when his narrator observes:

> I turn that way—I'm inside
> the Vietnam Veterans Memorial
> again, depending on the light
> to make a difference.

Shedding light on the truth of existence is important, as much in real life as it is in the literary lives of Morrison's and Komunyakaa's soldiers. Existence is proof of life, and warfare demands a confrontation with mortality because not everyone returns from the battle intact—psychologically or physically.

My father did not fight in the Vietnam War. Soon after receiving his draft notice, he headed over to the enlistment office to request deferment. He was treated like they had never heard the word deferment before and processed like any other draftee, with a medical exam, shots, and paperwork. Ultimately, however, as a college student, husband, and father his deployment was deferred. He reminded me that this was a war during which a lot of Black men, largely from Southern states, were sent off to battle. This alarm was raised publicly by Martin Luther King Jr. in his speech "Why I Am Opposed to the War in Vietnam." In this speech, King makes the following observation:

> We were taking the black young men who had been crippled by society and sending them 8,000 miles away to guarantee liberties in Southeast Asia which they had not found in southwest Georgia and East Harlem. So, we have been repeatedly faced with a cruel irony of watching Negro and white boys on TV screens as they kill and die together for a nation that has been unable to seat them together in the same schoolroom.

Earlier in his speech, King obliquely refers to this racial inequity as an aspect of the "superficial patriotism" ignored by proponents of the war. It was an era when Americans began to question a patriotism that raised so many ethical issues in the face of domestic hypocrisy around race equity and economic reform. Here again are the echoes of Komunyakaa's "Facing It," which elide the Black face of the narrator with a White vet and grieving mother. The bullets of war did not discriminate against who they took, and the grieving touched all races and genders.

Over the past few years, I have found myself using Ocean Vuong's *Night Sky with Exit Wounds*, a collection which also deals with the Vietnam War, regularly in my creative writing workshops. For me, Vuong's poem "Of Thee I Sing" evokes just as much conversation about patriotism as it does American exceptionalism and immigration. We often think of American patriotism as having a monolithic ethos, but there is always a political understory. American exceptionalism is the perception of America as a nation where any dream can become manifest based on the successful historic separation of European immigrants from their British colonial masters in 1776. In the poem "Of Thee I Sing," Vuong shatters the narrative of American exceptionalism through his chronicle of the assassination of John F. Kennedy from the point of view of his wife, Jacqueline Kennedy. Vuong slows down time to highlight these connections in the post-rifle shot moments of Kennedy's assassination: "I'm reaching across the trunk / for a shard of your memory,

/ the one where we kiss & the nation / glitters." In these precious seconds, the state of the nation is tied to a literal and figurative romanticization of the first couple as metonym for nation. In the lines "But I'm a good / citizen, surrounded by Jesus" readers are struck by the reference of allegiance to one nation tied to a monotheistic god. Vuong also invokes the limitless vistas of the nation with its green fields and endless blue skies before delivering the poem's final blow: "My one white glove, glistening pink—with all / our American dreams." In these lines he reveals the utter desecration of a nation that continues to see itself as invincible, a nation clearly forgetting that the hallmarks of America were always improvisation and non-traditionalism, a progressive framework for change, not invincibility.

Like the limbs and bodies lost in the obdurate granite of Komunyakaa's Vietnam Veterans Memorial, Vuong highlights the loss of national innocence in the murder of a fallen American president. The timeliness of Vuong's poem delivers in the complicated layering of his lyric, including the nature of the evil interloper revealed as the unseen catalyst of the whole event. We recognize this evil all too well. Somehow Vuong's bird's-eye view of Kennedy's assassination takes on new meaning in an era where the assassin is no longer exceptional. Historically, we have tracked his move from presidential cavalcade to Lorraine Motel balcony. When we were not looking, he entered the rural as well as the suburban high school, and even breached the university classroom. He singlehandedly created the phenomenon of the lockdown drill, institutional-wide emergency alert, and the mantra "run, hide, fight."

Yes, we bemoan the plots of national villains, actively resist the monikers new or normal. Like soldiers, we search for revelation and grounding following unforeseen events. Our search for unity still involves a simultaneous groping to redefine patriotism. Patriotism, by definition, is a love of country: in the words of Vuong's Jacqueline Kennedy, "They have a good citizen / in me. I love my country." Like the Vietnamese American creator of this poem, a nation benefits when it embraces new ways of interpreting American history. Vuong nudges the nation to resist traditionalist values which depend on outmoded, romantic national narratives. We become spellbound. We listen and watch intently as an immigrant Vietnamese poet retells the American tale of the nation's loss of an Irish president, also the descendent of immigrants. We believe him when he intuits that the "dream" must be built on something more substantial, and know it will take every ounce of our humanity to get there.

"Facing It" is really a poem of reconciliation. It is a poem in a collection that takes readers through various iterations of war to arrive at a conclusion that involves a confrontation with the here and now. Today, when most Americans think about war, they might predictably consider the acts of domestic terrorism that have reinvigorated nationwide discussion of gun control. These tragic events have made Americans think about conflict and community in different ways. We have come to know too well the emphatic red-letter graphics of breaking news alerts that arrest us in our tracks. We know we must face the lurid details of violence until, finally, headshots flash onto our screens; the contemporary soldiers on a battlefield we never could have imagined.

WORKS CITED

King, Martin Luther. "Why I Am Opposed to the War in Vietnam." April 30, 1967, Riverside Church, New York. YouTube, www.youtube.com/watch ?v=zyE4eo_leX8.

Komunyakaa, Yusef. *Dien Cai Dau*. Middletown, Connecticut: Wesleyan University Press, 1988.

Morrison, Toni. *Sula*. New York: Plume, 1973.

Vuong, Ocean. *Night Sky With Exit Wounds*. Port Townsend, Washington: Copper Canyon Press, 2016.

TRANSLATING FOOTSTEPS

Poems After Komunyakaa

DAN ALBERGOTTI

Shovel to the Maggot

on two lines from Komunyakaa

You're almost nothing, so goddamned little
I can hardly believe you're the master
of everything. Yet here you are, god of
every soul that flickers off on this earth,

twisting through what remains, eating with no
mouth more than a toothy crown. You are one
regal worm. And then, a fly. That's what gets
me—how you transcend this, how you get to

wing away like some angel to heaven,
leaving thousands of stone-etched names without
bodies behind. Yet before that going,
you're just a dark tunnel we all go through.

Merciless god, Yusef knew someday you
would carry him too. Still, he praised you first.

Rattlesnake

after "February in Sydney"

In our blue hour, a rattlesnake slides
from its sleep, becoming less
sculpture than sculptress, drowsing
along its own length, sensuous
as an opera glove touching a man's face;
in a jazz club in the city, a cloud
looms over brass, the masculine trio
separate—isolated, improvising—
the dregs of an audience
nodding with a peace found never
at home, in bed, in arms, but
here, in the ash of five am, with strangers,
watered-down whiskey,
ice cubes on the cusp of tears,
a perfume called *eau de vie*
like venom hung in fangs, tremor of
cymbals on the high-hat, performance
of its percussive trick, a bluesy
slithering giving solace to the soloist.

En el trayecto a Hoi An

Nadie *patea el aire & desaparece* en los túneles
ni *cuestiona cada raíz*
los turistas prefieren las vistas panorámicas

Las cuevas crecen alaridos de sus bocas
helechos que cubren el *río de tinieblas*
mientras perros errantes se lamen el pelaje de miel

El verdor *forzado hacia adelante*
por alguna necesidad alguna urgencia
rueda quinientos metros hacia abajo
y se sumerge en el mar del Sur de China

Arriba del paso de Hai Van
una novia se eleva *como un ángel*
posa en una redonda plataforma
sobre un búnker encima de un montículo
—huellas de bala y artillería visible en las paredes—
la estructura completa un cake de bodas

El fotógrafo *tira del gatillo* y los captura
mientras otra novia en blanco
su amplia falda y su pareja esperan turno

La mujer sobre el cake gira su rostro
perfil de precisión que corta el viento
mirada que reposa en ese *azul imaginado*
ese horizonte.

Nota: las frases en itálicas fueron tomadas del poem "Tunnels," del libro *Dien Cai Dau* de Yusef Komunyakaa. Traducción de Lucía Orellana Damacela.

Facing It

Again, a seminar in England.
Again, I'm teaching the poem.

Again I explain to a room
of 18-, 19-year-old Brits

the Vietnam War,
the memorial's glossy,

reflective black granite,
and then the names,

the names numbering
58,022

(here, one and another sweet
intake of breath).

I project an image of the memorial
onto white wall, and now

I deliver, voice as vehicle.
I'm not looking at the page.

I'm watching the students
sit and shift in the poem.

Afterwards, we linger at the memorial,
lean toward our ghostly faces,

find in them
someone else's name.

October

after "Ode to the Maggot"

I dreamed my mother died
a second time. I was surprised
to hear myself beg for her
life, as I have, while awake,
for the lives of others I've loved.
Imagine all those I have not
begged mercy for:
from them, do I ask forgiveness?

Yesterday rose light pooled below
turning maples. Today, leaves fallen,
their light lifts instead, like steam
from a pot of crawdads. I walked
inside the light both times,
expecting my skin to flush, nature
working its change on the body,
as it does in life and death.

I understand the purpose of the maggot
and the metaphor of heaven.
That mercy is brief and surprising,
that change is long, and surprising.

YOLANDA J. FRANKLIN

A Cento for Langston's Blues

from Komunyakaa's "Langston Hughes + Poetry = The Blues"

We weigh the most innovative voices at the axis. So,
voices hold and reshape the tongue and heart of poetry.
American-ness, at the center, has endured even. The Negro,
speaks, plumbs the muddy bosom of the Mississippi,
praises the Euphrates and the Congo, taking readers
on a tour through African heritage, focuses racial tensions
in America. Like the pulse and throb of vision driven by
an acute sense of beauty and tragedy in America's history:
life as an artist and individual, avenue from the blues.
Words somehow embrace the aria of music's divining
rod quivered over the bedrock of the blues: short lines,
syncopated insistence, and urgency. Art has to have tension.
It is simultaneous laughter and crying, orates jagged lyricism
and modulation—movement that sidesteps contemplation
but invites action/motion. Confrontation in the blues
seems to set out to take poetry off the page and toss it
up into air we breathe. In essence, the blues chants
to parallel improvisation in the lives of African Americans,
speaks daring joy, is more than images, is celebration
and revolution, in the same breath addresses the future,
forging possibility: a new black culture in literature, music,
and the arts that light on the tongue. Just mentioning her
name is enough. The blues, proclaims a jagged rhythm,
complex—it filters through the lenses of laughter with crying.

To Idleness, an Ode

And if my idleness is a result
of uncomfortable mud, then cast me
no sovereign, nor fill my flask

with brandy from your father's mantle.
Brother, we are both cut from the same
crude fabric. You needn't be reminded

of our shared lineage. What you see
is not my habitat, but only the nature
of my meanderings. Whereas history

granted you kindly with a legend
sung in schools across the land.
Mine's a folktale, a cautionary one.

Laxity may not be a virtue, but in spite of it,
I've courted failure far better than you.
And while on the subject of possibilities,

have your letters switched into German?
Has anyone knocked on your door
lately with a basket of dark bread?

Headless

you only like white-looking Black
girls she stated / the way a statement
and beg can hold each other
the way we'd just finished holding in the

humiliation of my parent's basement /
it's cold down there in November
and space heaters don't do shit
when accusatory palms turn calamity

frostbit / enough to make you question
your keepers / question the maps on
your palms and whether there's actual royalty
in those tracks / *touch me like you*

touch them redbones she called for /
like she'd known about the first time I'd seen
Apollonia topless in *Purple Rain* / she'd known
how my slight body was flooded in praise

Summer Ends with a Line
by Yusef Komunyakaa

It begins in memory—
the yellowjacket tender
as a splinter landing
near my palm, looking for a sip
of cider, & with it
I could fall back through
the seasons, windmill my way
past the sonata of humming wings
as if these harmonics might come from
my own lips, bullets of song
that sting when remembered.
When the edge of summer
brushes the threshold fall,
I want to kneel inside
the cooler night & wait for the chill
to descend dark as blacktop
& I'll clutch a bit of asphalt
that still breathes the heat of the day,
then turn my back on summer,
this one & all those that have come before
until I get to when you died: July,
splayed as wide as a century, split
like a lily, forever holy though
in a second-hand kind of way.
Each year, when I make it to fall,
I mistrust the calendar
and worry the devil has fiddled
with time or that you have shrunk
so small I only catch sight of you
in my dreams. There, I've already

hidden all the knives and scissors,
nothing for you to use
against yourself. Your skin
even then is papery,
the gray of a wasp's nest,
still unraveling.

After Reading "Anodyne"
by Yusef Komunyakaa

I am too skinny
for this body.
I mean, I walk.
I eat vegetables
and lots of fruit.
I bend my knees
at dawn to say
my prayers.
At the beach
I watch
the bikini-clad
strut along
the shoreline.
I strut too,
but I do stop,
often, to pick
up seashells.
I mean, I know
I look good.
I make love
with the lights
on, naked,
and sometimes
forget to put
on appropriate
clothes for
"company, show
too much ass"
or so I've been told.
I don't believe it.

My thighs
knocking against
each other
are drums
announcing
my arrival.
I never just enter.
I always arrive.

Crossing a City Highway at 3 a.m. in the Coyote Head Nebula, IRAS 15541-5349

From the eighth floor, I'm experimenting
with looking down from above. Who knows what
the right word is: observation, mandate,

apex predator. They lifted the mask
mandates and all the city's predators
catch coughs. And no one asks the right questions,

no one looks up. I'm up here, I don't say,
hook, line, and sinker—up, down, and every
where at once. I try out a predator's

posture, aiming my muscles at the dust,
infraredding at what's ahead. Fox-faced,
cow-coated red, I try on all the masks.

A mask is looking down at a distance.
Eight floors up in the city, looking down
is a mask, an unleashed animal with

or without a hand. The fox says, slam, dunk,
and hook, you're asking questions animals
wouldn't know to ask. Who's to say what kind

of scent you leave behind you, what you are
weaving and remixing for the Spitzer's
lens. Who knows what might track you home, walking

dead or lightning fast and amorous, light
years away and up and up to the eighth
floor. These are the questions, the fox says, they

wouldn't think to ask. In response, I say,
counting the nebulas, I'm laying out
around the sidestreets a circle of right

words and traps. I say, anyway, I don't
think like an animal. In the city,
I don't ask questions, don't see what comes next.

At the Vietnam Memorial Wall Circa 2018

In response to Yusef Komunyakaa's "Facing It," 1988

My sneakers fresh in the granite's reflection
A Nike swoop hovering above dead names
Black mirror mirrors my skin's reflection
I'm empty / Alone / I'm walking

A Trump supporter pushes aside her children
A family of MAGA hats cocked backwards
Her daughters crowned in the colors of America
Like tribal tattoos across the bodies of warriors

I swallow the spit in my mouth
Swallowing the staleness of history
I tiptoe with caution /
This backwards grave / My conscience
The holding place for martyrs /
A pathway I seek for refuge

To mourn
A portal
Reality
For bodies
For freedom / For six miles
No two acres / I'm separated
Myself / This memorial
I'm ignorant

58,022 names
A blade of grass peeks over memorialized slates.
Epigraphs written on stone tablets like Moses's commandments.

A White mother scolds her young daughters
Manners and freedom / peace and manners
Drop from mouth like breadcrumbs / It's unclear

I walk past them with the stone's progression
Each step / my silent protest

What about the border; families deported,
The anthem; being stopped at a red light
The wall he said he would build
Dammit I said I wouldn't do this

Patriotism my bowl of famine

I'm walking / I'm lost
In names as if walking through smoke from burning buildings

It's quiet / It's dim / Smoke rises like a phoenix
A park ranger lectures a small class of eagers
Her cursor points but her words go mute

I walk inside the serif end of the names
Caldron / Carter / Moses / Williamson
She points into the distance

I see platoons / gun smoke & helicopters
A city on fire /

I try to mourn
But my eyes harden to grit like chewed stone

I see police in riot gear
My freedom like a match on the horizon.
Burning / Smoke as thick as haze
I hear the name Gray and chants of justice / peace / & purge

It's quiet / dark
I'm lonely

I walk outside the sad stone
At the center
Connecting this east wing
of this Veteran Memorial Wall to its west.

I step inside the stone again
A boy in khaki shorts offers me a rock
It's heavy and dark like a lie

I reach out to grab the rock but my arm
is outside the stone again
With two fingers I graze the name John Author
Patriotism engraved into 36-year-old rock

Inside the stone a crowd chants
No JUSTICE No PEACE
No JUSTICE No PEACE
No JUSTICE No PEACE

The white mother and her children's lips vibrate
to that same cadence outside the stone window
It's quiet / Their lips as stiff as coffins
A whisper of our country / our freedom
As pale as cirrus clouds / our crooked agenda
No . . . wait

They're saying grandpa's name is right there
I'm empty again

What Does an Immigrant's Daughter
Know of War

caribbean wars have a romance to them
language lurking in every horror
Martí & his poet's hands strangling the reigns
steering a stallion towards death   dying
a line from his poem face outstretched
     before the midday sun
in Lares, un grito is different from un llanto
melancholy and sacrificio are twins & no one
ever dies with regret on a battlefield enclosed
in mango trees. so when Yusef wrote *at daybreak*
     she burns like a piece of paper
my lips became soot-stained, & so did my childish
philosophies
     a soldier kissing his beloved at dawn
     the same soldier returning unharmed
     as though fire could be exorcised
     as though war were not a stained glass window
        breaking in every room

once I saw my father slip into the addicting smokey
simmer of a crack-pipe & he may have whispered
     Perejil   *Perejil*
his tongue a casualty of war
     as it hung there soft & slack in his mouth—

MALIK NOËL-FERDINAND

Ode to the Flute

for Yusef Komunyakaa, Léon Sainte-Rose,
& Chris Abani

Ghazal, I hacked you for your stem's
archaic notes, for how sound it seemed

to be swayed outside the inborn
enjambments of your thick nodes. Burn
the dead branches in the backyard.
For his soul, my wife said to me.
You know, it wasn't envy that swept
me off my feet when I felt the sweet
breeze of your frondescence under the moon.
Years ago, I played you as an Igbo
griot exposed the smooth bounces of your tone
at the bare bottom of Venice lagoon,
before you broke into this plain polished
embouchure. But now I am tapping holes,
as if mapping the old Kalinago's

hollow routes in the marrow of my bones.
Roots cannot grow back from the aria

of a mild flute. You've been punctuated
by charcoal, wrought iron, and chord. Then breath

would make everything live again, as lips
remember the tenderness of the dew,

and the fugitive's fingertips mimic
the alliterations of the macaw

soft feathers along the mellifluous
bamboo stuff of the poem that in awe,

I plead you to govern. Incredulous
anthem of this island, would you flourish across
the ravines of the spearhead serpent? Babylons
up hills. Babylons down burgs. Babylons and gas.
Babylons beating. Babylons and the dia-
phanous shields of their gaze. Babylons inside we,
doomed by the aperture of the citizens' ir-
resistible babble. So, I had no nation
there but the quiet tears of its intonation,
no dasheen but the leafy flesh of its shadow
ka doudoumé, which flutters like a sweet darling.
Palanché. Palanché cheù moin. Palanché. Lift
up my heart. *Palanché cö moin.* Lift my chin up.
Palanché. Cheù. Cö. Palanché pays a. Cheer
up the country with the hoists of my cheated heart.
　　　Now my native tongue has exhaled this tribute through
　　　the susurrus groove of your arched grove,
　　　fill the forest & flow like a *jacquot*.

Self-Portrait in Flesh and Stone

Before the war, my father slid shoehorns between the lips of discount loafers and socked heels.

If the shoe fits, so the story goes, the true identity of the cinder-shrouded girl is known.

Persephone swallowed the seeds and her mother bent fallowed.

My father's mother had nine mouths to feed, ten if she counted herself.

Cronus ate his first five kids and then a stone.

The memorial is cut from polished black granite and cuts into the earth.

My father's name is not cut into the stone but still I see my reflection in its surface.

I tell you, it says in the Book of Luke, *if these remain silent, the stones would cry out.*

My father used to have a mouth on him, but now he reads the Bible and doesn't cuss.

Soldiers in the trenches passed the time sucking on cigarettes and the occasional fruitcake from home until their mouths clouded with rot and they called this trench mouth.

The 56th Dental Detachment, Phu Bai Dental Clinic, was the name of my father's unit.

A dentist once said to Gloria Anzaldúa, *We're going to have to do something about your tongue.*

I inherited my father's gutter mouth, which is not the same as trench mouth.

Soldiers dug 25,000 miles of trenches along the Western Front.

The Viet Cong required North Vietnamese villagers to dig three feet of the Cu Chi Tunnels each day, and this is where they burrowed to escape the bombs bursting in air.

I once pulled myself out of a depression by swallowing herbs and walking each day down the thin slit that cut across the winter-stripped field.

Persephone pulled the narcissus from its root and the dark mouth sucked her down.

There is a photo of my father pulling a rotten tooth from the mouth of a Vietnamese boy.

The trenches would flood and the soldiers would stand for long stretches in the muck unable to remove their wet socks and boots and their feet would soften to rot and they called this trench foot.

I put my foot in my mouth nearly every day.

Gloria Anzaldúa asks questions that are really refusals, *How do you tame a wild tongue, how do you bridle and saddle it? How do you make it lie down?*

In a 1969 photograph by Horst Faas, a young South Vietnamese woman covers her opened mouth as she stares into a mass grave where she fears her father's body lies.

Many mammals will eat the placenta of their newborns, but some Mexican women I know bury theirs near the hearth.

In 1967, Dang Thi Lanh sang and danced and cooked and crawled and dug with a short hoe and gave birth to her daughter in the Cu Chi Tunnels.

Cronus devoured his children and still his son came back and cast him down.

The soldiers would hump through the monsoon-soaked marsh until their feet bloomed with jungle rot.

My body and my father's body and Plath's body, *Head-stone quiet, jostled by nothing / Only the mouth-hole piped out, / Importunate cricket // In a quarry of silences.*

That time I put my foot in my mouth and asked my father what it was like over there.

My father has never eaten a pomegranate though he has spent time on the other side and its shadow darkens his return.

A mama bird will chew the worm and partially digest it before spitting it out into the mouth of her young and in this way the baby bird is fed.

My father in Phu Bai fingering the dark.

I am surprised sometimes by what comes out of my mouth, so I have to watch my tongue.

Those nights I watched my father's mouth when he dozed off in the recliner to make sure he didn't choke on his tongue during his nightly seizures.

Sometimes the rot was so far advanced they had to amputate the foot to save the man.

I try to swallow the truth but still, like Cronus, it comes out of my mouth anyway.

Yusef Komunyakaa returned from Vietnam and visited the memorial and wrote, *I'm stone. I'm flesh.*

As a defensive strategy, trenches followed a zigzag pattern and never a straight line.

Back home my father slips a hand under the lifted tongue and buffs the black leather until it shines with his reflection, and this is how he meets each week, emptied shoes laid out.

Love Letters for Tío Manolo

"sat in the quiet brutality"
"My Father's Love Letters," Yusef Komunyakaa

Friday nights he'd crack a can of Heineken
play Las Mejores Canciones de Camilo Sesto
after coming home from the factory to read
the latest batch of letters his wife sent with
Carla who just got her visa. She complained
the letters made her purse heavy. She didn't
want them in her luggage for fear the
blocks of queso Geo and bottles of Brugal
would overpower the Maja perfume misted
over the envelopes. Each letter, a plea for
mercy, folded hands to chest, knees sore
from endless prayer. Rolled from under the
pressure of her ballpoint pen: *perdóname,*
mi corazón es tuyo, te extraño, vuelve a mi.
Camilo's crooning broke the brutal silence
that heavied the air of Tío's rented room. Each
letter ending with a pink lipstick kiss. The same
shade he found on his better-looking brother's
neck the night he caught them coiled between
streetlight and shadow. None of her words
ever made the swelling of his right knuckle go
down. Her nose recast in one swift crack. Lost
between each sentence until the sunset pushed
itself through the opened window. Camilo's
voice a vigil as Tío Manolo held each letter
over a lighter, her lipstick: dancing to smoke.

Half-Mast Days

"I said I wouldn't dammit: No tears."
"Facing It," Yusef Komunyakaa

I cannot make out my face
in the white board.
I am plexiglass. I'm kevlar.

My students titter behind me.
Desk legs groan.
There's a scrum over
outlets. They all need
their phones plugged
in these days.

They've just had a lock-down drill.
Practiced staying quiet. Crouching.
Pressing themselves flat and still
against classroom walls.
Dark eyed rabbits in a hutch.
Waiting
for an all clear.

They know memorials.
Stuffed bears. Melted candles.
Vigils. Marches.
I am wiping away
the evidence of the last teacher's
lessons but
the words linger
I can just make out
Remember
Take-Aways

Make-up
Do Now

This is our memorial:
teachers & students.
Faded names on
a wall, letters of smoke;

thrown aways
muted under
the cicada call of shell casings
& final sales.

To my left;
movement.
my
co-teacher runs a hand across
her face wiping away tears
No
She's pushing her braids
back.

I turn fully from the board:
A student is hunched
underneath her desk
frantic.
No
She's fishing for a pen.

On Passing, or How to Stare at a Kardashian's Bum Without Blinking

after Lois Maïlou Jones's Nude Study, *the 2014* Paper *cover,*
& Komunyakaa's "More Girl Than Boy"

Look closer. Realize it's not remarkable.
She knows its lumps lack luster, dreams
Of lips thick & plump as every inch of you,
Yes, you: Not man enough for a Black man except
In secret, when no one's recording the contours
But him, not woman enough for a Black man,
Either. How to be his good ~~boy~~ girl, not question
Or make one move he doesn't order. Mimic her
As she purrs *yeeeeees!* Moans *sir.* Wauls *whose am I*
If not your blank canvas, pure & ~~*non*~~*white as margarine?*
We (almost) did it, Joe. Write that check ~~your~~ my ass
Can't cash. Meme me. I'll steal from you while looking
Through you, dead ~~to me~~, in your eyes. I'm 'pose to pose
As you even if it costs you everything, even your life.

Ode to a Thread of Spider-Silk Between a Dead and Living Tree

after Yusef Komunyakaa

Tripwire. String tuned to the infinite
music of time. Translucent epitaph
on the air. I walked into the late day

heat to witness this prism of light
pulled from the body like a soul
trembling in the breeze. Abandoned line

of poetry—warning to gnats and mayflies
the faded underscore of a no trespassing sign
or property marker camouflaged

depending on how I turn my eyes. Feast
or famine, an outstretched hand
could knock you down, though I've walked

headfirst into you before and felt panic
stir up from the spine, the last buzz
of breath we share before the end.

Acknowledgments

Doug Anderson, "Colonial Album." Previously published in *Blues for Unemployed Secret Police* (Curbstone Books, 2000).

Dr. Scott Bailey, "What Walking Brings." Finalist for the 2022 Saints + Sinners Poetry Contest as part of the Saints + Sinners LGBTQ Literary Festival, a program of the Tennessee Williams/New Orleans Literary Festival. Previously published in the anthology *Saints + Sinners 2021 and 2022 New Poetry from the Festival* (Rebel Satori Press, 2022).

Reginald Dwayne Betts, "Dear Yusef." Previously published in *Book Post*, August 2021.

Paula Bohince, "Rattlesnake." Previously published in *Brilliant Corners*, Summer 2018.

Curtis L. Crisler, "Superheroes Born by a Black Nerd." Previously published in *Indiana Nocturnes Our Rural and Urban Patchwork* (Nebo Publishing, 2019).

Toi Derricotte, "Beauty, Victory, and Survival in the Poetry of Yusef Komunyakaa." Previously published in *Callaloo* as "Seeing and Re-Seeing," Summer 2005.

Martín Espada, "Not Words But Hands." Previously published in *The Republic of Poetry* (Norton, 2006).

Kathy Fagan, "October." Previously published in *Magma* 79, Spring 2021.

Derrick Harriell, "Headless." Previously published in *Come Kingdom* (Louisiana State University Press, 2022).

Terrance Hayes, "Everyday Mojo Letters to Yusef Komunyakaa." Previously published in the *Boston Review*, June 2021.

Valerie Jean, "After Reading 'Anodyne' by Yusef Komunyakaa." Previously self-published in the chapbook *Threads*, 2001.

Jacqueline Johnson, "Laugh." Previously published in *Main Street Rag*, 2015.

Adrian Matejka, "Off the Rim." Previously published in *Callaloo*, Summer 2005.

John Murillo, "Dear Yusef," was previously published in *Kontemporary Amerikan Poetry* (Four Way Books, 2020).

Deborah Paredez, "Self-Portrait in Flesh and Stone." Previously published in *Year of the Dog* (BOA Editions, 2020).

Gregory Pardlo, "Dear Yusef Komunyakaa: On *Neon Vernacular* and the Half-Life of Double Consciousness." Previously published in *Literary Hub*, August 2019.

Ed Pavlić, "'Modern Man in the Pepperpot': The Black Musical Substructure of Yusef Komunyakaa's Poetic Thought." Previously published in *The Black Scholar*, 2013.

Lynne Thompson, "3/4 Jazz." Previously published in *Air/Light Magazine*, September 2020.

J.D. Scrimgeour, "Bloomington." Previously published in *Michigan Quarterly Review* 63, no. 1, Winter 2023.

Charlie Veric, "A Poet Is Addressing My Loneliness." Previously published in *Histories: Poems* (Ateneo de Manila University Press, 2015).

Artress Bethany White, "'Facing It': Of Soldiers, Patriotism, and Literary Resistance." Previously published in *Survivor's Guilt: Essays on Race and American Identity* (New Rivers Press, 2022).

Contributors

Dan Albergotti is the author of *The Boatloads* (BOA Editions, 2008) and *Millennial Teeth* (Southern Illinois University Press, 2014), as well as the chapbooks *Of Air and Earth* and *Circa MMXX* (Unicorn Press, 2019 and 2022, respectively). His third full-length collection, *Candy*, will be published by Louisiana State University Press in 2024. His poems have appeared in *32 Poems*, *The Cincinnati Review*, *Copper Nickel*, *Ecotone*, *The Southern Review*, *Best American Poetry*, and *The Pushcart Prize*, as well as other journals and anthologies. He has taught at Coastal Carolina University since 2005 and now lives in Tampa, Florida.

Doug Anderson has four poetry collections, including *The Moon Reflected Fire*, winner of the Kate Tufts Discovery Award. His most recent collection, *Undress, She Said*, was published in 2022. His memoir *Keep Your Head Down: Vietnam, the Sixties, and a Journey of Self-Discovery* was published in 2009. He has received fellowships from the National Endowment for the Arts and the Massachusetts Cultural Council. He has taught at Emerson and Smith Colleges, the University of Massachusetts, and the MFA programs at Pacific University and Bennington College. Anderson has been an affiliate of the William Joiner Institute for the Study of War and Social Consequences at the University of Massachusetts in Boston.

Scott Bailey is the author of *Thus Spake Gigolo* (NYQ Books). His poems have appeared in *Epiphany*, *Jabberwock Review*, *Meridian*, *Subtropics*, *The Journal*, *The Southeast Review*, and *Verse Daily*, among others. A Queer poet from Mississippi, he received an MFA from New York University and a PhD from Florida State University. He lives in the French Quarter of New Orleans, where he is an editor for Tulane University School of Medicine. To contact him, visit www.cscottbailey.com.

Margo Berdeshevsky, NYC born, writes in Paris. Her most recent collection is *Kneel Said the Night (a hybrid book in half-notes)* from Sundress Publications. Her forthcoming collection is *It Is Still Beautiful to Hear the Heart Beat* from Salmon Poetry. She is the author of *Before the Drought*, finalist for the National Poetry Series, *Between Soul & Stone*, *But a Passage in Wilderness*, and *Beautiful Soon Enough*, recipient of the first Ronald Sukenick Innovative Fiction Award. Other honors include the Thomas Merton Poetry of the Sacred Award and the Robert H. Winner Memorial Award from Poetry Society of America. http://margoberdeshevsky.com/.

Reginald Dwayne Betts is the founder and director of the Freedom Reads. A poet and lawyer, he is the author of four books. A 2021 MacArthur Fellow, his latest collection of poetry, *Felon*, was awarded the American Book Award and an NAACP Image Award. He holds a JD from Yale Law School.

Paula Bohince is the author of three collections, with poems in the *New Yorker*, the *New York Review of Books*, *Best American Poetry*, and elsewhere. She has received NEA Fellowships in Creative Writing and in Translation, the Raiziss/de Palchi Fellowship from the Academy of American Poets, the Amy Lowell Poetry Travelling Scholarship, and the John Montague International Poetry Fellowship in Ireland. She has an MFA from New York University and lives in Pennsylvania.

Emily Brandt is the author of the poetry collection *Falsehood*, as well as three chapbooks. She is a co-founding editor of *No, Dear*, curator of the LINEAGE reading series at Wendy's Subway, and member of the video-art collective Temp.Files. She earned her BA in psychology, English, and women's studies from Boston University, her MEd from Pace University, and an MFA from New York University, where she facilitated the Veterans Writing Workshop. She's of Sicilian, Polish, and Ukrainian descent, and lives in Brooklyn.

Nicole Cooley grew up in New Orleans and is the author of six books of poems, most recently *Mother Water Ash* (LSU Press, 2024) and *Of Marriage* (Alice James Books, 2018) and *Girl After Girl After Girl* (LSU Press, 2017), as well as a novel and two chapbooks. She is a professor in the MFA program in creative writing and literary translation at Queens College, City University of New York.

Curtis L. Crisler was born and raised in Gary, Indiana. Crisler's *Doing Drive Bys on How to Love in the Midwest* is forthcoming. He and Kevin McKelvey created *Indiana Nocturnes: Our Rural and Urban Patchwork*. His other poetry books are *THe GReY aLBuM [PoeMS], Don't Moan So Much (Stevie): A Poetry Musiquarium, "This" Ameri-can-ah, Pulling Scabs, Tough Boy Sonatas* (illustrated by the late Floyd Cooper), and *Dreamist: a mixed-genre novel*. He lives in Fort Wayne, Indiana, and is a professor of English at Purdue University Fort Wayne. He can be contacted at poetcrisler.com.

Lucía E. Orellana Damacela was born in Guayaquil, Ecuador. She has published *Extrañamiento* (2023), *InHERent* (2020), *Longevity River* (2019), *Sea of Rocks* (2018), and *Life Lines* (2018). Her work has appeared in both English and Spanish in *Tin House, Pank, Carve Magazine,* the *Bitter Oleander,* the *Acentos Review,* and elsewhere. Lucía has a PhD in social psychology from Loyola University Chicago, and has taught at the Universidad Católica de Guayaquil and at New York University, where she completed an MFA in creative writing in Spanish.

Tyree Daye is a poet from Youngsville, North Carolina, and an assistant professor at UNC–Chapel Hill. He is the author of two poetry collections *River Hymns*, a 2017 APR/Honickman First Book Prize winner, and *Cardinal* from Copper Canyon Press in 2020. Daye is a Cave Canem fellow. Daye won the 2019 Palm Beach Poetry Festival Langston Hughes Fellowship and 2019 Diana and Simon Raab Writer-In-Residence at UC Santa Barbara, and is a 2019 Kate Tufts Finalist. Daye was also awarded a 2019 Whiting Writers Award.

Toi Derricotte's sixth collection of poetry, *"I": New and Selected Poems,* was shortlisted for the 2019 National Book Award. She was awarded the Pegasus Award from the Poetry Foundation in 2023, the Wallace Stevens Award from the Academy of American Poets in 2021, and the Frost Medal from the Poetry Society of America in 2020. With Cornelius Eady, she co-founded Cave Canem, a home for the many voices of African American poetry, in 1996.

Joel Dias-Porter (aka DJ Renegade) is originally from Pittsburgh, and currently resides in South Jersey. The 1998 and 1999 Haiku Slam Champion, his poems have been published in *Poetry, Mead, Best American Poetry 2014, Callaloo, Antioch Review, Red Brick Review,* and the anthologies *Short Fuse, Role Call, Def Poetry Jam, 360 Degrees of Black Poetry, Slam (The Book), Poetry Nation, Beyond the Frontier,* and *Catch a Fire.* A Cave Canem Fellow, he also received the Furious Flower "Emerging Poet Award" in 1995. His collection *Ideas of Improvisation* is out from Thread Makes Blanket Press (June 2022).

Martín Espada's latest book of poems is called *Floaters* (2021), winner of the National Book Award and a finalist for the *Los Angeles Times* Book Prize. Other collections of poems include *Vivas to Those Who Have Failed* (2016), *The Trouble Ball* (2011), and *Alabanza* (2003). He is the editor of *What Saves Us: Poems of Empathy and Outrage in the Age of Trump* (2019). He has received the Ruth Lilly Poetry Prize, the Shelley Memorial Award, the Robert Creeley Award, an Academy of American Poets Fellowship, a Letras Boricuas Fellowship, and a Guggenheim Fellowship. He teaches at the University of Massachusetts in Amherst.

Originally from Normal, Illinois, **Carrie Etter** has lived in England since 2001 and is a member of the creative writing faculty of the University of Bristol. She has published four collections, most recently *The Weather in Normal* (UK: Seren; US: Station Hill, 2018), a Poetry Book Society Recommendation. Individual poems have appeared in the *Boston Review,* the *Iowa Review, The New Statesman,* the *Penguin Book of the Prose Poem,* and the *Times Literary Supplement.* She also writes short fiction, essays, and reviews.

Kathy Fagan's sixth poetry collection is *Bad Hobby* (Milkweed Editions, 2022). Her previous book, *Sycamore* (Milkweed, 2017), was a finalist for the 2018 Kingsley Tufts Award. She has been awarded Guggenheim and NEA fellowships and her work has appeared in venues such as the *New York Times Sunday Magazine, Poetry, The Nation, The New Republic, The Kenyon Review,* the Academy of American Poets *Poem-A-Day* series, the *Pushcart Prize Anthology,* and *Best American Poetry.* Fagan co-founded the MFA program at The Ohio State University, where she teaches poetry and co-edits *The Journal*/OSU Press Wheeler Poetry Prize Series.

Carolyn Forché's first volume, *Gathering the Tribes,* winner of the Yale Series of Younger Poets Prize, was followed by *The Country Between Us, The Angel of History,* and *Blue Hour.* Her most recent collection is *In the Lateness of the World.* She is also the author of the memoir *What You Have Heard Is True,* which was nominated for the 2019 National Book Award. Her anthology *Against Forgetting* has been praised by Nelson Mandela as "itself a blow against tyranny, against prejudice, against injustice," and was followed by the 2014 anthology *The Poetry of Witness.*

Yolanda J. Franklin's *Blood Vinyls* (Anhinga Press) is a debut poetry collection that Roxane Gay insists is a "must-must-must read." A five-time Fulbright Scholar Award Finalist, Franklin is also a Cave Canem, Callaloo, and VONA Fellow. Her poems appear or are set to appear in *Frontier Magazine, Sugar House Review, Southern Humanities Review,* and *The Langston Hughes Review.* Franklin is a full-time English professor in Atlanta. She collects original-press vinyl and can be found at her favorite coffee shop, Square Mug Café in Railroad Square, enjoying a drink the baristas named after her.

Washington, DC's **Brian Gilmore** is both bard and barrister, and the author of four collections of poetry including, *come see about me marvin,* a Michigan Notable Book Award winner for 2020. He is also the author of *We Didn't Know Any Gangsters,* a 2014 NAACP Image Award nominee. The author of numerous essays, law review articles, and short stories on a variety of political and cultural topics, he has been a regular contributor to the *Progressive Magazine* for the past twenty years. He is currently senior lecturer at the University College Park in the Law and Society Program.

Eugene Gloria is the author of *Sightseer in This Killing City,* winner of the Indiana Authors Award, *My Favorite Warlord,* winner of the Anisfield-Wolf Book Award, *Hoodlum Birds,* and *Drivers at the Short-Time Motel,* a National Poetry Series selection and recipient of the Asian American Literary Award. He is the John Rabb Emison Professor of Creative and Performing Arts and an English professor at DePauw University.

Jennifer Grotz is the author of four books of poetry, most recently *Still Falling.* Also a translator from French and Polish, her co-translation with

Piotr Sommer of Jerzy Ficowski's *Everything I Don't Know* received the PEN Award for Best Book of Poetry in Translation in 2022. Her poems have appeared in five volumes of the *Best American Poetry* series and have been published in venues such as the *New Yorker, The Nation, Poetry,* the *New York Times Magazine,* and the *New York Review of Books.* In addition to teaching at the University of Rochester, she directs the Bread Loaf Writers' Conferences.

Myronn Hardy is the author of, most recently, *Aurora Americana.* His poems have appeared in the *New York Times Magazine, The New Republic, Ploughshares, Poetry,* the *Georgia Review, The Baffler,* and elsewhere. He teaches at Bates College.

Derrick Harriell is the Ottilie Schillig Associate Professor of English and African American Studies at the University of Mississippi. His previous collections of poems include *Stripper in Wonderland, Come Kingdom, Cotton,* and *Ropes,* winner of the 2014 Mississippi Institute of Arts and Letters Poetry Book Award.

Terrance Hayes's recent publications include *American Sonnets for My Past and Future Assassin* and a book of drawings and essays, *To Float In the Space Between: A Life and Work in Conversation with the Life and Work of Etheridge Knight* . A collection of poems, *So to Speak,* and collection of essays, *Watch Your Language: Visual and Literary Reflections on a Century of American Poetry,* were released in 2023. He is a professor of English at New York University.

Didi Jackson is the author of *Moon Jar* and the forthcoming collection *My Infinity.* Her poems have appeared in *American Poetry Review,* the *New Yorker,* and *Virginia Quarterly Review,* among other publications. Her chapbook *Slag and Fortune* was published by Floating Wolf Quarterly. She has had poems selected for *Best American Poetry, The Slow Down* with Tracy K. Smith, and *Together in Sudden Strangeness: America's Poets Respond to the Pandemic.* She is the recipient of the Robert H. Winner Memorial Award from the Poetry Society of America and was a finalist for the Meringoff Prize in Poetry.

Linda Susan Jackson is the author of *Truth Be Told* (Four Way Books, 2024) and *What Yellow Sounds Like* (Tia Chucha Press), a finalist for the National Poetry Series and the Paterson Prize. She has received fellowships from the Cave Canem Foundation, the New York Foundation for the Arts, Calabash International Literary Festival, Soul Mountain Writers Retreat, and The Frost Place. Her work has appeared in *Brilliant Corners*, the *Harvard Review*, the *Los Angeles Review*, *Obsidian*, and *Ploughshares*, among others, and has been featured on the Academy of American Poets *Poem-a-Day* series. Now retired, she was an associate professor of English at Medgar Evers College/City University of New York.

Major Jackson is the author of six books of poetry, most recently *Razzle Dazzle: New & Selected Poems* and a collection of critical essays, *A Beat Beyond: The Selected Prose of Major Jackson*, edited by Amor Kohli. He lives in Nashville, Tennessee, where he is the Gertrude Conaway Vanderbilt Chair in the Humanities at Vanderbilt University. He serves as the poetry editor of the *Harvard Review*.

Jennifer Jean's poetry collections include *VOZ*, *Object Lesson*, and *The Fool*. Her teaching resource book is *Object Lesson: A Guide to Writing Poetry*. She has received honors, residencies, and fellowships from the Kenyon Review Writers Workshop, DISQUIET/Dzanc Books, the Massachusetts Cultural Council, the Her Story Is collective, the Academy of American Poets, and the Women's Federation for World Peace. Additionally, her poems and co-translations have appeared in *Poetry*, *Rattle*, *The Common*, *Waxwing*, *On the Seawall*, and elsewhere. She is the senior program manager of 24PearlStreet, the Fine Arts Work Center's online writing program.

Valerie Jean is a poet/writer now living in Frederick, Maryland. She has an MFA from the University of Maryland, College Park. She is a Cave Canem fellow, having graduated with the first class in 1998. She continues to seek beauty, joy, and peace.

Jacqueline Johnson is a multi-disciplinary artist creating in poetry, fiction, and fiber arts. She is the author of *A Woman's Season* (Main Street Rag Press) and *A Gathering of Mother Tongues* (White Pine Press), winner of the Third Annual White Pine Press Poetry Award. Her works in progress include *The Privilege of Memory*, a novel, and *How to Stop a Hurricane*, a collection of short stories. She is a graduate of New York University and the City University of New York. A native of Philadelphia, she resides in Brooklyn.

Melissa C. Johnson is a poet and academic administrator. She serves as associate vice provost and associate dean for undergraduate education at the Pennsylvania State University. Her second poetry chapbook, *Cancer Voodoo*, was published by Diode Editions in 2022.

Meghan Kemp-Gee is the author of *The Animal in the Room* (Coach House Books, 2023), as well as the poetry chapbooks *What I Meant to Ask* and *Things to Buy in New Brunswick*. She also co-created the webcomic *Contested Strip* and the graphic novel *One More Year*.

Zachary Kluckman is a nationally ranked slam poet with work appearing in print worldwide, including in *New York Quarterly*, *New Writing Scotland*, *Cutthroat*, *Crab Creek Review*, *Blue Mountain Review*, and *Arts & Letters*. A multi–award-winning writer and performer, Kluckman was recently named a finalist for the Subnivean Poetry Awards judged by Kazim Ali. His first collection, *The Animals in Our Flesh* (Red Mountain Press, 2012), won the Red Mountain Press National Poetry Prize. His newest collection, *Rearview Funhouse*, was published by Eyewear Publishing in 2023.

Wallace Lane is a poet, writer, author, and creative director from Baltimore. He received his MFA in creative writing and publishing arts from the University of Baltimore in May 2017. His debut collection of poetry, entitled *Jordan Year*, was also released in 2017. He works as an English and creative writing instructor with Baltimore City public schools. He is also part of the Baltimore Banner's Creatives in Residence program, which amplifies the work of artists and writers from the Baltimore region.

Matthew Lippman's collection *Mesmerizingly Sadly Beautiful* was the recipient of the 2018 Levis Prize and was published by Four Way Books in 2020. His new collection is *We Are All Sleeping with Our Sneakers On* (Four Way Books, 2024).

Anne Marie Macari is the author of five books of poems, including *Heaven Beneath* and *Red Deer*. Her first book, *Ivory Cradle*, won the APR/Honickman First Book Prize in 2000, chosen by Robert Creeley. Her poems and essays have been widely published.

Adrian Matejka is the author of seven books, including a mixed-media collection inspired by Funkadelic, *Standing on the Verge & Maggot Brain* (Third Man Books, 2021), and a collection of poems, *Somebody Else Sold the World* (Penguin, 2021), which was a finalist for the 2022 UNT Rilke Prize. His first graphic novel, *Last On His Feet* (Liveright), was published in 2023. He is the editor of *Poetry* magazine.

Sebastian Matthews (sebastianmatthews.com) is the author of the memoir-in-essays *Beyond Repair: Living in a Fractured State* and a hybrid collection, *Beginner's Guide to a Head-on Collision*. His other publications include two books of poems, the memoir *In My Father's Footsteps*, and the collage novel *The Life & Times of American Crow*. Along with Stanley Plumly, he edited *Search Party: The Collected Poems of William Matthews*. He is the host of *Jazz Hybrid*, a music and talk show out of Asheville, North Carolina, livestreaming at wpvmfm.org. He leads workshops for the Great Smokies Writing Program at UNC–Asheville.

Kenneth May was a student of Yusef Komunyakaa's at Indiana University in Bloomington from 1988 to 1991 and a member of the last Free People's Poetry Workshop led by Etheridge Knight in Indianapolis from 1989 to 1991. Since 1996, Kenneth has lived in Busan, South Korea. He is the founder and creative director of The Liquid Arts Network, an art collective dedicated since November 11, 2000 to presenting art, supporting artists, and connecting communities.

Jeffrey McDaniel is the author of seven books of poetry, most recently *Thin Ice Olympics* (Write Bloody, 2022). Other books include *Holiday in the Islands of Grief* (University of Pittsburgh Press, 2020), *Chapel of Inadvertent Joy* (Pittsburgh, 2013), *The Endarkenment* (Pittsburgh, 2008), *The Splinter Factory* (Manic D Press, 2002), *The Forgiveness Parade* (Manic D, 1998), and *Alibi School* (Manic D, 1995). McDaniel's poems have appeared in numerous places, including the *New Yorker*, the

American Poetry Review, the *New York Times*, and *Best American Poetry 1994, 2010*, and *2019*. Recipient of an NEA fellowship, he teaches at Sarah Lawrence College.

Philip Metres is the author of ten books, including *Shrapnel Maps* (2020) and *The Sound of Listening: Poetry as Refuge and Resistance* (2018). His work has garnered a Guggenheim Fellowship, a Lannan Fellowship, two National Endowment for the Arts fellowships, and three Arab American Book Awards. He is professor of English and director of the Peace, Justice, and Human Rights program at John Carroll University, and a core faculty at Vermont College of Fine Arts. He cherishes the independent study he did with Yusef Komunyakaa, working on Russian poetry translations, back in Bloomington, Indiana, a lifetime ago.

Dante Micheaux is the author of *Circus* (Indolent Books, 2018), which won the *Four Quartets* Prize from the Poetry Society of America and the T. S. Eliot Foundation, and *Amorous Shepherd* (Sheep Meadow Press, 2010). His poems and translations have appeared in *African American Review*, the *American Poetry Review, Callaloo, Literary Imagination, Poem-A-Day, Poetry, Poetry London, PN Review*, and *Tongue*, among other journals and anthologies. Micheaux's other honors include the *Ambit* Magazine Poetry Prize, and fellowships from the *New York Times* Foundation and the Cave Canem Foundation, where he is director of programs.

Yesenia Montilla is an Afro-Latina poet and a daughter of immigrants. She received her MFA from Drew University in poetry and poetry in translation. She is a CantoMundo graduate fellow and a 2020 New York Foundation for the Arts fellow. Her work has been published in the Academy of American Poets' Poem-a-Day series, *Prairie Schooner, Gulf Coast*, and *Best American Poetry 2021* and *2022*. Her first collection, *The Pink Box*, is published by Willow Books and was longlisted for a PEN award. Her second collection *Muse Found in a Colonized Body* (2022) was published by Four Way Books. Find her at www.yeseniamontilla.com.

Jonathan Moody received his MFA from the University of Pittsburgh. He has received a Cave Canem fellowship and has been published in journals such as *African-American Poetry Review, Borderlands*, the *Boston Review, Crab Orchard Review*, the *Harvard Review*, and other publications. Moody's second collection, *Olympic Butter Gold*, was the recipient of the 2014 Cave Canem/Northwestern University Press Poetry Prize. He lives in Pearland, Texas, with his wife and three sons, and teaches AP English at South Houston High School.

John Murillo is the author of the poetry collections *Up Jump the Boogie* and *Kontemporary Amerikan Poetry*. His honors include the 2021 Kingsley Tufts Poetry Award, the Four Quartets Prize from the Academy of American Poets and the T. S. Eliot Foundation, two Pushcart Prizes, the J. Howard and Barbara M.J. Wood Prize from the Poetry Foundation, fellowships from the National Endowment for the Arts, the Bread Loaf Writers' Conference, the Fine Arts Work Center, Cave Canem Foundation, and the Wisconsin Institute for Creative Writing, and his work has been included in *Best American Poetry 2017, 2019*, and *2020*. He is an associate professor of English at Wesleyan University.

Malik Noël-Ferdinand is associate professor (*maître de conférences*) in comparative literature at Université des Antilles in Martinique, where he teaches world literature and Creole culture. His research focuses on postcolonial literature, translation, and poetry. He has published articles about the works of Reinaldo Arenas, Toto Bissainthe, Dionne Brand, Aimé Césaire, Suzanne Césaire, Patrick Chamoiseau, Monchoachi, Serge Patient, Caryl Phillips, Djanet Sears, Derek Walcott, and Alexis Wright. He has won the *Kalbas Lò* prize for Creole-language creole in 1997 and 2000. His most recent academic projects embrace the forms of creative critical writing.

Sharon Olds is one of Yusef Komunyakaa's happy colleagues at New York University. Her most recent book is *Balladz*, a finalist for the National Book Award. *Arias* (2019) was shortlisted for the 2020 Griffin Poetry Prize, and *Stag's Leap* (2012) received the Pulitzer Prize and England's T. S. Eliot Prize. Olds is the Erich Maria Remarque Professor of Creative Writing at NYU's Graduate Creative Writing Program, where she helped to found workshop programs for residents of Coler/Isidor Goldwater Hospital, and for veterans of the wars in Iraq and Afghanistan.

Gregory Pardlo is the author of *Digest*, winner of the 2015 Pulitzer Prize for Poetry. His other books include *Totem*, winner of the *American Poetry Review*/Honickman Prize and *Air Traffic*, a memoir in essays. His honors include fellowships from the New York Public Library's Cullman Center, the New York Foundation for the Arts, the National Endowment for the Arts, and the Guggenheim Foundation. He is co-director of the Institute for the Study of Global Racial Justice at Rutgers University-Camden, and a visiting professor of creative writing at NYU Abu Dhabi.

Deborah Paredez is a poet, scholar, and cultural critic. Her most recent poetry collection, *Year of the Dog* (BOA Editions 2020), was a *New York Times* "New and Notable Poetry Book" and winner of the 2020 Writers' League of Texas Poetry Book Award. She is a professor of creative writing and ethnic studies at Columbia University and the co-founder of CantoMundo, a national organization dedicated to Latinx poets and poetry. Her book of literary nonfiction, *American Diva*, is forthcoming from Norton.

Ed Pavlić is author of more than a dozen books written across and between genres, most recently *Call It In the Air* (2022), *Outward: Adrienne Rich's Expanding Solitudes* (2021), *Another Kind of Madness* (2019), and *Who Can Afford to Improvise?: James Baldwin and Black Music, the Lyric and the Listeners* (2016). He is Distinguished Research Professor of English and African American Studies at the University of Georgia.

Jennifer Richter's first collection *Threshold* was chosen by Natasha Trethewey chose as a winner in the Crab Orchard Series in Poetry; her second collection, *No Acute Distress*, was a Crab Orchard Series Editor's Selection, and both books were named Oregon Book Award finalists. New work from her forthcoming collection, *Dear Future*, has been featured in *ZYZZYVA*, *The Account*, the *Massachusetts Review*, and the *Missouri Review*. Richter was awarded a Wallace Stegner Fellowship and Jones Lectureship in Poetry by Stanford University; she currently teaches in Oregon State University's MFA program.

Peggy Robles-Alvarado is a Jerome Hill Foundation Fellow in Literature, a BRIO award winner, and a three-time International Latino Book

Award winner who authored *Conversations with My Skin* and *Homage to the Warrior Women*. She has received fellowships from the Latinx Playwrights Circle, The Dramatic Question Theater, CantoMundo, Desert Nights, The Frost Place, and NALAC. She has been featured in HBO Habla Women, the Lincoln Center, the Smithsonian Institute, and the Dodge Poetry Festival. Through Robleswrites Productions Inc., she created Lalibreta.online and The Abuela Stories Project. Her poetry appears on Poets.org and has been published in several anthologies, including *The Breakbeat Poets, Volume 4: LatiNext*. For more, please visit Robleswrites.com.

Hannah Baker Saltmarsh has published a book of poems, *Hysterical Water* (University of Georgia Press, 2021), and a book of literary criticism, *Male Poets and the Agon of the Mother: Contexts in Confessional and Post-Confessional Poetry* (University of South Carolina Press, 2019). She is currently working on an essay about Toni Morrison's inventive, creative fictional daughters, and a piece about the political poetry of motherhood in works by Lucille Clifton, Audre Lorde, and Adrienne Rich. Her second poetry book manuscript, entitled *cures for deep wounds*, concerns motherhood, feminisms, illness, healing, and environmental wounds.

J.D. Scrimgeour is the author of five books of poetry and two books of nonfiction, including the AWP Award-winner *Themes For English B: A Professor's Education In & Out of Class*. With musician Philip Swanson, he released a CD of poetry and music, *Ogunquit & Other Works*, which includes a reading of a poem of Yusef Komunyakaa's set to music. He teaches at Salem State University in Salem, Massachusetts, a city where some of his ancestors were put to death for witchcraft and others sat on the jury that found them guilty.

Nicole Sealey is the author of *The Ferguson Report: An Erasure*, an excerpt from which was awarded a Forward Prize; *Ordinary Beast*, finalist for the Hurston/Wright Legacy and PEN Open Book Awards; and *The Animal After Whom Other Animals Are Named*, winner of the Drinking Gourd Prize. Her honors include the Arts and Hodder Fellowships from Princeton University, a Cullman Fellowship, a Rome Prize, the Stanley Kunitz Memorial Prize, and fellowships from the National Endowment for the Arts and the New York Foundation for the Arts. She teaches in New York University's MFA Writers Workshop in Paris program.

Lynne Thompson has been the 2021–22 Poet Laureate of the City of Los Angeles and received a Poet Laureate Fellowship from the Academy of American Poets in 2022. She is the author of four collections of poetry: *Beg No Pardon, Start with a Small Guitar, Fretwork,* and *Blue on a Blue Palette* (BOA Editions, 2024). Her recent work can be found in *Pleiades, New England Review, Ploughshares,* and *Best American Poetry.*

Charlie Samuya Veric is a poet, scholar, and curator. A fellow of the Johannesburg Institute for Advanced Study and the Stellenbosch Institute for Advanced Study, he is the author of bestselling and critically acclaimed poetry collections, including *Histories* (Ateneo de Manila University Press), *Boyhood: A Long Lyric* (Ateneo de Manila University Press), *The Love of a Certain Age* (University of the Philippines Press), and most recently, *No Country* (University of the Philippines Press). He holds a PhD in American Studies from Yale University and teaches at the Ateneo de Manila University.

Shari Wagner is a former Indiana Poet Laureate (2016–2017) and the author of three books of poems: *Evening Chore, The Harmonist at Nightfall,* and most recently *The Farm Wife's Almanac.* Her poems have appeared in many places, including *American Life in Poetry, The Writer's Almanac, North American Review, Shenandoah,* the anthology *A Cappella: Mennonite Voices in Poetry,* and the Indiana Repertory Theatre's production of *Finding Home: Indiana at 200.* Wagner has an MFA in creative writing from Indiana University at Bloomington, where she had the privilege of studying under Yusef Komunyakaa.

Derrick Weston Brown, a Charlotte, North Carolina, native, holds an MFA in creative writing from American University. He was the first Poet-in-Residence of Busboys and Poets. He is a former Cave Canem and VONA fellow, and his first book, *Wisdom Teeth,* was released in 2011 by PM Press.. He is an adjunct professor of composition and literature at Prince George's Community College and is on the creative writing faculty at the Duke Ellington School of the Arts. He resides in Mount Rainier, Maryland.

Artress Bethany White is a poet, essayist, and literary critic, and associate professor of English at East Stroudsburg University. She received the Trio Award for her poetry collection, *My Afmerica* (Trio House Press, 2019). Her book *Survivor's Guilt: Essays on Race and American Identity* (New Rivers Press) received a 2022 Next Generation Finalist Indie Book Award. Her prose and poetry have appeared in *Poetry*, the *Harvard Review, Ecotone, Birmingham Poetry Review,* and in the anthology *Why I Wrote This Poem: 62 Poets on Creating Their Works* (McFarland, 2023). She is nonfiction editor at the literary magazine *Pangyrus*.

L. Lamar Wilson's documentary poetics animate *Sacrilegion* (Carolina Wren Press, 2013) and *The Changing Same*, a collaboration with Rada Film Group and POV Short that has aired perennially on PBS since 2019. He teaches creative writing, African American poetics, and film studies at Florida State University and in the Mississippi University for Women's low-residency MFA program.

Matthew Wimberley is the author of two collections of poetry, *Daniel Boone's Window* (2021) and *All the Great Territories* (2020). Winner of the Weatherford Award from the Appalachian Studies Association and a grant from the North Carolina Arts Council, his work has appeared most recently in the *Adroit Journal, Blackbird,* and the *Threepenny Review*. A graduate of NYU's MFA program where he was a Starworks Fellow, Wimberley lives in the Blue Ridge Mountains and is an assistant professor of English.

Emily Jungmin Yoon is the author of *A Cruelty Special to Our Species* (Ecco, 2018) and *Ordinary Misfortunes* (Tupelo Press, 2017). She has also translated and edited a chapbook of poems, *Against Healing: Nine Korean Poets* (Tilted Axis, 2019). She currently serves as the poetry editor for *The Margins*, the digital magazine of the Asian American Writers' Workshop, and is an assistant professor in the East Asian Languages and Literatures department at the University of Hawaiʻi at Mānoa. Yoon's second full-length poetry collection *Find Me as the Creature I Am* will be published by Knopf in 2024.